CREATING WINNING MARKETING PLANS: PLANNING, STRATEGIES AND OBJECTIVES

Sidney J. Levy,
Editor

Excerpted Chapters from *The Dartnell Marketing Manager's Handbook, edited by Sidney J. Levy, George R. Frerichs and Howard L. Gordon, Third Edition,* 1994.

DARTNELL is a publisher serving the world of business with books, manuals, newsletters and bulletins, and training materials for executives, managers, supervisors, salespeople, financial officials, personnel executives, and office employees. Dartnell also produces management and sales training videos and audiocassettes, publishes many useful business forms, and many of its materials and films are available in languages other than English. Dartnell, established in 1917, serves the world's business community. For details, catalogs, and product information, write to:

THE DARTNELL CORPORATION
4660 N Ravenswood Ave
Chicago, IL 60640-4595, U.S.A.
or phone (800) 621-5463 in U.S. and Canada

This publication is designed to provide accurate and authoritative information in regard to the subject matter covered. It is sold with the understanding that the publisher is not engaged in rendering legal, accounting, or other professional service. If legal advice or other expert assistance is required, the services of a competent professional person should be sought.

> From a Declaration of Principles jointly
> adopted by a Committee of the American Bar
> Association and a Committee of Publishers

Copyright ©1996
in the United States, Canada and Britain by
THE DARTNELL CORPORATION

ISBN 0-85013-254-1

Library of Congress 96-083843

Printed in the United States of America

CONTENTS

FOREWORD

SIDNEY J. LEVY

In recent years the role of marketing planning has become recognized as critical to the successful performance of the organization. The growth of new businesses and the volatility experienced in a dramatically competitive global environment highlight the need for enhanced awareness of marketing. This need underlies the strong interest in the comprehensive volume Dartnell publishes as *The Marketing Manager's Handbook*. Its broad encyclopedic character enables readers to explore the field of marketing thought from several directions and at different levels. However, many people have expressed the desire for a convenient abridgement of the contents of the *Handbook* that is primarily focused on the topic of marketing planning and the creation of marketing plans. Therefore, this volume has been prepared as a collection of chapters that include significant discussions of the issues that must be dealt with in making marketing plans.

The content of these chapters will be helpful to readers with a variety of needs and goals. Nowadays there are many newcomers to the field of business who are either inventors or innovators. Perhaps they are starting a home business or are entrepreneurs with a fresh idea, or career changers who want to strike out on their own. Often, they feel inexperienced and uncertain, at a loss about how to think about the nature of a business or the kinds of things they should be planning and doing, or taking into account, in order to be successful. They may have narrow, stereotypical ideas about marketing, perhaps believing it is mainly just running advertisements or being an outgoing salesperson. Such readers will find much food for thought in this book. It will provide a sense of direction and many ideas to help them in their planning.

Similarly, managers with experience in other areas of business such as finance, accounting, or engineering, commonly find themselves moving into new or greater responsibilities that involve immersion in the marketing aspects of the enterprise. Their experience has commonly made them knowledgeable about many aspects of marketing, but they feel unevenly prepared and seek some clear expositions of the ideas they should be dealing with. Sometimes these people complain that they know some of the buzzwords used in marketing but do not truly understand what substance lies behind them, and how to apply them in meaningful ways.

There are also managers in the marketing area who are highly experienced, but have been primarily engaged in implementing the marketing planning done by other people. They have learned much from their firing line experience, and may initially feel confident to handle any duties requiring marketing know-how; but they often find that as they move up the line they need more preparation to handle the

v

larger perspectives that planning requires. Many specific marketing situations on the firing line do not lead to the consideration of major alternatives that sharp planners have to take into account. Perhaps one's organization has followed a narrow tradition or style of marketing management, and changing to another environment challenges the need for fresh thinking. Being a "new broom" can provoke a manager to look for stimulating analyses among the several topics that are involved in marketing planning.

The richness that such different readers will meet in this book comes about from several sources. First, it is designed to meet the needs of thoughtful managers seeking to understand what marketing planning is about; therefore it is not a simplistic "how-to-do-it" primer or workbook that leads one through checklists and standard actions that often do not fit the readers' situations. Second, the book's 14 chapters combine the work of 25 writers from numerous areas of expertise, and do not reflect only a single author's experience in a particular company or industry. Third, the quality of these writers is outstanding. They are established professionals, informed and up-to-date, and recognized as leaders in their areas of marketing. Fourth, the topics covered in these 14 chapters are wide-ranging, in recognition of the numerous elements involved in successful marketing planning. They show the value of having a broad awareness of the context within which marketing planning goes on, as well as the managerial activities required inside the organization. In addition to laying out basic processes and concepts, the volume is concerned with the impact of different contexts and forces that affect managers.

In this Foreword, to assist readers with an overview of the contents of *Creating Winning Marketing Plans*, I will comment on each of the chapters. The first chapter is by Harper W. Boyd, Jr. and Jean-Claude Larreche, and discusses the topic of "Setting Marketing Objectives." This topic is of course a fundamental one, critical to having clarity in one's planning. Its importance should not be underestimated; a recent survey among CEOs indicated that their most common regret as they contemplated their careers was that they did not think sufficiently about objectives. Also, in an earlier article on the subject, Harper Boyd and I researched some of the ways managers formulated their objectives and noticed the importance they placed on setting suitable ones, as well as the floundering tone visible among managers who confessed to lacking concrete statements of their company's marketing objectives. Here, Boyd and Larreche show how defining objectives differs from such ideas as goals and aims, helping readers to think about the specificity of their objectives. They also give special emphasis to the need to formulate an explicit statement of what business the organization is in; and they show how such a definition helps in making other strategic decisions about customers and how to relate to them.

Given the primary role played by customers in helping managers to develop their specific objectives, the text assists by providing content about customers. The second chapter, by Gregory S. Carpenter and Kent Nakamoto, is titled "Brand Dominance: Competitive Advantage Through Consumer Learning." These authors are richly qualified to discuss this topic, as they have been leaders in studying elements that contribute to the success of brands. The marketing planner is basically engaged in seeking competitive advantage; to accomplish this requires an understanding of how customers come to have certain preferences. Carpenter and Nakamoto have examined brands that stand out in the marketplace for their ability to gain substantial market share and to endure despite changes in the environment and challenges from new entries in the market. This success rests in customers' perceptions and their resulting choices when the dominant brand creates a preferred position. Successful brands act as role models, as avenues to seeing how their special status was achieved. The chapter is instructive in its implications for creating a brand and for understanding its importance to customers; and the authors also point out the hazards of merely imitating established brands.

The exploration of customer wants and needs is developed further in Chapter 3, by Richard R. Still, who discusses the topic of "Segmenting the Market." Given an interest in a market and its customers, the concept of market segmentation is regarded by many as the central necessity for giving focus to the development of that market. Too many marketing managers think vaguely about their customers as a large undifferentiated group, or they may exaggerate the generality of their potential audience. Professor Still points out the vast diversity in the marketplace and the resulting need to find meaningful groupings in it in order to communicate appropriately. Both Chapters 2 and 3 help the manager to think about a basic question, "Who is the customer?" They give content to the possibilities and types of segmentation that confront managers.

Chapter 4 presses to the forefront of modern marketing planning by presenting a highly informative discussion of "Database Marketing." The ability to locate and acquire precise information about customers is one of the major technical advances in marketing, and there is a high and widespread desire to learn about database marketing. Robert C. Blattberg stands out for his leadership in exploring the field of database marketing, both in developing its theory and in working on its practical application with specific organizations. He and Lynn C. Unglaub, who is associated with him in his consulting firm, present here a comprehensive explanation of what database marketing involves, how it arose, how it compares to other marketing approaches, and how it is applied. Understanding the point of view laid out in this chapter will add greatly to the manager's sophistication with its focus on both retaining the customer and maximizing the lifetime value of the customer.

As the manager is encouraged to think intently about customers in developing marketing plans, specific questions often arise about how to proceed, what techniques to use, what kinds of inquiry to carry out, and how to relate these issues to one's own organization. Chapter 5 assists in answering such questions by showing how to go about analyzing the market position of one's brand. It is written by Paul Green, one of the foremost workers in the field of marketing, joined here by John L. McMennamin and Shahrzad Amirani. They lay out in useful detail how to diagnose and map one's place in the market through applying specific methods of measurement that bring out consumers' perceptions, comparisons of users and non-users, etc. They illustrate the general value of their approaches by using examples of different customer groups, such as housewives and physicians.

The planning process continues logically from formulating objectives through numerous ideas about analyzing the market to a consideration of the means available for action. The process of marketing planning is interwoven and integrative, in that new information acts in a feedback manner to affect the objectives and the focus for planning that changing environments require. As managers make specific decisions about the directions in which to go, they use the marketing elements that are termed the marketing mix. Two distinguished contributors to explaining the marketing mix are William Lazer and M. Bixby Cooper in Chapter 6, "Developing the Organization's Marketing Mix." They indicate that although the marketing mix has traditionally been referred to simply as the Four P's—product, price, place, and promotion—the realities are more complex. The possibilities inherent in developing an effective marketing mix are numerous, with various levels and trade-offs to be taken into account in linking the organization and its markets.

Chapter 7 is titled "The Marketing Decision," written by William F. O'Dell and David K. Hardin. In their long years of experience at Market Facts, Inc., the well-known marketing research company, they have observed a large number of managers involved in marketing planning in varied situations. This experience has sensitized them to the nature of decision making. The ability to make appropriate decisions, a substantial challenge, characterizes the superior manager. O'Dell and Hardin offer insights into this process and help in working with it at various stages. These include identifying problems, recognizing alternatives, establishing criteria, and evaluating the alternatives enroute to a decision.

As marketing planning is taking form, through delineating objectives, analyzing consumers' perceptions, and moving through the decision-making process, the manager is engaged in determining marketing strategies. This is an area that is especially appealing for managers to learn about, as they often feel uncertain about what marketing strategies actually are and how to determine which strategies are suitable to their problems. In Chapter 8, Robert A. Lynn explains various kinds of marketing strategies and how they relate to the tactics that serve to implement them. He gives examples of various strategic approaches and raises questions that managers can ask themselves to help decide what is best for their situation.

The heart of marketing planning lies in the core issues presented in Chapters 1 through 8, and are largely about how to put forth one's company, product, and brand, and how to use the elements of the marketing mix to achieve which strategic objectives. But these decisions go on in an environment that requires managers to be sensitive to other forces and influences affecting their offerings. Laws, technology, special segments, managerial technique, and corporate settings are issues that are pressing in their own ways. They have impact on all marketing managers even when they may seem the responsibilities of other managers.

Regardless of the kind of business one is in, whether dealing with consumers, retailers, dealers, professionals, products, or services, the requirements of the law are ever-present. Lately, the role of law has come markedly to the fore, with much emphasis on litigation and its challenges to marketing offerings. Some regulations demand action: for example, the recently standardized nutrition information that must appear on food package labels. Other laws prohibit actions: for example, price-fixing. And still others are permissive: Although brand infringement is illegal, the government does not police it for managers, and they must take the initiative to protect their brands against infringement.

Chapters 9 and 10 both deal with the legal environment in which the business is conducted. H. Keith Hunt is an authority on public policy issues and their impact on managers. His chapter, titled "Government Regulation and the Marketing Manager: Developing a Perspective," points out the role of regulation and how managers might understand it. Hunt makes an important plea for the manager to understand rules not only for how they impinge on him or her, but also from the point of view of others in the marketplace as well. Such an understanding is especially valuable for operating in the adversary system that is characteristic in the United States, and for fully recognizing its benefits as well as its frustrations.

William L. Trombetta, a most knowledgeable attorney and scholar, elaborates on Keith Hunt's guidance, with a significant discussion of "Substantive and Procedural Changes in Antitrust Law: Implications for Marketing Management." He points out and explains recent profound changes in antitrust law that importantly affect marketing practitioners. Some of these matters seem technical, and marketing managers may wish not to be bothered with them. However, while these matters—and the cases Trombetta uses to illustrate his points—are issues for lawyers and judges to debate, the marketing managers must also be cognizant of them as part of their everyday actions and decisions about strategic planning and marketing research. That is necessary in order to lay a good basis for discovery—a suitable "paper trail"—as well as to avoid litigation.

Chapter 11 is by Nigel F. Piercy and William D. Giles, internationally known analysts of the marketing planning process. Their discussion is titled "Managing the Market Planning Process: The Search for Continuous Competitive Renewal." They offer a stimulating and provocative challenge to the market planning activity they see represented in the conventional model that addresses formulating a marketing plan as an overly narrow goal. They take the reader through a variety of issues that serve to embed the marketing plan in an ongoing advantage-seeking process. They contrast the conventional model—and what goes wrong with it—with fresh thinking about the design of the process and how the organization should be handling it. They emphasize the importance of iteration, whereby the planning process becomes essentially continuous.

Most marketing involves the distribution of the many products used to feed, house, and clothe people, with the vast varieties of substances and equipment now available to do that. The many choices people can make intensifies competition and the necessary alertness to what people want and how they want it. Such markets are regarded as demand-driven. But what of products that people are wary of, do not seem to want initially, or whose usefulness does not seem immediately apparent? John K. Ryans, Jr. and William L. Shanklin, who have devoted themselves to studying high technology and its marketing, are especially sensitive to the situation they describe in Chapter 12, "Marketing to Nonexistent Markets." Here, they point to the frequent but still special circumstances in which the classical goal of meeting consumer needs and demands seems less relevant, when the product is so new, innovative, and high-risk that consumers cannot be handled in the conventional ways. Ryans and Shanklin refer to the "supply-side marketing" that is then necessary, and to the different kinds of thinking and marketing research that are more suited to the situation. In support of their analysis, they list eight "corporate masters of innovation" and the basic philosophies that appear to characterize them and their success.

One of the most remarkable developments in the marketing field is the use of electronic scanning at the point-of-sale, in itself an example of the role of a technology that has come to have widespread acceptance and value. The authors of Chapter 13 present an unusually competent description of this technology. John C. Totten is a vice president, analytical and technical products, with Nielsen Market Research, and has years of experience at Procter & Gamble and Information Resources, Inc. He and Mike Duffy, director of forecasting and planning at Kraft General Foods, Inc., draw upon their extensive involvement and deep understanding of this technology and its application. They explain clearly what the scanning method is, and how it is used by retailers and manufacturers. Although the subject is a technical one, the authors are skilled in exposition and presentation. With several exhibits and practical examples, they lay out the numerous kinds of data that are accumulated, the kinds of reports generated, and the variety of purposes that can be pursued. They show the usefulness of the information for planning along the way, and also directly address the role that it can play in strategic planning. It is evident that like other technologies, scanning has gained increasing types of application, and that with added experience new uses will come along to assist in marketing planning.

The final chapter, "Evaluating and Controlling Marketing Performance," is by Philip Kotler, who is known world-wide for his top marketing textbook and his many contributions to the field. In Chapter 14 he discusses marketing planning from the viewpoint of the controls necessary to sustaining the organization's marketing activities. He takes account of four major categories of control: annual planning, profitability, efficiency, and strategic controls. Each of these categories has its own requirements for information, analysis, and interpretation. Kotler discusses concretely the forms of data to be acquired and the concepts that help to organize them, such as market share, customer satisfaction, marketing mix efficiencies, and the marketing audit. His chapter also includes two instruments he recommends for data gathering: a Marketing-Effectiveness Rating Instrument and the components of a Marketing Audit. He illustrates how recommendations can grow out of the findings.

It seems evident that the material in this volume includes a wealth of information and guidance to marketing managers. The range of ideas can bring along the beginning manager and stimulate the thinking of the most experienced. Collectively, the authors convey a sense of the importance of marketing planning, its vastly ramified character and sense of possibility, and an orientation to helping the reader solve problems.

ABOUT THE EDITOR

Sidney J. Levy is professor emeritus of Behavioral Science in Management and professor of Marketing at the Kellogg Graduate School of Management at Northwestern University. Previously, he was A. Montgomery Ward Professor of Marketing (1983) and Charles H. Kellstadt Distinguished Professor (1986).

Levy, who earned his Ph.D. from the Committee on Human Development at the University of Chicago, is a licensed psychologist in Illinois and a member of the American Marketing Association. As a principal with Social Research, Inc., Levy has directed and participated in research for major corporations, media, and various public and private agencies. During 1991, he served as president of the Association for Consumer Research.

Among other distinctions, Levy was named AMA/Irwin Distinguished Marketing Educator in 1988 and, in 1982, received the Fellow Award from the Association for Consumer Research.

Levy's articles have been widely anthologized; those of special significance to marketers include "The Product and the Brand," "Symbols for Sale," "Social Class and Life Style," and "Broadening the Concept of Marketing," and other articles appearing in the *Journal of Marketing* and *Journal of Retailing*, as well as in numerous books on marketing and its effects on society.

CREATING WINNING MARKETING PLANS: PLANNING, STRATEGIES AND OBJECTIVES

Sidney J. Levy, Editor

Harper W. Boyd, Jr.
Donaghey Distinguished Professor of Marketing
College of Business Administration
University of Arkansas (Little Rock)

Jean-Claude Larreche
Professor of Marketing
European Institute of Management (INSEAD)
Fontainebleau, France

CHAPTER 1

SETTING MARKETING OBJECTIVES

The setting of the firm's objectives is the first step in the strategic planning process. It is critically important since objectives serve as guidelines for all levels of managers in their decision-making activities and particularly those relating to the allocation of the firm's resources. Over the years business scholars have argued about what constitutes a set of viable objectives for a firm. These scholars represent four different schools of thought—those taking an economic point of view, those advocating a market or customer stance, those favoring social benefits, and those representing an organizational approach. Our discussion will focus on the first two concepts although all four must be utilized if the firm is to be successful.

Corporate objectives impact both strategy and operating decisions. In the case of the former, they do so largely in terms of the nature and scope of the businesses the firm pursues over time. From this emerges a definition of the business which is based largely on how the firm perceives the opportunities and threats facing its various product-market entries. Since, for a variety of reasons (e.g., the product life cycle) the firm will likely alter its investment emphasis with respect to one or more of its entries, its business definition will change over time. This, in turn, may affect the firm's choice of objectives. Thus, there is a strong interrelationship between objectives, strategy, and business definition.

Operating decisions are influenced by corporate objectives in the way managers formulate objectives for their areas of responsibility in their efforts to attain higher level objectives. There is, therefore, a hierarchy of objectives in any business organization. If, for example, a firm deems it necessary to sell a full line of products to the total U.S. market (business definition) in order to obtain its profitability objectives, then this will surely affect those decisions pertaining to channels of distribution, the sales force, advertising, and physical distribution.

It has long been recognized that corporate objectives influence both strategic and operating decisions. It has only been recently, however, that the linkages between objectives, business definition, and strategy have been explored in any depth. While each of these subjects is a worthy topic of discussion in its own right, it is their totality that is critical to the most managers. The purpose of this chapter is, therefore, to explore these linkages and to do so from the point of view of how they direct the firm's resource allocation process as well as serve as the basis for the organization's structure and its direction, motivation, and control.

GOALS VERSUS OBJECTIVES

There is considerable confusion in the literature between *goals* and *objectives*. Some writers use the two terms interchangeably along with *purposes* and *ends*. Others differentiate on the basis that objectives serve as the means by which goals are obtained while still others argue just the opposite. For our purpose a goal is defined as an open-ended statement which is expressed in broad terms describing some "state" the firm wishes to achieve. It is not bounded in time nor is it specific in any measurement sense. Such statements as being "a good corporate citizen," "a fair employer," "serving customers with high-quality products," and a "maximizer of profits" are examples.

Objectives, on the other hand, are measures of desired results and, as such, are comprised of four components—the desired attribute or result, a progress index, a target measure, and the time frame within which the target is to be achieved. Hofer and Schendel provide examples of some typical business objectives in Table 1.

The main value of a goal is that it is useful as a way of arriving at an objective. For example, the goal of a high quality product can be made into an objective by indicating its specific attributes or, as in the above table, relating it to competition. Goals also have merit in providing motivation to managers and employees. The AT&T goal of building a ". . . good, cheap, fast, worldwide telephone service for everyone" is cited as such an example.[1]

TABLE 1.

Possible Attributes	Possible Indexes	Targets and Time Frame		
		Year 1	Year 2	Year 3
Growth	$ Sales	$100 mil.	$120 mil.	$140 mil.
	Unit sales	X units	1.10 X units	1.20 X units
Efficiency	$ Profits	10 mil.	12 mil.	15 mil.
	Profits/sales	.10	.10	.10
Utilization of resources	ROI	.15	.15	.16
	ROE	.25	.26	.27
Contribution to owners	Dividends	$1.00/share	$1.10/share	$1.30/share
	EPS	$2.00/share	$2.40/share	$2.80/share
Contribution to customers	Price, quality reliability	Equal or better than competition	Equal or better than competition	Equal or better than competition
Contributions to employees	Wage rate employment stability	$3.50 @ hr. < 5% turning	$3.74 @ hr. < 4% turning	$4.00 @ hr. < 4% turning
Contributions to society	Taxes paid, scholarships, etc.	$10 mil. $100,000	$12 mil. $120,000	$16 mil. $120,000

Source: Charles W. Hofer and Dan Schendel, *Strategy Formulation: Analytical Concepts* (New York: West Publishing Company, 1978), p. 21.

Most firms have multiple objectives. Drucker, in an effort to balance the long run versus the short run, advocates that firms have objectives in eight key areas. These are market standing, profitability, innovation, productivity, physical and financial resources, manager performance and development, worker performance and attitude, and public responsibility.[2] The use of multiple objectives raises the question of internal consistency; that is, the obtaining of one objective must not preclude the obtaining of any other objective. For example, an improvement in market share in a fast growth situation is not likely to be accompanied by increased profits and a more positive cash flow. Further, objectives must be consistent with "reality"; e.g., if the ROI objective is twice that experienced on average by the industry, then there would be good reason to question its validity. In a similar vein the objectives must be "logical" in terms of the firm's resources and the anticipated dynamics of the environments in which it operates.

ECONOMIC OBJECTIVES

Typically the firm's overriding objectives are stated in economic terms. This assumes that profit maximization is the firm's primary consideration or rationale for existence. This is understandable, given that historically the firm has been viewed as an economic unit—the efficiency of which is measured on the basis of the returns generated by the capital invested. Indeed, the very essence of micro-economic theory is premised on the assumption that the rational firm will seek to maximize the return on its capital. Disagreement among those who adhere to the profit maximization school is mainly centered on which efficiency measures to use.

There are, of course, many business scholars who assert strongly that a firm's social responsibility goes far beyond profit maximization. They challenge Friedman who believes that any business objective other than that of profit maximization will undermine the foundation of our free society.[3] The social objectives argument that the market place should not be the sole means for judging the contributions made by a firm to society is hard to ignore.[4] The problem is that if the firm's primary objective is not economic, then how does it determine how best to allocate its resources?

Given the depth and complexity of social problems, most firms would be hard pressed to determine what would be the best way to attempt to solve them. Thus, we urge that social responsibilities over and beyond those concerned with the firm's legal (regulatory) framework not be made part of its business objectives. Rather, we suggest that the firm *first* strive to maximize its profitability and *second* to undertake to discharge those social responsibilities—either alone or in concert with others—which are acceptable to its various stockholders.

PROFITABILITY MEASURES AS
ALLOCATION CRITERIA

Economic objectives are usually expressed in terms of one or more profitability measures such as return on investment (either equity or total assets), earnings per share, profit after taxes, and profits as a percentage of net sales. Some companies state their longer term objectives in the form of variables which, if achieved, will lead to greater profits; e.g., increased sales or market share. Some elaborate their objectives in the form of debt-equity ratios, dividends, and debt retirement. Most factor a per annum growth rate into their sales and profit-after-taxes measures. Because of the high cost of capital and inflation, more and more companies are including cash flow among their set of economic objectives. Some managers will trade off a higher cash flow for a lower rate of return given the difficulty of effecting change without cash. When the firm's future environment is uncertain, managers will opt for flexibility objectives which typically include R&D strength, number of fertile technologies in which the firm has expertise, number of independent segments serviced, and liquidity.

While almost all companies use a variety of economic measures, the dominant one is concerned with profitability as determined on the basis of either equity or total assets employed. Any chief executive officer has to have as one of the primary objectives a "satisfactory" return to the stockholder. This is typically expressed as a return on equity or earnings per share. A return on assets employed or managed measure is used as a way of guiding and evaluating the firm's profit center or strategic business unit managers. The logic here is that the manager of such a unit should be responsible for earning a satisfactory return on the assets granted to the division. Thus, the manager and the subordinates are highly motivated to generate maximum profits—and, of course, expect to be rewarded accordingly.

Given the firm's overall profitability objective—a return on investment measure—the typical procedure is to factor it into the firm's capital budgeting system in an attempt to discriminate between investment requests within and between strategic business units. Inevitably, the use of a single rate of return measure will mean that some divisions will not be successful in obtaining their "share" of the corporation's resources. This will prove dysfunctional to those divisions which are mandated to grow or "turn around" as a result of the strategic plan which is based largely on the opportunities and threats emerging from the changing environment. Quite obviously the overall rate also affects the decision as to what businesses the firm wishes to pursue; i.e., its business definition. Thus, we note the interdependence between objectives and business definition and the need to link them strategically.

There is also the operational question of how the assets managed figure is derived. One obvious problem is that the use of a single rate of return measure of a strategic business unit's performance is that it does not discriminate between investments which bear different risks; e.g., an inventory build-up can typically be liquidated more easily than can an increase in machinery and equipment. Nor does a single rate treat costs as part of an interdependent system. Thus, new machinery could well improve quality and thereby lower sales and service costs. Further, when a gross book value is used as the basis for determining the worth of assets employed, the manager involved could improve performance by scrapping a fixed asset which still has a value or by lowering his inventory even if this lowered sales. If net book value is used, then a unit's investment base declines over time, thereby providing an automatic increase in the division's return on investment.

The use of such measures as the basis for reward and punishment causes many unit managers to take actions which are more oriented towards the short than the long run. Thus, managers may sacrifice future earnings to show a satisfactory short-term profit by reducing R&D, sales, and advertising expenses.

MEASURING FUTURE PROFITABILITY

The inherent problem with the use of "long-run profit maximization" (the present value of future profits) as the firm's primary economic objective is that at best it is difficult to measure *present* profits. Even when this is accomplished satisfactorily, the results may not be a good indication of future profits. As we have earlier noted, it is not overly difficult to improve short-term profitability in ways which may seriously endanger longer-term profits.

In the long run a firm's profitability is largely a function of how it copes with the impact of environmental changes on its investment units. It does so by altering its present allocations between units and by adding and/or subtracting products, markets, or both. In making its investment decisions the firm is guided by its assessment of the investment climate for each unit as well as its relative ability (distinctive competency) to exploit it. If we define investment units as product-market relationships, then what is needed is a measure of the relationship between them. Market share is increasingly used as such a measure since it ties the product directly to the market served and, in the process, tells something about the firm's competitive position. Market share can, therefore, be used as a strategic market objective in its own right and as such is directional in nature in terms of the investments to be made.

Market share is determined by dividing company sales of a given product by industry sales for the market served. Share data can be computed using physical units or dollars. While the former "method" is preferred because of the precision possible, the latter is often used because of its ready availability from secondary sources. The difficulty here is that one is not always sure of what level of product-type aggregation is involved.

For market share to serve as a valid indicator of longer-term profitability, it would have to be highly correlated with return on investment. While it has long been believed that such was true, it was not until the PIMS (Profit Impact of Marketing Strategies) study that we had strong empirical evidence over a wide range of businesses to not only verify this conclusion, but to shed light on why it occurred.[5]

The PIMS study found that absolute market share was strongly correlated with product profitability as measured by pretax ROI. On the average each difference of 10 share points is associated with a difference of about 5 ROI percentage points (see Exhibit 1 for these relationships).

There are several commonsense explanations why we would, on average, expect high share businesses to yield higher ROI's than low share businesses. First, there is the assumed inverse relationship between share and per unit costs due to scale and learning effects. The Boston Consulting Group has combined these two effects into what they call the "experience curve." Their proposition is that every time the firm's accumulated sales double per unit costs (based on value added) drop between 20 and 30% as expressed in real dollars. Thus, cumulative relative share (firm's share divided by that of the industry leader) will be closely correlated with relative per unit costs and have a direct bearing on profitability.

EXHIBIT 1. Relationship between Market Share (Absolute) and Pretax ROI

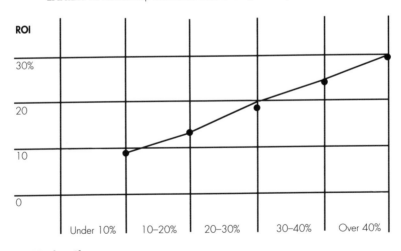

Market Share

Source: Robert D. Buzzell, Bradley T. Gale, and Ralph G.M. Sultan, "Market share—A Key to Profitability, " *Harvard Business Review*, January-February, 1975, p. 98.

A second reason why higher profitability derives from high share is a better "fit" between the product and the served market. This can be due to higher product quality in a physical sense and/or better services. Often the higher perceived quality permits charging a premium price. And, third, there is the possibility of market power which enables the dominant firm to earn higher profits because of its ability to police the industry (administer prices) and bargain more effectively with suppliers.

It must be noted that the above fails to take into account the position of the product in the life cycle. Yet stage in the life cycle should affect both profitability and cash flow. Thus, products with high shares during the growth stage will tend to generate negative cash flows and lower profitability than will the same product during the mature stage. Also, different kinds and amounts of expenditures are associated with different stages in the product life cycle. This is certainly the case with such marketing costs as those having to do with product development, advertising, channel/account development, and the building of a sales force.

Despite this difficulty market share is used by some managers as a proxy measure for future profitability and hence serves as the basis for setting objectives. The latter are stated in the form of "change"; i.e., increasing, holding, or harvesting share. The former is most likely to be adopted when the market is growing while the holding or maintaining relates to a stable market situation. Harvesting or disinvestment is recommended mainly when the market is declining or when the firm cannot finance the necessary growth required to make the product viable on a relative cost basis.

The use of market share measures as objectives, however, inevitably gives rise to the thorny question of how the firm defines its business, and, in particular, its served markets. Without such a definition a market share measure cannot even be calculated. It is also true that business definition affects the choice of a given share objective as is the case when a firm redefines its product-market scope to take advantage of opportunities presented in the form of new segments. Under such conditions the firm would inevitably set new share and cash flow objectives. This is not to suggest that objectives do not affect business definition since profitability is at the heart of any investment decision relating to the scope and direction of the business. Because objectives and business definition are so highly interrelated, it is necessary to discuss the latter subject further. This is the purpose of the next section.

BUSINESS DEFINITION

Objectives are important in setting the level of economic performance the firm seeks to attain. For them to be used effectively requires a resource allocation process which permits the firm to deploy its resources across its investment centers in its efforts to achieve success.

In the aggregate these centers define the firm's business. Thus, from an operational point of view, objectives and a definition of the business are inseparable.

Business definition—sometimes called business purpose or concept of the business—has long been of interest to marketing scholars. Drucker and Levitt, in particular, have advocated the dominance of the market place in such a definition. The former argues persuasively that the purpose of the firm is to ". . . create a customer."[6] Levitt elaborates this notion by urging firms to define themselves not in terms of the products they sell, but by the functions such products perform. Since needs remain relatively constant over time while products are often rendered obsolete by technological change, such a concept helps ensure the firm's continuing vitality. Thus, it is argued, had the railroads conceptualized themselves as being in the transportation rather than in the railroad business, they would have continued to prosper.[7]

The difficulty with defining a business solely on the basis of product function lies in its lack of specificity. To define a firm's business as being "transportation" is to do so in such a generalized way as to make it impossible for management to formulate strategy. Does being in the "transportation" business imply a product line consisting of trains, cars, trucks, ships, airplanes, taxis, busses, and helicopters serving a variety of customer groups including individuals, families, business firms, and the government?[8]

The strategy literature—starting in the mid 1960s—sought to provide greater specificity by defining a business in terms of its product-market scope. Following along these lines the end goal of the strategic planning process was conceptualized as being a best yield portfolio or mix of products and markets.[9] This view of the business and the strategic planning process implicitly recognizes product-market relationships as investment units; further, that their aggregation represents a definition of the business which changes over time.

BUSINESS DEFINITION DIMENSIONS

In more recent years attempts have been made to define the business in ways which will provide the firm with a competitive superiority based largely on the dynamics of the firm's product-market environment. In particular, there has been increasing awareness of market segments as a way of defining and understanding market opportunities and threats. For the most part the dimensions used include customer groups (market segments), customer needs, products, and technology. The use of these dimensions is an extension of product-market scope since markets can be defined in terms of needs and products in terms of their technology. This elaboration is, however, important since it provides a way of integrating products and markets and, in the process, understanding their relationships from the customer's point of view.

If segments can be defined, first, in terms of their needs and, second, on the basis of their identifying characteristics (e.g., demographics, lifestyle, and geographical location), then the first two dimensions can be merged. Needs can be defined in either broad (generic) or specific terms. The more general the need is stated the more difficult it is for the firm to deploy its resources; e.g., almost everyone needs "transportation," but in what form?

A definition of needs—if it is to be useful—must be specific as to what goals/objectives the consumer wishes to attain and/or what problem solutions are being sought. Since most consumers use a system consisting of labor, products, and machines to "solve" a problem, the ascertainment of needs—there is usually more than one—in measurable form is rarely easy. Further, needs will often vary depending upon the use environment.

Some illustrations may help clarify the above. Consumers, in general, have the need to clean their teeth. They do so in an effort to attain such goals as those pertaining to appearance (white teeth), health (tooth decay prevention), and social acceptance (lack of mouth odor). In the case of overseas travel such needs as time in route, safety, comfort, and the convenience and punctuality of departure and arrival times, are presumably critical to most passengers. In a similar way food packers have a need to protect their product in transit and in storage against damage, loss of freshness and appearance, taste deterioration and shrinkage.

In an effort to solve a problem, the consumer (either household or industrial) employs a decision process which matches products to needs. This consists of the development of choice criteria by which needs are translated into a set of ideal choice criteria. The latter reflect the product characteristics or attributes the consumer feels are necessary to meet his/her needs. Product alternatives are, therefore, evaluated on the basis of whether they possess the desired attributes as well as the extent to which each is of value to the consumer. For certain needs, the above process takes place within different use settings, thereby giving rise to different choice criteria.

Given the above, need segments can be derived at a number of different levels of aggregation; e.g., use environment, product class, product type, and brand levels. In the case of our transportation example, segments (groups of potential customers) could be structured around business versus vacation and international versus domestic travel (different use situations), product class (airplane, ships, railroads, and automobiles), product type (international versus domestic carrier and plane type—747/DC10/L1011 versus 707/DC8), and brand (TWA, Pan Am, BA, and Air France). The existence of a given segment would be based on the extent to which a sufficient size group possessed a different set of choice criteria. The size of the segment would depend upon the extent to which the firm deemed it necessary to have high homogeneity within versus heterogeneity between segments. One can, of course, carry segmentation too far. Segments must be large enough to justify the economics required to be treated differently.

If we first segment on the basis of different choice criteria (presence of different attributes and/or different values attached to individual attributes), then we need to identify the individuals belonging to each segment. The resulting groups are called operational segments. For consumer goods these are mostly based on demographics, lifestyle, and geography while for industrial products these are based on account size and geography.

The choice criteria of the various segments provide the basis for the firm's product line decisions as well as those pertaining to the physical (including price) and service dimensions of the individual product. The closer the product's characteristics are perceived to be similar to the choice criteria of the target segment, the higher the probability of its being purchased. Brand share should, therefore, be closely tied to the brand's relative rating vis-à-vis the choice criteria.

Technology in a broad sense can be thought of as the resources (including skills) required to design, manufacture, and market that "utility package" which best meets the needs (choice criteria) of a customer group (segment). It needs to be emphasized here that technology does apply to marketing. This is particularly true for many consumer goods where the determinants of market share are largely those skills related to product design and product development, advertising, and merchandising. Thought of in this light the choice of products and their characteristics become a function of how technology is applied to meeting needs. Thus, we can drop product(s) as one of the business definition dimensions.

Hopefully, the above discussion has provided a way of linking customer groups, customer needs, and technology both conceptually and operationally. Collectively they serve as the essence of how a business defines itself. The tighter the linkages the more precise the definition and the greater the chance for the business definition to be successful. What has not yet been discussed, however, is the extent to which the firm wishes to engage in serving multiple customer needs and customer groups. Usually referred to in terms of "scope," such decisions clearly affect the business definition and are the subject of the next section.

SCOPE AND BUSINESS DEFINITION

Most business definitions have typically relied on some kind of a product-market *scope* measure. Abell elaborates this concept by advocating that businesses be defined by applying scope and differentiation measures to the three dimensions. "Scope" he defines on the basis of being focused or narrow with respect to customers served, their needs, and the technologies employed.[10] Differentiation has two meanings; first, the extent to which a business treats one or more of the three dimensions differently and, second, the extent of difference between the offerings of two or more competitors. Clearly the first meaning is simply another way of implying broad scope.

Perhaps a more meaningful way of looking at a way of classifying alternative business definitions is to apply only the focus and differentiation (first meaning) to the three dimensions. This simpler typology omits the extent to which the firm differentiates itself from competitors. One can argue that the decision to do this makes no great difference since competitive offerings have already been taken into account in the way the firm has differentiated its offerings across its segments. Further, a firm will take competitive offerings into account in deciding which business definition to opt for.

The modified typology contains eight different ways of defining the business as follows:

Business Definition Category	Customer Groups	Customer Needs	Technologies
1.	Focused	Focused	Focused
2.	Focused	Focused	Differentiated
3.	Focused	Differentiated	Focused
4.	Focused	Differentiated	Differentiated
5.	Differentiated	Focused	Focused
6.	Differentiated	Focused	Differentiated
7.	Differentiated	Differentiated	Focused
8.	Differentiated	Differentiated	Differentiated

Most businesses start out by using a highly-focused approach. Some firms continue to employ such a narrow scope even though it involves high risk since a change in any of the dimensions can pose a substantial threat. Examples here include specialized suppliers to the automobile industry. Success is largely a function of volume, the ability to reap the benefits of the experience curve, and a product which is closely linked to buyer specifications. The more unique the need and tailored the product, the greater the protection afforded the high share seller since little or no cost advantages will accrue to firms servicing broader groups and/or needs.

Category two consists of using two or more technologies to service a customer group, the members of which have the same needs. This can happen when a business is in a state of transition regarding its technologies (e.g., electronic versus mechanical). The use of more than technology is present in tennis today where players are confronted with an array of wood, plastic, and metal rackets. In such a case one could argue that groups and their needs are too broadly defined; that segments exist, but cannot be defined operationally.

Category three is concerned with servicing the multiple needs of a single customer group using a single technology. Examples here include the increased versatility built into hand-held calculators, hi-fi units which both record and play, and security systems which guard against fire and theft. Closely-related technologies are used by many companies to generate a host of products serving different yet related needs of the same group; e.g., laundry and cleaning products.

Category four is less focused than the earlier three since different technologies are used to service different needs of the same customer group. Examples include many household products companies which sell a variety of product classes to the American housewife; e.g., P&G, which sells laundry, paper, food, and beverage items; Gillette, which sells razors and personal care items to men; and General Electric, which sells both small and major appliances besides radios and television sets to much the same households.

Category five involves selling essentially the same product to meet the same needs of a variety of customer groups. Examples include firms selling such products as office supplies, paper, metals, plastics, electric motors, and computers across customer groups (end users). Most large packaged food and beverage companies sell to both households and commercial customers.

Category six involves the use of different technologies to service the same need of multiple groups. Of necessity this definition requires a broad definition of need. The use of specially formulated paints (protective coatings), and the production of a variety of floor (cork, vinyl, and wood) and wall coverings (paint and wallpaper) are examples here.

Category seven seeks to serve the multiple needs of more than one customer group via one product. Versatility is the order of the day here; e.g., tractors which can fulfill a variety of needs for farmers and road builders. The last category involves differences across all three dimensions and is more likely to apply at the corporate rather than the business level.

The weakness in the business definition classification scheme discussed lies in its inability to specify the degree of difference existing between multiple customer groups, needs, and technologies. The broader the definitions the less the differences. In contrast the more a firm tends to define its customer groups on the basis of their choice criteria the more precise will be the business definition and the greater the number of customer groups.

Business definitions can and do change over time primarily because of market evolution. Thus, a focused definition is appropriate early on in the product life cycle, but its relevancy decreases over time as market fragmentation occurs. Clearly, the more differentiated the firm the more life cycles are involved, thereby in turn affecting business definition. In any event, using the same framework as discussed above enables the firm to redefine itself. Thus, change can occur in seven ways:[11]

1. In customer groups
2. In customer needs
3. In technologies
4. In customer groups and customer needs
5. In customer groups and technologies
6. In customer needs and technologies
7. In all three

When thought of in terms of change, the business mix the firm aspires to becomes an objective in its own right. It is certainly directional in nature with respect to investments even to the extent of defining—at least broadly—where and how they must be made. If strategy is thought of largely as a change in product-market scope, then any change in business definition derives from strategy. The two—strategy and business definition—are, therefore, intimately related.

A precise definition of the business is critical if the proper functional area strategy decisions are to be made. The more broadly a firm defines itself the greater the impact is likely to be on marketing. This is particularly true with regard to its advertising, sales, and distribution strategies. If segments are defined using choice criteria, then the strategies relating to the servicing of the need(s) are more easily defined; i.e., the basis used for linking customer groups and their needs is highly diagnostic and facilitates the development of viable R&D, product and product line, price, channels, advertising, and personal selling decisions.

SUMMARY AND CONCLUSIONS

Marketing plays a key role in the establishment of the firm's objectives. Traditionally, these have been defined using a variety of economic measures of which some index of profitability is the single most important measure. Because of the difficulties inherent in forecasting future profitability, many firms have turned to the use of market share as a proxy measure of future profitability. Thus, objectives are often stated in terms of increasing share, maintaining share, and harvesting. The PIMS report shows that there is a high positive correlation between market share and pretax return on investment.

Market share measures require a precise understanding of both products and markets serviced. These, in turn, form the basis for the way the business defines itself. Indeed, without such a definition it is hardly possible for the firm to determine market share and the profitability of its product-market investment units. Thus, there is a strong interrelationship between objectives and business definition.

The most recent thinking centers on the use of three dimensions (customer group, customer needs, and technology) as the bases for defining a business. When scope (focus versus differentiation) measures are applied to these three dimensions, then seven different business definitions emerge, each of which has its own advantages and disadvantages.

The tighter the firm is able to link the three dimensions the more likely it is to have a business definition which leads to success and is capable of changing to meet new opportunities and threats. Further, business definition is essential if the proper functional area strategies are to emerge. This is particularly true in marketing where critically important strategic decisions pertaining to product, price, channels, advertising, and personal selling must be made.

NOTES

1. Charles H. Granger, "The Hierarchy of Objectives," *Harvard Business Review*, May–June, 1964, p. 66.
2. Peter F. Drucker, *The Practice of Management* (New York: Harper and Row, 1954).
3. Milton Friedman, *Capitalism and Freedom* (Chicago: The University of Chicago Press, 1962), p. 133.
4. Andrew Shonfield, *Modern Capitalism: The Changing Balance of Public and Private Power* (New York: Oxford University Press, 1965), p. 227.
5. Robert D. Buzzel, Bradley T. Gale, and Ralph G. M. Sulton, "Marketing Share—A Key to Profitability," *Harvard Business Review*, January–February, 1975. Also see Strategic Planning Institute, "Market Position: Build, Hold or Harvest," Pimsletter number 3 (Cambridge, MA, 1977).
6. Drucker, *op. cit.*, p. 37.
7. Theodore Levitt, *Innovation in Marketing: New Perspective for Profit and Growth* (New York: McGraw-Hill, 1962), pp. 63–71.
8. H. Igor Ansoff, *Corporate Strategy* (New York: McGraw-Hill, 1965), p. 107.
9. Charles O. Rossotti, "Two Concepts of Long-Range Planning: A Special Commentary" (Boston: The Boston Consulting Group, N.D.).
10. Derek F. Abell, *Defining the Business* (Englewood Cliffs, N.J.: Prentice-Hall, Inc., 1980), Chapter 7. 11. *Ibid.*

REFERENCES

Roger W. Brooksbank, *Marketing Intelligence and Planning*, "Marketing Planning: A Seven-Stage Process," 1990, pp. 21–28.

Yash P. Gupta, Subhash C. Lonial, W. Glynn Mangold, *International Journal of Operations and Production Management*, "An Examination of the Relationship between Marketing Strategy and Marketing Objectives," 1991, pp. 33–43.

Gregory S. Carpenter
Associate Professor of Marketing
Richard M. Clewett Research Professor
J. L. Kellogg Graduate School of Management
Northwestern University
Evanston, Illinois

Kent Nakamoto
Assistant Professor of Marketing
Graduate School of Business
University of Colorado
Boulder, Colorado

CHAPTER 2

BRAND DOMINANCE: COMPETITIVE ADVANTAGE THROUGH CONSUMER LEARNING

INTRODUCTION

In many markets, competition produces a remarkable outcome: One brand outsells all others not just for a short time but sometimes for decades. Wrigley's chewing gum, Gerber baby food, Kleenex tissues, and others have retained the largest shares of their markets for years. Empirical studies demonstrate that this observation is true among brands that dominate a market early in its life—so-called market pioneers (Robinson and Fornell 1985; Urban, et al. 1986)—and among high market share brands in general (Hambrick, MacMillan, and Day 1982).

The persistent dominance of these brands challenges the traditional view of competition, in which successful brands attract new competitors offering improved products or, at the very least, equivalent products at lower prices, eventually reducing the dominant brand's market share. Indeed, dominant brands retain their high market shares *despite* successful new product introductions, shifting consumer tastes, and changing technology. Some even thrive as a result of new competition. Coca-Cola's market share, for instance, *increased* following the initiation of the so-called cola wars by Pepsi with its Pepsi Challenge.

We explore what creates and sustains such an enduring advantage in this chapter. Our explanation focuses on consumer preference and choice. The traditional view of consumer choice in markets dominated by a single brand is that buyers choose brands based on actual or perceived attributes and price relationships according to their (fixed, predetermined) preferences (Schmalensee 1982). Of course actual consumer behavior in these markets is much more complex. The dominant brand is perceptually distinctive, adding complexity to simple assessments of attributes and price. Buyer preferences are affected by the order in which buyers learn about brands (Carpenter and Nakamoto 1989), and consumer tastes are neither predetermined nor fixed (Tversky, Sattath, and Slovic 1988). We are not born with brand preferences but *learn* our preferences through experiences with brands. This process, called *preference formation*, is central to the creation of buyer preferences, resulting in a persistent competitive advantage for a dominant brand. The following paragraphs describe this preference formation process and how brand dominance influences it, creating such an advantage.

Once a competitive advantage is created one must ask, What sustains it? What protects a dominant brand, for instance, from low-priced competitors offering equivalent products (so-called me-too brands)? We turn to the competitive implications of consumer preference formation to address this question. At the heart of any explanation for dominant brand advantage is a model of consumer decision making. In the traditional view of competition where buyers choose based on simple attribute-price relationships according to fixed preferences, a high market share can be sustained if competitors offering more value can be deterred from entering the market (Encaoua, Geroski, and Jacquemin 1986).

In contrast, a consumer preference formation view of competition suggests a very different competitive process. Rather than having fixed, predetermined preferences, buyers *learn* their preferences, and the process of preference formation creates a preference structure favoring the dominant brand. This learning process, more complex than simple attribute-price comparisons, is strongly influenced by the dominant brand. It can *define* the ideal product and become the standard of comparison for all other brands, affecting the perceived value of every brand. Moreover, this preference structure, once created, is difficult to alter. Therefore, consumer learning yields a preference structure that favors the dominant brand, is slow to change, and is difficult for competitors to alter, producing a persistent dominant brand advantage.

We will explore consumer preference formation and its competitive implications in three stages. First, we will consider how brand dominance influences the formation of consumer preferences. We will consider how initial experiences with a brand influence subsequent brand preference and the role of brand dominance in that process. Next, we will discuss how that same process creates consumer preferences that make reducing the high share of the dominant brand difficult for competitors. Finally, we will explore the strategic implications of consumer preference formation and the competitive advantage it creates.

CONSUMER PREFERENCE FORMATION

Consumer Learning

Memory for product information or past usage experience has a profound impact on consumer decisions. For example, knowledgeable consumers appear to rely more heavily on brands as foci for organizing product information and on categories and subcategories as bases for grouping brands (Bettman 1986; Johnson and Russo 1984; Sujan 1985). In addition, choice experience results in selective retention of brand information favoring chosen brands (Biehal and Chakravarti 1982). This selective retention continues to favor previously chosen brands even if a previously inferior brand is improved through addition of a new attribute (Biehal and Chakravarti 1983). Thus choice affects memory, and memory in turn affects choice.

Because of this ongoing interaction of experience and preference, the order of a consumer's product experiences can affect choices over time. Changing the order of experiences, even if they are the same in aggregate, changes product perceptions and preferences. Brands a consumer is exposed to first influence the structure of the consumer's preferences in the category and can become perceptually and preferentially dominant for the consumer. Two archetypal situations in which order of experience plays a significant role are especially interesting. In the first case, consumers enter a market consisting of a largely fixed set of brands; in the second case, brands sequentially enter a largely stable market of consumers. The first case is typical of mature markets, and the second case is more likely to be found in emerging markets or emerging segments of mature markets.

Sequential Consumer Entry. Consider a market in which new consumers enter, older ones exit, but the available brands are largely stable. One example is the toothpaste market; although new brands have successfully entered, the major brands remain largely the same, and new consumers are constantly entering the market. If one brand dominates such a market, an entering consumer's initial product experiences are likely to include it because of its wide availability and common use. An extreme version of this would occur if one's experience were limited to a single brand for an extended period of time. For instance, one might grow up in a household where one brand is regularly used for whatever reason (e.g., a "Crest household"). Exposure to a dominant brand will bias learning. Growing up in a Crest household will lead to a different learning experience with regard to toothpaste than growing up in a household where either a variety of brands or one other brand was regularly used.

Sequential Brand Entry. Another important situation is that presented by brands sequentially entering a market consisting of a static set of customers. Consumers' initial experiences will be limited to early entering brands by default. These brands can significantly affect the consumer learning experience. In the nondairy dessert toppings market, for instance, eighteen years elapsed between the introduction of Cool Whip and a comparable competitor. The category was defined by Cool Whip, and consumers' knowledge of it was biased by that limited definition of the category. Regardless of whether learning is biased by buyers or brands sequentially entering the market, early consumer experience is limited to a specific subset of the brands ultimately available and experienced in the category.

Consumer Learning and Preference

Consumer learning about the category is likely to bias preferences in favor of this subset of brands for two reasons. First, prior to experience, consumers may know little about the importance of attributes ortheir ideal combination. For example, one hundred years ago, few people were likely to have strong opinions about how sweet or carbonated a cola should be. A successful early entrant can have a major influence on how attributes are valued and on the ideal attribute combination. Coca-Cola, for example, may have had a significant impact in its early years on the formation and evolution of individuals' preferences for colas. This influence shifts individuals' preferences to favor the brands tried first.

Second, these brands are likely to be strongly associated with and highly representative of the category and, therefore, highly salient. Exemplar theories of categorization (Medin and Schaffer 1978; Medin, Altom, and Murphy 1984) suggest that these brands become exemplars or "standards" against which new brands are compared. Moreover, for goal-directed categories (of which product categories would be one example), the "goodness" of an item as a member of the category is a function of the relative proximity of an object's features to category ideals and the frequency with which an item has been experienced as a member of the category (Barsalou 1985). Brands experienced first will likely be seen as ideal (because preferences form around them) and they will have been experienced more frequently than others, so they can become strong standards of comparison.

This is especially true in product categories where the contribution of product attributes or features to overall brand value and the ideal attribute combination are ambiguous. For example, if one purchases a down quilt and receives a certain measure of value from it, the contribution of the percentage of goose down fill to that overall value is ambiguous. Other examples include the flavoring of soft drinks, features of computer programs, and combinations of ingredients in vitamins. Under these conditions, brands that consumers sample first, whether because of a brand's early market entry or its current high market share, will be favored. The impact of experience on consumer preferences will be much lower if the value of attributes and their ideal combination are unambiguous or readily observed.

Preference Structure

To see how early trial affects preference more formally, consider a consumer's experience before and after trial. Prior to trial, consumer preferences are likely to be weakly formed because the category is novel. The value of an individual attribute or the superiority of one attribute combination over another may not be obvious even if buyers have objective information on brand attributes (Howard 1989; Howard and Sheth 1969). Consider home robots, an emerging market. Few buyers know much about the relative value of home robot attributes or of the ideal combination of them. As a result, individuals may be indifferent about alternatives within a relevant range. In a two-attribute market the distribution of ideal points or vectors across consumers would be approximately uniform, as shown in Exhibit 1a. The average ideal will be located in the center of the market, as shown in Exhibit 1b. Attribute weights used to value brands will also be tentative.

Buyers update their preferences through trial. Sampling an early entrant in an emerging market or the dominant brand in an established market, a consumer may associate a successful outcome with the attribute combination of the tried brand, lacking information to the contrary (Meyer 1987). In doing so, buyers develop a naive theory relating brand attributes to value, which advertising and repeat purchasing reinforce (Hoch and Ha 1986; Deighton 1984). Having used one home robot model that is highly rugged for extensive outdoor use, for instance, one might infer that one's satisfaction is due in large measure to the robot's unique attributes; continued use and advertising reinforce this belief. Thus buyers learn through trial how to value attribute combinations, but if a trial is limited to a dominant brand, updated preferences will favor it.

Consumer learning leads individuals to shift their ideal points toward the position of the tried brand, as shown in Exhibit 2. Both the

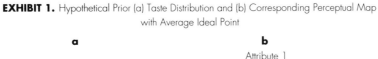

EXHIBIT 1. Hypothetical Prior (a) Taste Distribution and (b) Corresponding Perceptual Map with Average Ideal Point

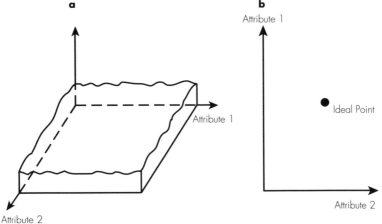

EXHIBIT 2. Hypothetical (a) Taste Distribution and (b) Perceptual Map Updated after Trial
of the Dominant Brand

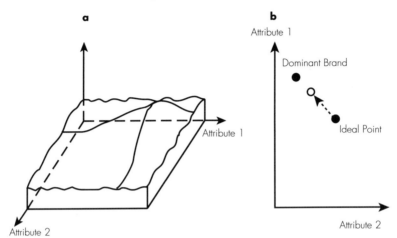

taste distribution and average ideal point shift toward the brand's location. This shift occurs *independent of the brand's characteristics*
because of the ambiguity in attribute valuation.

This shift in preferences also defines attribute trade-offs buyers
use, which is the relative importance of attributes in product evaluation. For example, in Exhibit 2, the location of the dominant brand
implies that attribute 1 should be more important in evaluation than
attribute 2. Again, the attribute importances favor the trade-offs adopted by the dominant brand. Consistent with this mechanism, Carpenter
and Nakamoto (1989, Study 1) found that the location of the average
ideal point for consumers shifts in the direction of the location of the
dominant (or pioneering) brand. In addition, they showed (Study 2)
that the relative importance weights of attributes reflect the strengths of
the dominant brand.

In sum, the processes of consumer learning and preference formation lead to rules of competition, reflecting consumer preferences,
slanted in favor of a dominant brand. The dominant brand has not so
much *found* a preferred position as *created* one.

COMPETITIVE ADVANTAGE

Perceptual Distinctiveness

Dominant brands have an additional important advantage over later entering competitors—perceptual distinctiveness. Because they are experienced, first, and perhaps more often, dominant brands attain *category dominance* (Farquhar, Herr, and Fazio 1990). They are more naturally salient for the typical consumer—strongly associated with and highly representative of the product category. Indeed, they are often *cognitively inseparable* from the category and come to mind more quickly and reliably than other brands when the category is mentioned (e.g., Kleenex tissues, Levi's jeans). As such, these brands become *cognitive referents* for consumers (Medin and Schaffer 1978; Sujan 1985).

Recent studies present evidence consistent with this general view. Kardes and Kalyanaram (1990) cite information integration findings showing that the amount of information in memory regarding a brand will influence the extremity of its evaluation and the consumer's confidence in that evaluation. They show that the brand first encountered has an advantage both in terms of recall of brand information and preference over later encountered brands, even if a later encountered brand is superior. Consumers simply have more information about dominant brands in memory, and it is more accessible, increasing evaluation of these brands at the cost of later entering brands about which consumers retain less information.

Competitive Implications

The competitive implications of category dominance are profound. It makes the preferred position occupied by the dominant brand very difficult to assail. A me-too product, despite its similarity to the dominant brand, will suffer in comparison. The more similar the me-too and dominant brands, the *greater* the relative prominence of the dominant brand. Thus preferences for the dominant brand are *asymmetric*; greater similarity between a competitor and the dominant brand *increases* valuation of the dominant brand and *decreases* valuation of the competitor. In the case of a me-too brand, this is because the me-too brand derives its identity from the dominant brand, and this similarity reduces any distinctive value of the me-too brand. It is different simply because it is not the dominant brand, but since it has no distinctive competence it is inferior.

Consistent with this analysis, Carpenter and Nakamoto (1989, Study 1) found that the greater the perceived similarity between the dominant brand and a later entrant, the greater the preference advantage of the dominant brand. Moreover, compared to differentiated later entrants, me-too brands' price discounts were less valued (Study 2).

Brown and Lattin (1990) found further consistent evidence in market data—the longer a dominant brand preceded its competitors in the market, that is the longer consumers learned about it alone, the greater its competitive advantage.

Persistence

Once this preference structure is established, why does it persist? At one level the preference structure can be viewed as a schema, and once established consumers have no incentive to relearn these preferences. For instance, once we learn how to value home robot attributes, we have no incentive to revisit our decision and change preferences. Moreover, schema are difficult to alter even if consumers are confronted with disconfirming information (Bettman 1986; Fiske and Taylor 1984). If a competitor seeks to change the preference structure by suggesting that consumers are using the "wrong" criteria to evaluate brands, consumers will be reluctant to change preferences. Effecting change requires that a competitor present consumers with *overwhelming* evidence that a new preference structure is needed. For a nondominant brand, presenting such evidence is a daunting task. The preference structure established by the dominant brand often persists as a result.

An Example

This preference formation process and the resulting competitive advantage are well illustrated by Vaseline, which was introduced in 1880 and advertised as a healing agent of unsurpassed purity. Sampling Vaseline, a translucent, highly pure gel, buyers learned that its attributes produced an effective wound preparation and, generalizing from this observation, inferred that the effectiveness of petroleum jelly lies in its translucence and purity (in contrast to the competing black coal tar derivatives of the time). Subsequent trials and advertising of course confirmed this conjecture. Thus translucence came to be favored over opacity and gained more importance in brand evaluation. Moreover, all later brands were compared to Vaseline and found wanting even if identical simply because they were not Vaseline. This has produced a lasting competitive advantage.

STRATEGIC IMPLICATIONS

The implications of consumer preference formation for competitive marketing strategy are significant. Competitive advantage is traditionally viewed as arising from entry or mobility barriers erected by established firms through capacity expansion, advertising, or other strategic investments designed to make competition more costly for later entrants and thus deter competition (Encaoua, Geroski, and Jacquemin 1986; Porter 1985). So long as a cost differential persists, competitors will be deterred, and a high market share will be sustained.

Entry barriers can arise from a number of sources including product positioning (Lane 1980; Prescott and Visscher 1977). An early entrant may adopt the "best" market position, leaving smaller or less attractive segments for others. Located in less attractive positions, these smaller brands are at a competitive disadvantage, leading to the continued dominance of one brand if they cannot easily reposition. Switching costs created by uncertainty about later entrants' quality can have a similar impact on competition. If trial of the dominant brand is successful, trying an alternative is risky, forcing later entrants to cut prices or offer some premium to compensate for risk and induce trial. So long as trial of later entrants remains low and their quality remains unknown, the dominant brand will retain its high market share (Schmalensee 1982).

Empirical studies show that entry barriers are an important source of competitive advantage (Robinson and Fornell 1985), but they also show that dominant brand advantages exist in markets where traditional entry barriers do not exclude competition. For example, Urban et al. (1986) show that Miller's Lite Beer retains its advantage even though conventional entry or mobility barriers did not deter competitors such as Budweiser and Schlitz. Buyers are aware of both brands, and brands can reposition. Thus competitive advantage must be sustained by something more than entry or mobility barriers.

Competitive advantage, in a consumer preference formation framework, arises because a brand influences the evolution of preferences and creates a *preference asymmetry* in doing so. Achieving market dominance, possibly by early successful entry, provides the opportunity to define the ideal combination of attributes and to create an asymmetric preference structure that limits the impact of competitors on the dominant brand's market share. The resulting competitive advantage persists even in cases where strategic investments are ineffective at creating cost differences and entry barriers in the traditional sense.

A particularly vivid example of the difference in approach is provided by the case of me-too brands. Conventional analysis argues that me-too brands fail because of ruinous price competition; picking a position near the dominant brand and competing on price leads to lower prices for all and the elimination of high profits. In contrast, in a consumer learning framework, me-too strategies do not provoke a disastrous price war. Having positioned near the dominant brand with a low price, a me-too brand earns low profit. In fact, it poses no real threat to the dominant brand; it derives its identity from the dominant brand, but offering nothing unique except a low price (and that is not of central importance), a me-too brand will sell poorly (Carpenter and Nakamoto 1990). Thus me-too brands do not "fail" so much as languish.

CONCLUSION

Consumer preference formation suggests a view of competition and strategy that differs significantly from the conventional view. Brand dominance, in that view, indicates exceptional profits, attracts new competitors, leads to lower prices, and eliminates dominant brand advantage. Brand strategy is designed to erect barriers to that competition.

A consumer-learning view reflects a very different world. Brand dominance influences the evolution of buyer preferences and creates a *preference asymmetry* that persists because of the persistence of that learning. Competitive entry places little pressure on a dominant brand. Preferences are asymmetric, so greater similarity between a competitor and the dominant brand *increases* rather than *decreases* the dominant brand's market share. The dominant brand's market share advantage persists as a result.

Most fundamentally, this suggests a different view of competition in which brands *battle over* consumer preferences rather than simply responding to them. Competition in such a world becomes a struggle to define consumer preferences with the winner receiving a tremendously valuable asset—a favorable, asymmetric preference structure—producing a persistent dominant brand advantage.

REFERENCES

Barsalou, Lawrence W. 1985. Ideals, central tendency, and frequency of instantiation as determinants of graded structure in categories. *Journal of Experimental Psychology: Learning, Memory and Cognition*, 11 (October):629–55.

Bettman, James R. 1986. Consumer psychology. *Annual Review of Psychology*, 37:257–89.

Biehal, Gabriel, and Dipankar Chakravarti. 1983. Information accessibility as a moderator of consumer choice. *Journal of Consumer Research*, 10 (June):1–14.

_____ . 1982. Information presentation format and learning goals as determinants of consumer memory-retrieval and choice processes. *Journal of Consumer Research*, 8 (March):431–41.

Brown, Christina L., and James L. Lattin. 1990. Pioneering Advantage in Packaged Goods: The Headstart Effect. Working paper, Graduate School of Business, Stanford University, Stanford, CA.

Carpenter, Gregory S., and Kent Nakamoto. 1990. Competitive strategies for late entry into a market with a dominant brand. *Management Science*, 36:1268–78.

_____ . 1989. Consumer preference formation and pioneering advantage. *Journal of Marketing Research*, 26 (August):285–98.

Deighton, John. 1984. The interaction of advertising and evidence. *Journal of Consumer Research*, 11 (December):763–70.

Encaoua, David, Paul Geroski, and Alexis Jacquemin. 1986. Strategic competition and the persistence of dominant firms: A survey. In J. E. Stiglitz and G. G. Mathewson (eds.): *New Developments in the*

Analysis of Market Structure. Cambridge, MA: MIT Press.

Farquhar, Peter F., Paul M. Herr, and Russell H. Fazio. 1990. A relational model for category extensions of brands. *Advances in Consumer Research*, 17:856–60.

Kardes, Frank, and G. Kalyanaram. 1990. Consumer Learning and the Pioneering Advantage: An Information Integration Perspective. Working paper, College of Business Administration, University of Cincinnati, OH.

Hambrick, D. C., I. C. MacMillan, and D. L. Day. 1982. Strategic attributes and performance in the BCG matrix—A PIMS based analysis. *Academy of Management Journal*, 25:510–31.

Hoch, Stephen J., and Young-Won Ha. 1986. Consumer Learning: Advertising and the ambiguity of product experience. *Journal of Consumer Research*, 13 September:221–33.

Howard, John A. 1989. *Consumer Behavior in Marketing Strategy*. Englewood Cliffs, NJ: Prentice-Hall.

Howard, John A., and Jagdish N. Sheth. 1969. *The Theory of Consumer Behavior*. New York: Wiley & Sons.

Johnson, Eric J., and J. Edward Russo. 1984. Product familiarity and learning new information. *Journal of Consumer Research*, 13 September:221–33.

Lane, W. J. 1980. Product differentiation in a market with endogenous sequential entry. *Bell Journal of Economics*, 11 (Spring):237–60.

Medin, Douglas L., and Marguerite M. Schaffer. 1978. Context theory of classification learning. *Psychological Review*, 85 (May):207–38.

Meyer, Robert J. 1987. The learning of multiattribute judgment policies. *Journal of Consumer Research*, 14 (September):155–73.

Porter, Michael E. 1985. *Competitive Advantage*. New York: The Free Press.

Prescott, Edward C., and Michael Visscher. 1977. Sequential location among firms with foresight. *Bell Journal of Economics*, 8 (Autumn):378–93.

Robinson, William T., and Claes Fornell. 1985. Sources of market pioneer advantages in consumer goods industries. *Journal of Marketing Research*, 22 (August):305–18.

Schmalensee, Richard. 1982. Product differentiation advantages of pioneering brands. *American Economic Review*, 27:349–65.

Sujan, Mita. 1985. Consumer knowledge: Effects of evaluation strategies mediating consumer judgments. *Journal of Consumer Research*, 12 (June):31–46.

Tversky, Amos, Shmuel Sattath, and Paul Slovic. 1988. Contingent weighting in judgment and choice. *Psychological Bulletin*, 95:371–84.

Urban, Glen L., Theresa Carter, Steve Gaskin, and Zofia Mucha. 1986. Market share rewards to pioneering brands: An empirical analysis and strategic implications. *Management Science*, 32 (June):645–59.

Richard R. Still
Professor of Marketing & International Business
The University of Georgia

CHAPTER 3

SEGMENTING THE MARKET

Discussion in this chapter focuses on key aspects of market segmentation. The first three sections clarify the concepts of market and market segmentation and explain the two main approaches to market segmentation: demographic and psychographic. The fourth section considers certain problems in segmenting consumer and industrial markets. The fifth section analyzes marketing characteristics of goods and services as they influence the bases on which markets can be meaningfully segmented. The sixth section sets forth the implications for marketing decision makers.

MARKETS AND MARKET SEGMENTATION

Two of the most important and basic marketing concepts are those of "a market" and "market segmentation." A "market," according to the American Marketing Association, is the aggregate demand of the potential buyers of a product or service.[1] A market, in other words, represents the total demand of all those who might conceivably buy a particular product or service. But an aggregate demand, or total market, also is the sum of the demands of different *segments* of the market, each containing a group of buyers (or buying units) who share qualities or characteristics that make the segment different from other segments and of significance to the marketer. Thus, a market is not only the aggregate potential demand for a product but the sum of various demand subtotals, each representing the potential demand of a particular market segment.

Diversity, not uniformity, characterizes the markets for all products. No two buyers or potential buyers of any product are ever exactly alike in all respects. But groups of buyers do share certain characteristics that are meaningful to the marketer and which have implications for both the setting of market objectives and the formulation of marketing strategies. By grouping buyers sharing characteristics of marketing significance into market segments the marketer attains some degree of homogeneity, facilitating the analysis of each market segment's unique needs, wants, and desires and the tailoring of marketing strategies accordingly.

Meaning of Market Segmentation. The term "market segmentation" is used in two different senses. Many use the term to describe specific types of marketing strategies (or programs) designed to cultivate chosen market segments.[2] Others use the term to describe the process of identifying subsets of buyers with different buying desires or requirements.[3] "Market segmentation" is used here in the second sense; i.e., to refer to the marketer's efforts in searching for improved insights on markets.

Market segmentation is an analytical process that precedes market targeting; i.e., deciding which market segments to cultivate. It involves dividing up a product's total market into smaller and more homogeneous segments, any one or more of which might be designated as market targets requiring individually tailored marketing strategies. The distinctive features of each identified market segment, in other words, *may* make it profitable for the marketer to adapt the product and/or marketing programs so as to meet more precisely each segment's requirements. Market segmentation provides the marketer with improved insights on the market's nature, hence assisting in selecting target markets and in designing optimal marketing strategies.

Principle of Segmentation. One management consultant suggests a "principle of segmentation" that provides a helpful guide for practical marketers: *Segmenting the market is the process of grouping individuals whose expected reactions to the producer's marketing efforts will be similar during a specified time period.*[4] Thus, the aim of market segmentation is to identify groups of potential buyers who can be expected to respond similarly to given marketing moves (i.e., to changes in products, distribution, promotion, and price). Similar responses may be forthcoming for any of various reasons including comparable needs, wants, attitudes, interests, and lifestyles. Furthermore, the skilled segmenter recognizes that the characteristics of any market segment change over time because of shifts in needs, wants, competition, and other variables. A currently useful market segment in terms of response homogeneity can become relatively heterogeneous within a short time; therefore, in planning the cultivation of a given market segment, a definite limit should be set on the time period for implementation of marketing efforts.[5]

Whatever the basis used for segmenting the market, the resulting market segments should be groups of prospective buyers who are more like each other within the groups on all relevant dimensions than they are to members of other groups. Segmentation should aim for minimizing within-segment variance and maximizing between-segment variance.[6]

Requirements for Meaningful Market Segmentation. One key step in segmenting a market involves selecting the criteria to use in dividing up the market into segments; i.e., in determining the characteristics of prospective buyers that will produce the most meaningful and useful market segments. Kotler suggests three requirements for effective segmentation. The first is *measurability*, or the degree to which the size and purchasing power of the resulting segments can be measured. The second is *accessibility*, or the degree to which the resulting segments can be effectively reached and served. The third is *substantiality*, or the degree to which the segments are large and/or profitable enough to justify separate cultivation.[7] Bell suggests an important fourth requirement for meaningful segmentation—chosen segments should differ in their responsiveness to marketing efforts;[8] unless market segments respond uniquely to given marketing moves, they do not justify the expenditures required for planning and implementing individualized marketing strategies.

DEMOGRAPHIC SEGMENTATION

The most common approach to market segmentation seeks to identify groups of prospective buyers sharing selected demographic characteristics. Demographic segmentation, in other words, seeks to answer the question, "Who is the market?" Consumer markets are segmented on the basis of such demographic variables as geographic location, rate of product usage, income, age, sex, education, stage in the family life cycle, religion, race, and social class. Industrial markets are segmented demographically according to such variables as geographic location, kind of business, rate of product usage, and size of user.

Geographic Segmentation. The most widely-used form of demographic segmentation groups customers and prospects according to their geographic locations. Department stores in large cities, for instance, generally group their customers into local and out-of-town accounts. Some manufacturers selling regionally or nationally usually classify their customers by region—e.g., into those located east and west of Denver.

For many products, sufficient variations exist from place to place in buyer needs, wants, and preferences to justify geographic market segmentation. Furniture manufacturers, for instance, recognize that consumer preferences for different styles of furniture vary considerably region by region. Southern consumers typically exhibit a much stronger preference for traditionally-styled furniture than do Midwesterners, while large groups of consumers in the Far West prefer furniture styles showing oriental or Scandinavian influences. Similarly distinctive regional preferences exist for many grocery products, items of clothing, floor coverings, and paint.

Climatic differences justify geographic market segmentation for some products. Areas with long hot summers, for instance, are the most fertile markets for home and auto air conditioners. Areas with considerable snow and long winters are the best markets for winter sports equipment and snow blowers. Geographical differences in climate, in other words, sometimes cause variations in product-usage rates and the proportions of the population who need or want a particular product.

Regional variations in income cause some products but not others to find more fertile markets in some areas than they do in others. While to the maker of garbage cans, income differentials are of little significance, to the maker of garbage compactors, the higher income regions definitely represent the best market targets.

But statistics on regional income generally relate to per capita income; thus, even the maker of garbage compactors may find "pockets" of good prospects within a region that has low per capita income. Interregional variations in income are not as great as the differences between urban and rural incomes within a single region. Differences in per capita incomes in Atlanta and Philadelphia, for example, are not so great as differences in per capita incomes of residents of Atlanta and rural Georgia.

Segmentation by Rate of Product Usage. Many marketers segment their markets according to the amount of product consumed by different buyers. A grocery products manufacturer, for instance, divides the total market into five segments:

• present heavy users
• present light users who are potential heavy users
• present light users who are confirmed light users
• nonusers who are potential heavy users
• nonusers who are potential light users

For many consumer products, considerable variation exists in the product usage rates of heavy and light users. Most people, for instance, drink soft drinks occasionally, but less than a third of the population drink them at the rate of one glass or more per day, and this heavy-user group accounts for more than three-quarters of soft drink sales. Under a fifth of the homemakers use flour once a day or more, but they account for more than half of the flour used. Under 15% of the population make almost 75% of the long distance telephone calls.[9]

Companies segmenting their markets by rates of usage must identify the reasons for usage variations. Often the differences trace to such demographic factors as age, income, size of household, or stage in the family life cycle. The Quaker Oats Company, for example, found that the housewife's age and family size were the two main variables differentiating heavy from light users of Life, a ready-to-eat breakfast cereal. Housewives under 40 in families of five or more members were identified as "extremely important targets" (i.e., heavy users), while those 50 and over in families of one or two members were classed as "very inferior targets" (i.e., as either nonusers or very light users).[10]

PSYCHOGRAPHIC SEGMENTATION
Psychographic segmentation involves breaking down a market according to the life styles, personality characteristics, or buying motives of buyers. Distinctive life styles characterize the members of various subcultures, with new life styles continually developing and older life styles becoming obsolete with the passage of time. One writer describes a life style as "a vehicle through which we express ourselves" and "a way of telling the world which particular subcult or subcults we

belong to."[11] Some life styles; e.g., the Hippie, the Yippie, the Surfer, the Executive, and the Black Militant, are fairly easy to identify. Other life styles; e.g., the Sports Fan, the Do-It-Yourselfer, and the Compulsive Shopper, are somewhat more difficult to recognize.

Psychographic research aims to describe the human characteristics of consumers influencing their responses to marketing variables—products, packaging, media, and the like—that demographic character-istics alone do not explain.[12] Two major approaches to psychographic analysis have emerged. The first focuses on individual consumption patterns on the assumption that an individual expresses personality and projects chosen life style(s) through the products consumed. The second analyzes the individual in terms of activities, interests, opin-ions, and values as measures of life style. It has seen increasing use in supplementing demographic descriptions of consumer groups, but psy-chographic researchers differ as to the appropriate dimensions of life style.[13]

Most psychographic studies involve asking respondents to indi-cate on rating scales their degree of agreement with various statements. For instance, one researcher asked housewives to rate their agreement on a scale ranging from five to one with such statements as:

If there's a flu bug going around, I'm sure to catch it.
Once you've got a cold, there is very little you can do about it.

This study resulted in descriptions of four segments of the mar-ket for cold remedies:

Realists—not health fatalists, nor excessively concerned with protection or germs; view remedies positively, want something that is convenient and works, and do not feel the need for a doctor-recom-mended medicine.

Authority Seekers—doctor-and-prescription oriented. Neither fatalists nor stoics concerning health, but prefer the stamp of authority on what they do take.

Skeptics—have a low health concern, are least likely to resort to medication, and are highly skeptical of cold remedies.

Hypochondriacs—have high health concern, regard themselves as prone to any bug going around and tend to take medication at the first symptom. They do not look for strength in what they take, but need some mild authority reassurance.[14]

ULTIMATE CONSUMERS AND INDUSTRIAL USERS

The first step in segmenting the market for any product is to divide its prospective buyers into two broad categories: ultimate con-sumers and industrial users. The sole basis for classifying a buying unit as an ultimate consumer or an industrial user is the general reason for buying. Ultimate consumers buy for either their own or their households' personal consumption, while industrial users buy to further the production of other goods and services. The mass of ultimate consumers makes up the "consumer market" and the mass of industrial users the "industrial market."

Ultimate consumers and industrial users differ considerably in their buying patterns and behavior. Ultimate consumers buy in much smaller quantities and for consumption over shorter time intervals than do industrial buyers. Ultimate consumers are not as systematic buyers as are industrial users; some industrial users are profit-seeking enterprises, thus encouraging systematic buying procedures, while others are non-profit organizations whose operations are audited by outside authorities, which also encourages systematic buying procedures. Typically, too, ultimate consumers are part-time buyers, while industrial users employ professionals who devote their main efforts to buying. Furthermore, ultimate consumers spread their buying skills over a wide range of goods and services, while professionals specialize and have more chance to perfect their buying skills.

Segmenting Consumer Markets. In segmenting many consumer markets, the household is a more significant analytical unit than the individual. Some products, such as most groceries, although usually bought by individuals, are consumed by all household members. Other products, such as household appliances and automobiles, are purchased jointly by two or more members of a household and are used by all household members. In such instances, market segmentation, either according to demographic or psychographic variables, should be based on differences among households rather than among individuals.

Some consumer markets, however, are meaningfully segmented according to differences among individual consumers. Market segmentation along sexual lines, for instance, is meaningful for a wide variety of cosmetics, grooming aids, and clothing, with male and female market segments requiring different marketing strategies.

Talley reports an interesting case of market segmentation according to differences in individual consumers. The case concerns a producer of crystal glassware which had long focused its marketing efforts on the bride-to-be market, but its sales had topped out. After studying the market more closely, management concluded that three market segments existed for crystal: (1) the bride-to-be, (2) the matron, and (3) the "rich aunt." The matron market segment consists of women who had not been affluent enough to buy crystal at the time of marriage but whose buying power had grown subsequently to the point where they now could afford this type of purchase. The "rich aunt" market segment is made up of well-to-do relatives who buy gifts for brides. Marketing efforts were redirected, the two new market segments were tapped, and company sales and profits resumed their growth.[15]

Segmenting Industrial Markets. The four most common bases for segmenting industrial markets are (1) geographical location, (2) kind of business or activity, (3) customer size, and (4) usual purchasing procedure. Geographic segmentation generally is according to geographic clusters of buyers or by sales territories. Segmentation by kind of business or activity often is effected through the SIC system, which classifies all industrial users into 10 major categories which, in turn, are broken down into finer divisions. The SIC system is a way to break down an industrial market by kind of business or activity into relatively small, medium-size, or large market segments.[16] Most governmental agencies use the SIC system in presenting statistical data of interest to market analysts.

Industrial market segmentation by customer size is important. Industrial users range all the way from one- and two-person shops to huge organizations employing hundreds of thousands. Consequently, the size of industrial purchases varies greatly, and many industrial marketers segment their markets by customer size and use different marketing strategies to reach the individual segments.

When some buyers buy the product as original equipment and others buy it for replacement purposes, market segmentation according to usual purchasing procedure is meaningful. Original equipment buyers follow more complex buying procedures than if they were buying for replacement. Because of relative unfamiliarity and lack of experience with the product, the original equipment buyer demands fuller and more technical product information, oftentimes conducts an exhaustive study of possible suppliers and their offerings, and requires more company executives to "okay" the purchase. By contrast, when an item is being bought as a replacement, the buying decision is reached through routine procedures. Thus, adequate reasons exist for some marketers to divide their markets into original equipment (O.E.M.) and replacement market segments, and to individualize marketing strategies for each segment.

MARKETING CHARACTERISTICS OF GOODS AND SERVICES

Numerous marketing characteristics of goods and services influence the bases on which their markets can be meaningfully segmented, but three are important in so many situations as to deserve mentioning here. One concerns the degree of "customization" of the product. At one extreme, certain products, such as special-purpose machine tools and custom-tailored clothing, are literally "one of a kind" designed to fit each buyer's unique requirements; in such cases, each potential buyer, in effect, is a separate market segment. At the other extreme, some products, such as cement, are so highly standardized that it is meaningful to segment the market by grouping an extremely large number of buyers into a very few market segments according to such bases as buyer size and geographic location.

Brand loyalty is a second marketing characteristic that frequently provides a meaningful basis for segmentation. Most brands have certain customers who are extremely loyal, thus constituting a core market segment. But the brands also have other buyers who switch from brand to brand, and these comprise the fringe market segment. Whenever a brand has both brand-loyal and fringe buyers, segmentation on the basis of brand loyalty may prove meaningful in setting marketing objectives and in formulating strategy for the two quite different markets.

The product's stage in its life cycle is a third marketing characteristic that provides a meaningful basis for segmentation. At different stages in a product's life cycle, changes occur in the relative size and importance of different groups of buyers. In the market introduction or pioneering life cycle state, the product is bought by a small group of "innovators," those who are first to accept a radically new type of product. They are followed by the "early adopters," who, though not venturesome enough to try the adoption first, want to be among the early buyers. Gradually, members of groups making up the mass market (i.e., those in the "early" and "late" majorities) buy the product and it finally reaches market saturation. Others—the laggards—buy the product very late in its life cycle, after its market has begun to decline. Thus, it is often meaningful to identify target market segments at each stage in a product's life cycle. In the market pioneering stage, for instance, money and marketing effort are wasted if the marketer attempts simultaneous cultivation of the total market. Usually, it is more effective and less costly to concentrate early marketing efforts on the innovators, and shift later to the early adopters and to each of the following groups, one at a time.

IMPLICATIONS

For the marketing decision maker, there are six main implications of the preceding discussion.

1. Recognition that diversity, not uniformity, characterizes the total market and is a necessary preliminary to the realistic setting of marketing objectives and to the formulation of effective marketing strategy.

2. Market segmentation is most profitable when members of individual segments are alike in terms of their likely responses to different marketing moves. Unless market segments respond uniquely to given marketing moves, they do not justify expenditures for individually-tailored marketing strategies.

3. Demographic segmentation is most useful in answering the question "Who is the market?"

4. Psychographic segmentation is useful mainly in supplementing demographic descriptions of customer groups, since it helps in understanding and predicting buyer behavior.

5. Generally different approaches should be taken to the cultivation of consumer and industrial markets.

6. Various marketing characteristics of goods and services influence the bases on which their markets can be profitably segmented.

NOTES

1. Committee on Definitions, *Marketing Definitions* (Chicago: American Marketing Association, 1960), p. 15.

2. For example, see Wendell R. Smith, "Product Differentiation and Market Segmentation as Alternative Marketing Strategies," *Journal of Marketing*, Vol. 21 (July 1956), pp. 3–8.

3. For example, see Philip Kotler, *Marketing Management*, fourth edition (Englewood Cliffs, N.J.: Prentice-Hall, Inc., 1980), p. 195.

4. Steven C. Brandt, "Dissecting the Segmentation Syndrome," *Journal of Marketing*, Vol. 30 (October 1966), p. 25.

5. Brandt, same reference as footnote 4.

6. Martin Christopher, "Cluster Analysis and Market Segmentation," *British Journal of Marketing*, Vol. 3 (Summer 1969), p. 99.

7. Kotler, same reference as footnote 3, at pp. 205–206.

8. Martin L. Bell, *Marketing: Concepts and Strategy*, 3rd Ed. (Boston: Houghton Mifflin Co., 1979), p. 125.

9. Fred D. Reynolds and William D. Wells, *Consumer Behavior* (New York: McGraw-Hill Book Company, 1977), p. 390.

10. "The Quaker Oats Company—Life Cereal" case in Milton P. Brown, Richard N. Cardozo, Scott M. Cunningham, Walter J. Salmon, and Ralph G. M. Sultan, *Problems in Marketing*, 4th Ed. (New York: McGraw-Hill Book Company, 1968), pp. 181–182.

11. Alvin Toffler, *Future Shock*, Bantam Edition (New York: Bantam Books, Inc., 1971), p. 314.

12. Harold W. Berkman and Christopher Gilson, *Consumer Behavior* (Boston: Kent Publishing Company, 1981), p. 63.

13. Ronald E. Frank, William F. Massy, and Yoram Wind, *Market Segmentation* (Englewood Cliffs, N.J.: Prentice-Hall, Inc., 1972), pp. 58–59.

14. Ruth Ziff, "Psychographics for Market Segmentation," *Journal of Advertising Research*, Vol. 11 (April 1971), pp. 4–6.

15. Walter J. Talley, Jr., *The Profitable Product* (Englewood Cliffs, N.J.: Prentice-Hall, Inc., 1965), pp. 93–94.

16. For an explanation of the S.I.C. system, see Office of Management and Budget, *Standard Industrial Classification Manual*, 1972 (Washington: U.S. Government Printing Office, 1972).

Robert C. Blattberg
Polk Brothers Distinguished Professor of Retailing
Kellogg Graduate School of Management
Northwestern University
Evanston, Illinois

Lynn C. Unglaub
Vice President
Robert C. Blattberg Consultants
Chicago, Illinois

CHAPTER 4

DATABASE MARKETING

The use of data for marketing is as old as direct mail and catalog marketing. In the early days, direct mail marketers and catalog companies kept customer records on index cards. With the advent of computer technology, the industry leaders shifted their customer records to mainframe computers. The shift to database marketing came when firms began to use the power of the information to design and monitor marketing programs directed to these customers. Because it has been touted as a more efficient form of marketing, many traditional marketers have considered transforming themselves into database marketers.

The purpose of this chapter is to help the reader understand what database marketing is and what is required for a firm to use database marketing effectively. To help establish a perspective, the chapter begins with a brief history of database marketing. Database marketing is then defined and contrasted to traditional marketing. Next the key elements of database marketing are described. Inhibitors to becoming a database marketer are discussed and the chapter concludes by showing how the marketing function will need to change if the firm and its service providers want to become effective database marketers.

THE ANTECEDENTS OF DATABASE MARKETING

The foundation was laid for database marketing with the dawn of the mail order industry in the last century. As early as 1872 with the launch of the Montgomery Ward catalog and Richard Warren Sears' first sales of gold watches to railroad agents in 1886, companies were employing public delivery to inform potential customers of their offerings, to receive orders, and to deliver merchandise. Although the industrial revolution of the late 1800s made the mass production of consumer goods possible and brought down prices to the point where a majority of households could afford a variety of products manufactured outside the home, most consumers lived far away from major metropolitan areas where department stores were located. However, mail delivery was becoming increasingly reliable. Firms that began as small operations quickly blossomed into some of the biggest businesses in the United States.

By 1910, catalog companies had developed the "12-month prune rule" whereby customers who had not purchased anything for the past year were dropped from the mailing list. This was the beginning of database marketing. Over the next few decades, catalog companies realized that many households who purchased a few small items each year were unprofitable whereas a customer who purchased a major item every two years might be very profitable. Catalogers and direct mailers quickly learned that a detailed customer file became very important to reducing mailing costs.

To target prospects, R. L. Polk and Reuben H. Donnelley began to compile customer lists from external sources, including telephone directories, automobile registrations, and driver's license records. Although the information was rudimentary, Old American Insurance was successful during the 1940s at targeting older Americans with direct mail solicitations for life insurance through driver's license records. The records listed age, and people who drove cars were assumed to be affluent and mobile (and therefore in reasonably good health).

Unlike the mass appeal used by general merchandise companies, the efficient identification of new prospects was of profound importance to the direct mail industry. Companies like Market Compilation and Research Bureau and The Kleid Company emerged to help firms increase their customer base by selling them the lists of other companies' customers who were direct-mail responsive for related products.

THE EMERGENCE OF COMPUTER TECHNOLOGY

In 1963, the U.S. Postal Service introduced zip codes and rules requiring third-class mailers to not only label each piece of mail with the proper zip code, but to sort outgoing mail in zip code sequence. The labor costs required to comply with the new rules promised to be enormous. The industry adopted computerization of mailing lists as a solution. The introduction of computers in the direct mail industry led to major industry innovations in the ensuing decades. Many experts cite the computerization of the industry as the beginning of "true" database marketing.

In the 1960s, a number of direct mailers began to experiment with using zip codes and census tract information to predict buying behavior. From the 1960 census, the U.S. Census Bureau divided certain parts of the nation into 180 groupings and released basic demographic information on each one. O.E. McIntyre, a list management company, developed a system it created SIFT (Selection by Individual Families and Tracts), which combined geographical demographics with individual data from their list of 40 million names.

In the late 1960s, merge/purge programs became publicly available. Prior to this, it was almost impossible to avoid sending more than one solicitation to the same consumer or to abstain from sending acquisition offers to current customers. Merge/purge programs not only saved companies money by avoiding the mailing of duplicates, but they also changed the way direct mailers could target. Previously, mass direct mailers rented only large, broadly targeted mailing lists because combining a number of small lists resulted in many duplicates. With a merge/purge program, these marketers could combine many small lists and weed out duplicates, thereby permitting them to prospect a new universe of lists previously deemed too inefficient. Computerization also brought a deluge of personalized, computer-generated letters. Letters personalized only with a "Dear Mr. Jordan" salutation pulled as many as six times the responses as nonpersonalized offers in the mid 1960s. While creative approaches to personalization continue to work fairly well, complaints from a growing number of consumers over a perceived threat to their privacy is discouraging marketers from using personal information in their copy.

The Growth of Statistical Sophistication

A number of factors converged in the late 1960s and 1970s to make direct marketing much more scientific. Increasing postage costs made it impractical to send out mailings on a mass basis. More "niche" catalogs and mail order companies went into business, making the targeting of good prospects essential. A number of mathematicians became interested in the field, leading to more sophisticated statistical and financial analyses. These new techniques included lifetime value models that directed the level of investment a company could profitably make in each customer segment and scoring models developed using multiple regression, AID, or CHAID, which predicted the responsiveness of customers to new offers. Most of the new analytical techniques and technology were used on a piece-meal basis until the 1980s, when further reductions in computing costs and the sharing of information allowed companies to begin to implement more sophisticated, integrated programs.

The pace of innovation in computer technology quickened in the 1980s. Relational database technology made the storage, retrieval, and manipulation of massive warehouses of customer information feasible. The introduction and rapid growth of personal computers allowed marketing managers to conduct sophisticated analyses at their desktops. Not only did companies collect additional customer data, they began to use this information to understand their customers and predict their behavior. The era of database marketing had begun.

The Dawn of a New Era

In the 1990s, the focus of database marketing has begun to shift to relationship marketing. The concept suggests that by better understanding customers on an individual level and by delivering to them information and products targeted to their specific needs, marketers can develop long-term annuity streams that translate into substantial profits. This concept differs from traditional direct marketing that targets customers in segments and focuses more on attracting new customers than on retaining old ones. Relationship marketing uses improved technology to regularly communicate with the firm's customers and to base product offerings on the consumer's buying behavior. The saturation of products in the marketplace, increasing costs of targeting a mass audience, and consumer concerns over the environment and personal privacy require firms to concentrate on selling more to current customers and retaining those customers already loyal to the firm. Otherwise, the firm's marketing costs will skyrocket, putting the firm at risk economically.

DEFINITION OF DATABASE MARKETING

Database marketing is extremely difficult to define. If the definition is too narrow, it excludes many potentially interesting uses of databases for marketing; if it is too broad, all firms using any type of data will be considered database marketers. In this chapter, two definitions will be given and the reader can decide which is most appropriate. The first is a broad definition that encompasses more than just the use of a customer database to send promotional materials. The second definition is more narrow and more traditional. At the end of this section, we indicate which definition will be used throughout the remainder of this chapter.

Broad Definition of Database Marketing

The creation and use of databases in conjunction with information technology to improve the efficiency and effectiveness of marketing activities.

In examining this definition, we see that it includes the use of electronic point-of-sale (POS) data, not only customer-specific information, as well as other relevant marketing data used to design and develop marketing programs. Thus Procter and Gamble, Kraft-General Foods, and other leading package goods companies who use electronic POS data for measuring the effectiveness of marketing activities such as pricing and promotions are "database marketers" using this definition. This definition does not require database marketing to use a database to deliver marketing programs to the customer nor to use it to communicate with the customer. It does not even require that a customer database be employed. Thus employing this definition, any firm using databases to improve the efficiency and effectiveness of the marketing function is a database marketer.

It is important to recognize that using the broad definition greatly expands the types of activities that fit under the umbrella of database marketing. Promotional analysis, baseline development, and price elasticity modeling all conform to this broader definition. Marketing research is included in this definition. Many of the quantitative marketing models that have been created over the last twenty years would be tools of database marketing.

What is excluded from this definition? The answer is any research or marketing activity that does not directly translate into more efficient and effective marketing programs. For example, firms who use salespersons to call on accounts are *not* database marketers. If, on the other hand, the firm targets accounts and uses information to design the customer-salesperson interaction, then it fits this definition of database marketing.

Narrow Definition of Database Marketing
The use of internal and external customer databases in conjunction with information technology to develop and communicate individualized marketing programs.

The narrow definition of database marketing requires that a customer database be used to deliver marketing programs. The delivery may be through mail, phone, or direct contact. By using detailed internal customer files and external lists, firms can develop highly customized marketing programs directed to their customers. The factor that differentiates database marketers from direct marketers is the sophisticated use of information to design individual marketing programs. By obtaining and managing detailed customer behavior data in conjunction with promotional histories, database marketers can infer the types of products and services the customer is likely to buy, create targeted promotions directed to the customer based on historical responses, and produce special pricing. Traditional direct marketers do not have these capabilities because of their inability to process information rapidly and cost effectively. With a detailed customer history file, database marketers can create marketing programs that are highly individualized. The enabling factor is computer technology. While theoretically this can be done without computer technology, it is almost impossible to execute it. The major change that has made database marketing possible is low-cost, high-powered computer systems and software that make accessing the databases far easier. Statistical analysis programs have been developed which allow database marketers to score and target individual customers in much greater detail than was feasible for direct marketers twenty years ago.

Contrasting the narrow definition with the broad definition, the narrow definition greatly limits what activities fit under the umbrella of database marketing and who is a database marketer. It also raises the question of how revolutionary database marketing really is. This definition is clearly an extension of direct marketing with a greater emphasis on computer technology.

Definition Used in This Chapter
The definition that will be used throughout this chapter is the narrow definition. By limiting the scope of the chapter, we can focus on how information technology in combination with selected marketing programs can be used to create highly efficient, very targeted marketing programs that are only beginning to be used in a wide variety of

industries. While this approach to marketing will not fit every company, as the cost of database development declines and as the ability of firms to learn how to use one-on-one marketing strategies and tactics increases, the number of firms using database marketing will increase. Ironically, computer technology is enabling firms to revert back to the type of one-on-one marketing that firms conducted before it became cost-effective to mass market. The difference is that computer technology, not individual sales personnel, is designing and delivering the marketing "pitch."

DATABASE MARKETING VERSUS CONVENTIONAL MARKETING

Database marketing differs from conventional marketing both strategically and tactically. This section will focus on the strategic differences and the next section will focus on the tactical differences.

Focusing on the Lifetime Value of a Customer

One of the primary advantages of database marketing is that it enables the firm to compute the lifetime value of the customer, which is the discounted net profit the firm makes from a customer. The advantage of computing lifetime value of a customer is that it changes the focus and mission of the firm from product orientation to customer orientation. Concepts like brand equity and product positioning, which are at the heart of traditional marketing, while still very important, become less of a focus to the firm than the value of the customer franchise and how to maximize it. The firm's marketing and product activities are directed toward how it can change the customer's long-term value. This means that the firm will make or buy products or services that will enhance the relationship with the customer, and the firm will price and promote based on the long-term relationship with the customer.

To compute the lifetime value of a customer requires information such as the customer's purchase history, promotional history, and projected future purchases (dollars and frequency). The source of this information is a detailed customer history file that conventional marketers do not maintain, and hence they cannot compute the lifetime value of their customers.

We will consider an example to demonstrate the differences in decision making between a traditional marketer and a database marketer that can compute the impact of its marketing activities on the lifetime value of the customer. Consider a firm that issues an FSI (free standing insert) coupon that costs $7 per thousand and has a face value of $.40 plus $.10 handling charges. The coupon generates 20 purchases for every 1,000 sent. Of the 20 responses, 10 are customers who would have bought the product without the coupon, 5 are totally new customers to the product, and 5 are switchers from other brands who historically have bought the brand. The initial purchase made by a customer is $2.00. The retailer pays the manufacturer $1.50 for the product, and the incremental profit for the manufacturer is 67% resulting in a profit of $1.00. If one computes the initial profitability of the customer to the firm, we see that only ten purchases were incremental, and so they generate $10 in profits (to the manufacturer); but we must subtract the coupon redemption and distribution costs of $10 and $7, respectively, resulting in a net loss of $7 per thousand coupons issued. If one simply looks at the initial net profitability of the coupon, it is easy to conclude that it should not be run. However, there is also the long-term profit generated from the five new customers. Assume each of these customers will buy six more times, on average, over their lifetime, resulting in a net profit of $30 (6 x 5 x $1) minus the initial loss to acquire these customers of $7, which generates $23 in profit per thousand. However, without being able to calculate the long-term value of the program by tracking the buying behavior of individual customers, the firm will fail to determine the relevant economic return and reject the program. Thus the lifetime value calculation is critical to the economic analysis of marketing activities. Without it, the firm is far more likely to reject programs that generate long-term profits, which adversely affects the profitability of the firm.

Installed Base Marketing

Another critical difference is the firm's focus on the importance of selling more to existing customers. A rule of thumb is that it costs seven times as much to acquire a new customer as it does to sell additional products to an existing customer. The source of this rule of thumb is the economic analysis of direct mailers who separate their acquisition costs from their ongoing marketing costs. It is also known that multiple-time purchasers have much lower promotional and marketing costs than one-time buyers. Thus once a customer consistently does business with the firm, he or she has signalled a satisfaction level with the firm and is comfortable with its position, value, and customer service level.

Using the heuristic just described, it is clear that the firm should try to sell more to existing customers, which is called *installed base marketing*. Customer relationships have significant value because it is less expensive to sell new products and services to the firm's customers than to acquire new customers. Firms who try to understand how to sell more to existing customers because of the affinity they have established with them are likely to have lower marketing costs. Database marketing facilitates this strategy because through the availability of a detailed customer database, the firm is able to target current customers without having to invest in untargeted promotions and advertising. The smart database marketing firm is likely to focus on new products or services that it can sell to its customer base rather than developing new products or services for which its current customer base is not a particularly good target.

While selling to existing customers may seem obvious, contrast it to Procter and Gamble. It sells Tide to the household but does not necessarily sell additional products and services to the same customers. It uses, instead, the brand's franchise to create spin-off products such as Tide with Bleach. The difference is that Procter and Gamble is focused on the brand's equity and what else can be sold using the image and positioning of the brand versus using an installed base marketing strategy that focuses on the customer and how to sell more to the existing customer base. Clearly both can be successful strategies, but the database marketing firm has an advantage because it can always continue to expand its product line (brand equity) as well as acquire other products and services that appeal to its existing customer base (customer equity).

Shift From Mass to One-on-One Marketing

Marketing is entering a new era in which communication will no longer be one way from the manufacturer or seller to the customer but can become two way, when the buyer's needs can be directly or indirectly communicated to the seller. While this occurs now between a salesperson and a prospective customer, there is no systematic communication based on the historical customer-seller relationship. There is also no memory trace showing the promotions and marketing communications received by the consumer and the resulting behavior.

Because computers can be linked with telecommunications and other communication vehicles, it is now possible to begin developing one-on-one marketing vehicles that relate specifically to the customer's needs. The computer maintains and analyzes the information and then uses it to send customers information. Thus mass marketing tactics such as FSIs and network television are necessary only to the extent that targeted, specialized messages do not increase response rates enough to cover the higher distribution costs of targeted vehicles. Newspapers, network television, and even mass promotions have begun to feel the increased competition from one-on-one marketing campaigns designed around detailed customer information.

An example will help clarify the concept. Spiegel, a leading U.S. catalog company, can target customers based on recent purchase behavior. A customer that purchases a purse from Spiegel will receive different types of promotional material than a customer who purchases housewares from the catalog. Targeting based on purchase behavior leads to higher response rates and hence more efficient marketing execution.

The concept of developing a marketing program based on customer needs is not unique to database marketing but it is more cost-effective today because storage and access of customer purchase information is much cheaper. Ironically, good salespeople in prior generations kept card files of customers and then knew when to call the customer and what to offer. The difference is that through database marketing, one-on-one marketing can actually be executed for a mass market. Tailored products, advertising, copy, pricing, and promotions are based on historical information gathered and maintained about customers' behavior.

Efficiency and Effectiveness of Marketing Expenditures

As was implied in its definition, database marketing can lead to more efficient and effective marketing programs. Efficiency means that the same sales are generated through lower marketing expenditures; effectiveness means that the marketing program produces a higher response. Both are important.

Efficiency is created through detailed customer information. Suppose you were working for a securities firm selling stocks and bonds. You have two customers, both with a net worth of one million dollars. One owns a large portfolio of stocks and bonds ($500,000) and the other a portfolio of rare antiques and modern art ($500,000). Which one will be more responsive to a new stock offering? The odds clearly favor the customer with the stock and bond portfolio. Knowing customer behavior increases the firm's ability to target the relevant customers. Customer information directly affects marketing efficiency.

Effectiveness is improved through database marketing because it allows the firm to determine the relevant communications, products, pricing, and promotions to customers based on their past purchase and promotional responsiveness and relevant customer characteristics. American Express can offer cruise customers different types of promotions and copy based on their past behavior. If a customer has gone to the Caribbean every year for the last five, it is easy to target very specific types of promotions and copy to that customer. A customer who has changed venue every year but has also taken a yearly cruise will receive different copy and promotions. Effectiveness, just like efficiency, is enhanced with information.

Efficiency and effectiveness are enhanced through analysis of past marketing campaigns. Database marketing facilitates this because it focuses on the collection, maintenance, and analysis of response data. Time-Life is able to determine the cost-effectiveness of different television ads for its magazines because it can track the responses for each insertion through the toll-free numbers. By matching the toll-free number with the insertion ads, the lowest cost per order can be determined. Database marketing firms like Time-Life are able to produce more effective ads (higher response rates) and more efficient marketing programs (lower cost per thousand) because they are able to track their customers' buying behavior. This clearly gives them an advantage.

In summary, database marketing affects the strategy of the firm because it:

- focuses the firm on the lifetime value of the customer,
- concentrates on selling more to existing customers,
- makes it possible to use one-on-one marketing tactics to a mass market, and
- improves the effectiveness and efficiency of the firm's marketing programs.

A detailed customer database makes all of this possible. Conventional marketing firms are at a strategic disadvantage because they cannot execute the same strategies that a database marketing firm can.

ELEMENTS OF DATABASE MARKETING PROGRAMS

The components of a database marketing program—the media, offer, and package—are elements that distinguish database marketing from traditional marketing. The purpose of this section is to describe the major options in each of these areas and to discuss their application. In conventional marketing, the retail outlet is the marketplace; in database marketing, the media defines the marketplace. The various media options include direct mail, telemarketing, newspapers, magazines, co-ops, broadcast, and electronics. The offer is the motivation for the prospect to buy the product or service. Knowledge of the target audience is critical to structuring a successful offer. The alternatives in creative packages are limitless and therefore only the major types of packages will be discussed in this section.

The tactics used by database marketers are almost identical to those used by direct marketers. The difference is in database marketers' ability to target, customize, and monitor marketing programs. Analysis of internal customer files or external data sources provide database marketers with more sophisticated targeting. The ability to customize the messages or offers depends on the amount of information the firm has about the customer or prospect, and clearly database marketing expands the firm's ability to customize. Monitoring again is enhanced by tracking customer responses to specific marketing programs. Database marketing improves the efficiency and effectiveness of marketing tactics but does not change the vehicles used. The one caveat is that database marketers must monitor the response from any marketing programs.

The Media of Database Marketing

Telemarketing. Marketers are often surprised to learn that the telephone is probably the largest advertising media with over $45 billion a year in total expenditures. Experts estimate that this number is fairly evenly divided between outbound calls for selling and sales support activities and inbound calls for orders, inquiries, and customer service. Stone defines telemarketing as "the planned, professional, and measured use of telecommunications in sales and marketing activities" (1984). Each of these adjectives—*planned, professional, measured*—is important since successful telemarketing is not a boiler-room operation where ill-prepared operators canvass untargeted lists to push products. Although integration of telecommunication into a marketing program can dramatically increase its effectiveness, telemarketing is not inexpensive and therefore must be carefully planned and measured.

It is important to realize what benefits telemarketing can provide when deciding to incorporate it into a marketing program. Telemarketing provides immediate customer feedback so that the marketer can measure and project the effectiveness of the program. Because the communications are interactive, the caller can collect diagnostic information from the prospect to allow the marketer to modify the script or offer to improve the response rate. When integrated with a field salesforce, telemarketing can improve customer service and reinforce customer relationships.

The critical component that distinguishes a telemarketing program from other database marketing programs is the script. In writing the script, each contact should be viewed as a sales call and should contain each of the elements required for a call. These elements include

- removing the curse from the call and breaking the preoccupation barrier,
- introducing the caller and the company,
- qualifying the contact so that the call is not wasted,
- describing the product or service,
- summarizing the major benefits to the prospect,
- presenting the offer and trial close,
- handling objections and answering questions,
- repeating the order and all relevant information, and
- thanking the customer for the order.

A good script is flexible and provides a framework for the call but does not sound like a "canned pitch."

Although telemarketing is used for both consumer and business products, it has become especially important to business-to-business firms as they attempt to reduce selling costs. Although inbound telemarketing has long been recognized as an efficient means of handling leads, taking orders, and servicing customers, outbound telemarketing can also be integrated into the territory and account management activities of the sales force. Outbound telemarketing is an efficient means to generate and qualify leads, reactivate accounts, cross-sell new products, monitor inventory levels, and notify customers about special promotions or price changes.

Direct Mail. Mailing lists provide the media for direct mail. The list that generally proves most responsive and profitable is the company's own customer file, often referred to as the house list. The information maintained on the customer database is used to profile and segment the customers into groups that reflect their responsiveness to the company's assortment of products and offers. Profiles of customer segments are used to acquire external mailing lists with similar characteristics in order to prospect for new customers. There are two basic types of external lists: lists of customers, prospects, or subscribers from other companies and compiled lists. Lists from other direct response companies have one key advantage when compared to compiled lists— the names are those of direct response buyers. However, if your market is college students or new mothers, compiled lists will offer the largest universe.

The rental of names is generally negotiated through a list broker. The broker works for both the company that owns the list and the company renting the list, although his or her fee is paid by the list owner when a rental is arranged. With literally thousands of lists available, the broker can provide valuable insights into which lists represent the market the mailer is targeting. Names are rented for a one-time use; only the responders may be added to the company's in-house files. Firms that rent their house lists frequently or have many lists available for rent have begun to use list managers to deal with the numerous details associated with promoting and managing the rental process. The list manager handles contacts with brokers, bills the broker and collects payments, approves mailing pieces and dates, maintains the list, and processeses rental orders. The price range for most list rentals in 1992 was $40 to $60 per thousand names.

Magazine. Selection is the key to using magazines as the media for database marketing. Just as the location, whether Rodeo Drive or an outlet mall, creates an image and attracts a particular type of customer to a retail store, the readership of a magazine defines a market. High ticket collectibles may do well in *Smithsonian* and the *New Yorker* while moderately priced fashions perform well in publications like *Seventeen* and *Cosmopolitan*. Magazines provide a high number of exposures at a relatively low cost; however, the response rate, average order, and bad debt rate must be carefully tracked to manage the media profitably.

Broadcast. As the average American household substitutes its consumption of print media (i.e., newspapers and magazines) with hours of exposure to broadcast media (i.e., TV, cable, and radio), database marketers have adapted their media plans, offers, and strategies. Broadcast is now employed for all the classic database marketing tactics—direct selling, lead generation, support of other media, and outlet locator programs. Network broadcast TV can be extremely expensive and is rarely the most effective option for database marketing. The cost is based on the rating (i.e., percentage of households viewing the program), length of the ad, and time of day. An 18 rating means that 18 percent of the television households are watching the program. When the ratings for all the time periods in a schedule are combined, the sum is called the gross rating points or GRP. Advertisers focus on two measures of effectiveness: reach and frequency. *Reach* refers to the number of *different* households that see the message in a given timeframe and *frequency* refers to the number of times the message will be viewed. Broadcast time may be purchased by specific time slot—the most expensive—or ROS (run of station) with or without specified time of day. If demand for TV time is relatively low, it may also be purchased based on PI (payment per inquiry) or bonus to payout.

Radio offers an economical low-reach, high-frequency media. There are many more radio stations than TV stations in a market and each offers its own type of audience based on its programming. Understanding the profile of your customer or prospect is critical in selecting successful outlets and time of day. The relatively low cost of air time and commercial production also makes radio an attractive alternative for many database marketers.

Cable TV. The fastest growing media alternative in terms of dollars spent by all advertisers is cable TV. Cable TV looks like network broadcast but offers the database marketer an important advantage in that the cable TV audience is well defined. Cable operators maintain customer records that can be matched with demographic and psychographic information to profile their subscribers. There is also the chance to market the product, the audiences through the special interest cable channels like Arts & Entertainment or ESPN. Because cable time is more widely available and cheaper than network time, longer commercials can be created that tell a more complete story. This trend has led to the phenomena of "infomercials" that may be 30 minutes in duration.

Newspapers. In 1965, Time-Life Books proved that preprint was a viable direct marketing medium. Preprints now abound in four-color single-page and multipage formats. With daily circulation of over 70 million, newspapers offer an attractive channel for products with a mass appeal. Syndicated Sunday supplements such as *Parade* and *Family Weekly* offer a vehicle to reach millions of households in both primary and secondary metro markets at a relatively low cost. A third form of newspaper advertising is called ROP (run of paper). It is widely used by retailers, but has only proven cost-effective for database marketers who run small-space, low-cost ads over a long period of time with high frequency so that the number of impressions accumulate rapidly compared to cost.

Co-op. The largest mail co-op in the U.S. is Carol Wright, which is owned by Donnelley Marketing and distributed to more than 24 million households selected from the 70 million on Donnelley's household database. Carol Wright is primarily used by consumer packaged goods manufacturers to distribute cents-off coupons. Although direct mail is much more expensive on a cost-per-thousand basis to circulate coupons when compared to newspapers and FSIs, the redemption rate is generally two to three times greater. Instead of Carol Wright, database marketers tend to use mail order co-ops arranged by a consortium of database marketers and distributed to households that have proven to be mail responsive. Other database marketers have developed their own in-house co-op mailings, which spread their mailing costs across several offers. In general, co-op mailings pull one fourth the response rate of solo mailings, but they likewise cost about one fourth of a solo mailing.

Electronic Media. Stand-alone electronic media such as video cassettes, video discs, and computer discs including CDs have ushered in a revolution in database marketing. Database marketers are just beginning to tap the exciting potential of two-way electronic media such as Videotext, Prodigy, and two-way cable television.

The Offer in Database Marketing

The proposition the marketer makes to the prospect is referred to as *the offer.* The basic components of the offer for a product or service include product description, price, premium or incentive, guarantees, time limit, credit options, future obligations and options, additional charges, and optional features. Variations of these components that are used to motivate the prospect to buy include incentives such as sweepstakes and free gifts. Even the way an offer is stated can effect response rates. *Buy one get one free* generally draws a higher response than *50 percent off.*

With the wide variety of options available in creating the offer, it is important to clearly establish the objective of the program. The best offer to generate a sales lead may be very different from the most effective offer to attract new customers. It is also important to understand why a prospect is motivated to respond. The marketer can use a positive option like social approval or sensory gratification or a negative option like problem removal or avoidance.

The Package in Database Marketing

The classic direct mail package includes an outer envelope, letter, brochure, order form, reply envelope, and other inserts such as a free gift slip or product sheet.

Solo. The simplest form of a promotional offer is the solo. With this appeal, the marketer must explain the product and motivate the customer to respond with one exposure. The typical solo package includes a letter, brochure, reply card, or order form and return envelope.

Multistep. A variation of the solo promotion is the multistep promotion. For products that are too complicated or expensive to sell through a single mailing, it is often possible to generate a list of interested prospects through direct mail, magazines, or TV with responses provided by toll-free numbers, bingo cards, or reply cards. The sale is generally completed through a direct contact. Products typically sold in this manner include encyclopedias, financial services, and expensive exercise equipment.

Catalog. With a catalog, the marketer can offer an assortment of hundreds of products within a single mailing. Circulation costs are spread across many items, and the probability that the customer will find an appealing item is increased. Catalogs also enjoy a longer shelf life in the home than solo mailings. There are four basic types of catalogs: business-to-business catalogs, which primarily offer office equipment and supplies; full-line merchandise catalogs; retail catalogs like Neiman-Marcus, which are designed primarily to support store traffic; and specialty catalogs, which now form the most competitive, fastest growing segment of the catalog industry.

Continuity. An important and extremely profitable segment of the traditional direct marketing industry is continuity programs. Under these programs, the customer is shipped a product periodically against regular payments. Most continuity programs operate as a negative option under which the company continues to send products to the customer until the customer cancels the program. Books, records, video cassettes, and recipe cards are frequently sold through continuity programs. Leading companies in this segment include Time-Life Books and the Franklin Mint.

THE ECONOMICS OF DATABASE MARKETING

Database marketing is not viable for every firm. There are certain economic conditions required before a firm should invest in database marketing. This section will offer a brief example to illustrate when database marketing pays and when it does not. Some general principles are then identified when database marketing has the highest potential payout.

Example

Two alternative scenarios show when a detailed customer database increases the firm's profitability. We will use a traditional FSI coupon drop versus a database marketing targeted coupon to analyze the payout.

Scenario 1—We will return to our example from the "Database Marketing versus Conventional Marketing" of this chapter. An FSI coupon was dropped at a cost $7 per thousand, the face value of the coupon was $.40 plus $.10 handling costs, and the response rate was 2 percent. The profit for the manufacturer was $1.00 per unit sold. Fifty percent of the sales were incremental. For the current example, we will not assume any new buyers were attracted by the coupon. Under scenario 1, traditional couponing, the costs were $7 per 1,000 for distributing the coupon and $10 for redeeming it, totalling $17. The profits were $10 from incremental units sold and so the coupon drop resulted in a $7 loss.

Scenario 2—Suppose the firm was able to obtain a detailed list of its customers along with their purchasing behavior and then use this list to mail the coupon to infrequent users. The cost of this mailing is $250 per thousand. The response rate is 15%, and 90% of the units sold are assumed incremental. For scenario 2, the response rate increased significantly, but so did the cost of distributing the coupon. The coupon generated 150 responses per thousand. The distribution cost is $250 and the redemption cost is $75. The profit generated before distribution and redemption costs was $135 from the incremental units sold. After subtracting distribution and redemption costs, the net loss was $190. Thus while the direct mail coupon was more effective, it was less efficient and profits declined. Clearly database marketing did not pay off.

Using scenario 2, assume that the firm modifies its program to mail five different coupons for five unique products to a selected set of customers based on their buying behavior. The cost of the coupon distribution drops to $50 per coupon per thousand. What is the payout? It goes from a loss of $190 to a profit of $10. If the promotion cost drops significantly, then the use of database marketing can pay off.

When Is Database Marketing Most Effective and Efficient?

The previous example highlights one issue: the cost of targeting. However, there are several conditions required to make database marketing feasible:

1. The cost of targeting relative to mass marketing must not be inordinately high.
2. The average price of the product or service or its gross margin relative to the marketing cost must be high, which implies that database marketing is far less effective for low-ticket items unless there are multiple purchases made from the same promotional event.
3. The ability to group promotions (e.g., through catalogs, co-op mailings) is critical to the efficiency of database marketing because it decreases the cost of targeting.
4. The more rapid the repeat purchasing, the higher the economic payout of database marketing.

Given these requirements, which types of firms will be most effective at database marketing? The answer is firms such as catalog companies that can promote multiple items, thus decreasing promotional cost per item and increasing the average expenditure per promotional mailing; credit card and financial services companies that have long-term relationships with their customers and rapid repeat usage cycles; and business-to-business marketers such as Dell Computer that sell items such as microcomputers through the mail can succeed because the cost of promotion is low relative to the price of the item.

Firms can restructure their marketing strategies so they can meet the four requirements described. DEC is beginning to sell computers directly. Many business-to-business marketers are developing catalogs to substitute for direct selling. Procter and Gamble, Kraft, and Ocean Spray are testing a frequent-user card so that multiple promotions can be sent to customers based on their purchase behavior.

The economic equation of database marketing determines its viability. The clever firm restructures its marketing strategy to make the economic equation work for its products and services.

EXAMPLES OF DATABASE MARKETING FIRMS

The following section provides two case studies in database marketing. Each outlines the objectives of the company for its database marketing program, how the company created its database, and general applications.

Industry: Insurance
Company: USAA (United Services Automobile Association)
Case: Alternative sales channel and customer support

Background

USAA, founded in 1922, is a large insurance and diversified financial services firm based in San Antonio, Texas. It is made up of fifty-six subsidiaries and affiliates, and owns and manages over $20.1 billion in assets. Some of its products include property and casualty, life and health, and automobile insurance; no-load mutual funds; real estate investments; discount brokerage services; credit cards; deposit services; and consumer loans. USAA members insure one another and share in any profits realized by the company.

USAA's membership consists of active and former military officers and their dependents, which at present number over two million. While property and casualty insurance and the organization's buying services are only available to its members, the majority of remaining products are available to the general public. Although products are available to the general public, the mission of the company is to provide products and services that satisfy the needs of its members.

USAA's Objectives

According to the company, USAA's standing as one of the premier financial services providers is largely due to its emphasis on information technology. From its inception, USAA has conducted most of its business by mail and currently has no independent selling agents. The reason for this was necessity. The company was formed by a few military officers to provide each other with automobile insurance. The officers were having difficulty obtaining reasonable rates for their coverage because the traditional insurers felt that military officers were a significant risk. Because the officers were stationed throughout the United States and abroad, business had to be conducted by mail. This practice has proven to be an efficient, cost-effective means of serving its members. Because the target customers of the firm are military officers, the majority of whom are on active duty, stationed throughout the world and constantly being relocated, mail communication has proven not only cost-effective but logical. The firm sees its databases as vital in its pursuit of providing the lowest cost, highest quality products and services.

Collecting and Maintaining Database Information

As mentioned previously, USAA has been building customer files since its inception. Additional customers are largely recruited through word-of-mouth endorsements by the company's current members. This is possible because of the trust that exists between military officers. New client names are also obtained through university ROTC programs, the various military academies, and the direct commissioning offices. The company does not purchase commercial lists because they do not exist for its target market segment.

The company feels the quality and breadth of its data is unmatched within the industry. The reason for this is the willingness of its members to share extensive personal information with the company. This occurs because of the trust the company has developed with its members and because the company makes it clear to its members that the information is necessary to provide them with the best service possible. To foster this trust, USAA does not share data with any outside firms.

Initially, there are fifteen critical pieces of data collected. Database maintenance then becomes a constant and ongoing process. Every contact with its members and customers is a chance to update database information. In addition, to ensure the integrity of its data, the company sends out data update forms to 20 percent of its customers every year. The analogy the company uses is that database maintenance is like painting a bridge; you start at one end and by the time you finish, it is time to start again.

General Uses of Database Marketing

Because of their integrated information technology, all departments can access the central database that supports many applications including research and development, product promotion, and new product solicitation. The company strategically orients itself around "lifecycle needs" because it views its customers as being clients from "cradle to grave" (for twenty-five years or longer). The lifecycle need concept associates the company's products and services with different stages in its members' career and life. Therefore, product managers can target promotions toward that segment of the database that falls within the most likely user category of their product or service.

Information collected from customers can also provide vital input for the process of new product development. For example, feedback from members stored in the database showed that most of its members were using services provided by the American Automobile Association (AAA). USAA developed a travel product that was more competitively priced than AAA for its members. Another example of the powerful new product development application of the company's databases is the buying services provided by the company. Through database analysis, it was clear that the company's customers wanted low-cost, long-distance telephone service. Once the company was aware of this demand, USAA approached Sprint and obtained a low-cost primary service deal for its customers. USAA is the ultimate database marketer in that it leverages its relationship with its customers (affinity group) to offer new products and services as demanded by its members (installed base marketing).

Problems

The greatest challenge for USAA is providing quality customer service worldwide. It is the company's use of information technology that has enabled it to offer the range of products and services that its members demand.

Another challenge is the development of affinity between members and USAA, not specific agents. Because of the personalized nature of selling financial services, the company is organized so that a customer can speak with the same agent regarding any product if he or she so desires. While each agent cannot be an expert in every product, an agent can act as the point person with a particular customer and direct questions to the appropriate agents. Each promotion gives a toll-free number to call, or the customer can call any agent, including the one he or she has used previously, for information. Again, the information maintained in its databases allows the company to provide expert service. Its technology allows every agent to have access to the purchase and policy records of every member; therefore, regardless of which agent answers the call, he or she can speak intelligently to the customer about needs, previous products purchased, and the relationship of the new product or service to the customer's other products and services.

Industry:	Catalog
Company:	Spiegel
Case:	Strategic repositioning

Background

In 1905, Joseph Spiegel began operating from a location in Chicago selling inexpensive, utilitarian household goods and furniture to the working-class, immigrant population. By offering easy financing with low downpayments and reasonable monthly installments to the expanding middle class, the Spiegel catalog enjoyed steady growth throughout the first half of the century. Although Spiegel grew to become the fourth-largest catalog company in the United States (behind Sears, Montgomery Ward, and J.C. Penney), by the 1970s new forces were eroding Spiegel's traditional market. The number of working class families as a percentage of the population was beginning to decline, and discount stores and mass merchandisers were offering stiff competition for the remaining market.

Spiegel's Objectives

In 1976, Hank Johnson, the firm's new CEO, recognized a need for change more radical than merely altering the merchandise assortment or developing more efficient and effective tactics for marketing to the current customer base to shore up short-term profits. Johnson identified four trends—computers, toll-free numbers, working women, and accelerating social and economic change (Johnson 1990)—that shaped his strategy for transforming Spiegel from a downscale, me-too catalog to an upscale, unique specialty book. Johnson's objective was for Spiegel to become "the ultimate, convenient way to shop for the upper third of the households in the country, providing fashionable merchandise for adult women in those households."

Spiegel moved its headquarters to an upscale Chicago suburb to revitalize its image with its employees, suppliers, customers, and market. The 200 retail stores were closed. Hundreds of items including top sellers were dropped in order to stress fashion and quality rather than price. New catalogs were designed with a more lavish appeal and expensive appearance. The apparel books featured apparel from leading designers like Liz Claiborne, Norma Kamali, and Yves St. Laurent. Goods from Laura Ashley, Henredon, and Fieldcrest were featured in the home fashions catalogs.

Uses of Database Marketing

To acquire their new target customer, Spiegel had to go beyond the traditional catalog customer lists. Eighty percent of Spiegel's customer file did not fit the profile of the new target customer so Spiegel began compiling lists of relatively affluent, working women from other sources such as upscale magazine subscription lists. A preview catalog, "Discover Spiegel," which contained its best merchandise at the lowest possible cost, was used to entice the initial response. Catalog circulation was augmented with sophisticated print ads in fashion and interior design magazines that projected Spiegel's new image and offered the preview book (Johnson 1982).

Databases were critical in allowing Spiegel to track its customers, segment them, and determine their buying preferences. Spiegel began to offer specialty books that focused on a particular type of merchandise. Women who bought shoes were sent books featuring shoes and accessories. Customers who ordered linens were sent the housewares books. Target marketing to the upscale, working woman was becoming a reality for catalogers. Circulation was reduced from forty million to twenty million, but increasing response rates and order amounts drove higher earnings. Between 1976 and 1982, response rates rose from two to four percent and the average order tripled. By the mid 1980s, the desired minimum household income for a target household was $25,000 and the median income was $35,000 (Spiegel 1984).

Spiegel began to extend database marketing techniques beyond the traditional segmentation of customers based on RFM or the type of merchandise purchased. Spiegel surveyed a sample of its customers about their lifestyles, family structure, careers, and attitudes and then clustered the customers based on their answers. The clusters reflected a sense of style from the classic, traditional woman to the avant garde. The firm then analyzed the specific items that the women in each cluster had purchased. With the clustered items, Spiegel could look at the purchases of all the customers in its database and assign each customer to an appropriate style. Catalogs were then developed that offered an assortment of merchandise reflecting a particular style rather than a particular type of merchandise.

INHIBITORS TO SUCCESS

In addition to the economic obstacles described previously, the successful implementation of a database marketing program can be affected by a number of factors—some of which are beyond the control of the firms conducting these programs. The firm must recognize these inhibitors and ascertain whether they make it impossible for the firm to become a successful database marketer.

Acquiring Customer Information

Although many consumers are unclear about the amount and types of personal information that are being collected by credit bureaus, database marketers, and list compilers, their concern about the potential for invasion of privacy is growing. The language of the U.S. Constitution does not refer to any "right of privacy" in the commercial context, and it has never been articulated by any decision of the U.S. Supreme Court. In fact, the court has taken the position that the flow of information is crucial to a free economy (Posch 1988). However, legislation restricting invasive telemarketing practices and controlling the dissemination of data is being considered in almost every state. Congress is currently considering bills that would restrict access to credit agencies' databases and establish a federal data protection board that would regulate privately held databases. This growing level of concern among consumers may soon cut off some of the most important sources of data about customers. The three major credit agencies and the database marketing industry are working with the U.S. Office of Consumer Affairs to address these concerns through voluntary measures.

If sources are limited, data acquisition will become much more expensive. This places a premium on firms with large, detailed customer databases because these firms will be able to market to existing customers using purchase history information. Database marketing firms will have an advantage because they will have the information to concentrate on installed base marketing and will not need to rely on customer acquisition strategies.

Limitations Due to the Quantity and Quality of Data

Beyond the pending legislative restrictions on the exchange and collection of customer data are the practical obstacle of obtaining and retaining customer data. With order entry systems in catalog companies and scanner systems tied to frequent buyer programs in retailer companies, it is possible to capture and analyze the buying behavior of each customer. However, the massive size of these databases makes them expensive to store and process. Citicorp faced this problem when it tried to create frequent user programs for grocery retailers. The sheer size of the database was beyond its computer processing capabilities.

In addition to buying behavior, personal information about the customer such as his family structure, financial condition, lifestyle characteristics, attitudes, and demographics are required to complete an accurate profile. Some of this information can be purchased from data suppliers such as Donnelley Marketing and R. L. Polk, but the most accurate data usually come from self-reports through survey responses or telemarketing. Intensive effort is required to capture this information and then maintain its accuracy. Until marketers learn to use these data to create more accurate and predictive profiles of their customers, response rates to database marketing programs will stall and economic barriers to the implementation of these programs will remain intact.

Computer Literacy in the Marketing Organization

As cited in the brief history of database marketing that introduced this chapter, computerization is a necessary component. Many of the innovations in the field were driven by technology. Economic barriers to the adoption of powerful computer systems are decreasing as distributed processing capabilities are appearing on the manager's desktop. The constraining factor in the implementation of these capabilities is now the lack of computer literacy among marketing managers. The information systems department in an organization often lacks the experience in marketing applications required to fill this gap. Companies often turn to software and services provided by vendors and consultants to augment their internal expertise. However, the firms that develop analytical and computer skills within the marketing organization where critical decisions are made will build the strongest competitive advantage.

Marketing Organizations Are Slow to Change

Database marketing presents a new paradigm for the organization. Visions of marketing to the masses must be supplanted by marketing to the individual. In addition to new analytic skills and computer literacy, the organization must learn to develop new creative approaches, adopt new measurements and economic models, and work with new types of media to communicate to targeted customers. Service providers such as some advertising agencies have also had great difficulty in designing effective one-on-one programs. New paradigms are needed in pricing, communications programs, and product design. These types of systemic changes will diffuse slowly through the organization.

THE ORGANIZATIONAL IMPACT OF DATABASE MARKETING

If a firm makes a commitment to become a database marketer, it can no longer conduct business using the old organizational paradigms. This section begins by describing the organizational changes necessary for a firm to be an effective database marketer and ends with a table summarizing this section.

The New Marketing Organization: Customer Retention and Customer Acquisition Specialists

The marketing function has traditionally been focused on managing elements of the marketing mix such as pricing, promotions, advertising, and channel management, and there are staff departments whose responsibility it is to manage these activities (e.g., the advertising department). This will need to change as a firm moves to become a database marketer. The marketing function will need to be reorganized around (1) current customers and (2) customer acquisition. This bifurcation is necessary because each type of customer requires different types of marketing programs. Marketing to current customers requires concentrating on customer retention and installed base marketing. Marketing to prospects requires sophisticated offers, cost-effective media selection, and quality copy. The skills and programs necessary to market to these two segments is different and implies the need for separate organizations.

The New Marketing Research: Measurement and Management of Customer Affinity

The past thirty years have seen a strong orientation in marketing to product positioning. Many brands have developed a distinct positioning and this has catapulted them to category dominance. One such case is Marlboro cigarettes. Customers develop an image of a firm that is similar to its positioning but is usually softer and less focused. Sometimes this image is managed by the firm and sometimes it evolves by itself. Harley Davidson has a very distinctive image that has evolved over time, and now the firm is using this image to its advantage. It markets accessories consistent with the Harley Davidson image. A database marketing firm must learn to manage the affinity the customer has with it because this affinity offers an opportunity to develop a strong installed-base marketing program.

The need to understand the customer's affinity with the firm will require marketing research to shift its activities from brand attitudinal research to determining customer affinity. Affinity refers to the "unique" relationship the customer develops with the firm. AARP (American Association of Retired Persons), for example, has developed a very strong affinity with its members. It is quite different from a positioning that focuses the customer on the individual product or service. While attitudinal research is oriented toward advertising and understanding how it works, customer affinity research requires evaluating the types of products and services that are consistent with the customer's affinity with the firm. Can Toys R Us create summer camps for children? Can McDonald's sell clothing for children? Can L.L. Bean create a line of sports clothing to compete with Nike and Reebok? The answer depends on the affinity created by the firm with its customer. Since affinity is not tangible, the type of research required may be far less quantitative than current marketing research and may be more in the tradition of linguistic research which tries to understand the meaning of symbols and words that have connotations not easily discerned. Thus uncovering the boundaries of customer affinity is likely to be subtle and complex and less amenable to "scientific" discovery. Yet, it has significant consequences for the firm.

The New Marketing Services Function: Knowledge-Based Systems Experts

Database marketing, as its name implies, is very data intensive. This requires the ability to analyze and use information for decision making. In the consumer packaged goods industry, firms are beginning to use knowledge-based systems (related to expert systems) to help them work with the massive quantities of data that their brand managers and sales force must use. Cover Story and Sales Partner produced by Information Resources, Inc., and knowledge-based systems by McCann and Gallagher (1990) provide graphical computer-generated information that serves as the basis for marketing decisions. These systems take the information, use rules to search through the information for certain types of events, and then access statistical models to produce recommended marketing and sales actions. While in their infancy, these systems allow marketing mangers to identify key findings in the data without having to peruse the massive databases being generated.

As databases become larger, which is inevitable, the need for "smart systems" will increase. Database marketing firms, to take full advantage of their customer and marketing databases, need to develop automated analytical systems that can assist decision makers and analysts in working more effectively with the data. One important inhibitor to the successful use of marketing databases will be the inability of marketing managers to analyze them to develop tactics and strategies. Expert systems, artificial intelligence, and knowledge-based systems will be the primary way many firms will be able to gain a competitive advantage from their databases.

What does this imply about the types of information systems the organization will need to supply? The answer is that marketing will need a "knowledge-based systems" team to translate and transform data into computer delivery systems that simplify working with data. These systems are more sophisticated than traditional marketing decision support systems because they use expert systems/artificial intelligence to recommend decisions, not simply to provide easy access to data. Obviously, this expertise rarely exists in any organization and definitely not in marketing. Yet, it is critical to managing the use of information—the key to effective database marketing.

The New Agencies: Retention and Acquisition

As database marketing matures, there will be agencies who specialize in designing tactics and strategies to utilize (1) the firm's customer database and (2) outside data sources for customer acquisition. This implies that advertising and promotional agencies will be forced to change their orientation to concentrate on either retention or acquisition marketing so that they have the skills to be expert in a given type of marketing. New types of services firms with different names such as retention specialists or acquisition specialists will evolve. This change will redirect the strategies and tactics used. While concepts like positioning will still be important, so will special programs that "tie" the customer to the firm through frequent user cards, special services provided to customers, and regular communications focused on the customer's specific needs. This bifurcation of marketing activities implies that a fundamental change is required—agencies must recognize the differences in retention and acquisition marketing. Separate account teams, separate services, and separate (but integrated) strategies are needed. Can one agency provide these services? It is unlikely.

The New Accounting: Lifetime Value of the Customer

As discussed earlier, database marketing focuses the firm on customer retention and its importance to the long-term success of the firm. Firms will quickly learn that any erosion of its customer base is of paramount importance, and the firm must orient all of its activities around maintaining its customer base. General Motors, who in the 1980s lost significant market share while maintaining its short-run profitability, is a perfect case in point. In the 1970s, product quality slipped and the percentage of GM customers who purchased a second or replacement vehicle dropped. Had the firm had an accounting system that tracked the long-term value of General Motors' customers, the financial community and its directors would have learned that the company was in serious trouble. Unfortunately, profits lagged changing customer retention levels.

If a balance sheet item and a flow statement (similar to an income statement) were added that showed the value of the firm's customer franchise, executives would be forced to focus on customer retention and satisfaction to a greater extent than currently exists. The role of accounting is to provide this type of statement. This would then focus the marketing, production, and operations functions on retention strategies that include improved customer service, improved product quality, better value of the firm's products and service, relationship pricing, and other factors that determine whether the customer is willing to continue the relationship he or she has with the firm.

The New Focus of Product Development: Installed-Base Marketing

Installed-base marketing becomes critical to maximize the lifetime value of the customer. The integration of marketing and new product development is very important in being able to market successfully to an installed based. Marketing must be able to identify products and service the customer base wants and needs. New product development must concentrate on acquiring new products or services, rather than creating and producing them. Thus new product development must expand its flexibility to become a "systems integrator," which means taking components from other sources and putting them together as a product or service provided to the customer. Managing outsourcing for product development becomes a critical new function within the firm.

Operations and production must also be more closely aligned with marketing because they both greatly affect the lifetime value of the customer. If either provides poor value to the customer because its costs are too high, or because product or service quality is too low, then the long-term relationship with the customer is jeopardized. Currently, marketing is responsible for external relationships and production and operations for internal systems. The problem is that the two functions must be more tightly linked. Without a closer linkage through greater understanding of the customer's evaluation of the products and services of the firm, a key asset of the firm, the customer lifetime value will decline.

Comparison of the Old Marketing Organization to the New Database
Marketing Organization

Function	Traditional Marketing	Database Marketing
Marketing	Organized around the marketing mix	Organized around customer retention and customer acquistion
Marketing Research	Focused on consumer research and market size analysis	Focused on the measurement and management of customer affinity
Marketing Services	Directed to manage the firm's agency and outside vendor relationships	Provide knowledge-based system expertise
Outside Agencies	Organized around marketing mix functions	Organized around retention and acquisition
Accounting	Product oriented	Analyze and provide statements about the lifetime value of a customer
New Product Development	Product oriented	Become specialists in the acquisition and management of products to be sold to the installed customer base

REFERENCES

Johnson, Hank. 1990. *The Corporate Dream: Making It Big in Business.* New York: Carol Publishing Group.

Johnson, Henry. 1982. Spiegel's new winnin' spirit based on target marketing. *Direct Marketing.* August.

McCann, John M., and John P. Gallagher. 1990. *Expert Systems for Scanner Data Environments.* Boston: Kluwer Academic Publishers.

Posch, Robert J., Jr. How the law(s) of "privacy" impact your business. *Direct Marketing.* October, pp. 74–82.

Spiegel, Edward. 1984. Spiegel's turnaround—Net sales rocket to $516 million. *Direct Marketing.* April, pp. 40–57.

Stone, Bob. 1984. *Successful Direct Marketing Methods.* Chicago: Crain Books.

Paul E. Green
University of Pennsylvania
Philadelphia, Pennsylvania

John L. McMennamin
The Carnation Company
Los Angeles, California

Shahrzad Amirani
University of Texas at Arlington
Arlington, Texas

CHAPTER 5

MARKET POSITION ANALYSIS

Measuring the position of a firm's product or service in the minds of consumers—if not the touchstone to successful marketing—is crucial to the planning of most strategic efforts. Chemically similar products, for example, brands of aspirin or Vitamin C, may be perceived quite differently by the consumer. Conversely, chemically (or physically) differentiated brands might be perceived similarly if their differentiation occurs along dimensions that are not salient to the potential buyer.

Not surprisingly, managers are interested in buyers' perceptions of their brand, particularly if there are misperceptions that cast the product/service in an unfavorable light. Misperceptions can often be corrected through advertising/promotion. Interest in relationships between perceptions and "true" product profiles is becoming all the more important, given the growing trend toward comparative advertising. Indeed, the strategy of brand positioning is based on finding meaningful (and deliverable) advantages over competing brands.

Furthermore, brand preferences are obviously dependent on perceptions, since being able to distinguish between brands is a necessary condition for preferring one brand to another. Not surprisingly, consumers' preferences (and perceptions) are rarely homogeneous. The strategy of market segmentation attempts to capitalize on differences across submarkets in brand perceptions and preferences.

This chapter is concerned with the application of new procedures for measuring buyers' perceptions and preferences for brands and the implications of these measurements for the design and control of marketing strategy. First, a few brief examples are presented. Next, one problem—concerned with the development of promotional strategy for a laundry-type product—is discussed in some detail. The import of these new measurement techniques on the development of new products or services and the control of existing ones is briefly described.

The methodology to be discussed in this chapter has the rather esoteric name of *multidimensional scaling*. Without delving into technical details, these relatively recent techniques, developed by psychometricians and mathematical psychologists, permit the researcher to portray buyers' perceptions and evaluations geometrically. Brands (or suppliers) are represented as points in a geometric space whose axes can be described as frames of reference along which brands are compared perceptually.

People (e.g., consumers, retailers, corporate salespeople) can also be represented in these spaces. In this case, the point locations represent their perceptions of the *ideal* amounts of each dimension of the perceptual space—that is, those levels that they would most prefer to have in a product or service.

Over the last decade, multidimensional scaling and similar methods have undergone a rapid expansion in the variety of models and techniques. In particular, *correspondence analysis* has emerged as a popular type of scaling procedure. We conclude the chapter with a discussion of some of these newer developments and their role in market positioning.

SOME EXAMPLES

Soft Drink Slogans

A prominent producer of soft drinks wished to consider the adoption of a new slogan—one that would connote the distinctive features of the brand. The firm's advertising department had prepared 15 candidate slogans and the problem was which one should we choose?

A study of consumers' perceptions of these slogans and their association with various brands of soft drinks was undertaken. The study indicated that 11 of the 15 slogans were perceived as more closely associated with the images of one or more competitive brands than the firm's own brand. Had no comparison of brand-slogan congruence been attempted, it is conceivable that a slogan might have been chosen that would be more closely associated with a competitor's brand than with the company's own brand.

Computer Firm Images

A large producer of computers was concerned with the relationship between the physical characteristics of its hardware and data processors' perceptions. Computer models—the firm's and its competitors'—were first positioned geometrically in performance space (how long it would take the computer to perform multiplication, size of core, etc.). Perceptual judgments of computer model similarity were also obtained from the firm's sales personnel, its customers, and its noncustomers.

The sales personnel's perceptions agreed most closely with the objective (performance) positioning of the computer models. However, the firm's customer perceptions disagreed in significant ways with the sales personnel's perceptions, suggesting that the salespeople were not emphasizing certain performance characteristics of the company's line that would enhance customer satisfaction. Perceptions of the firm's noncustomers had relatively little correspondence with the true performance characteristics of its computers. Quite to the contrary, noncustomers perceived the firm's computer line as more or less undifferentiated from those of other firms.

The firm's noncustomers, to a large extent, evoked criteria other than physical performance in evaluating competitive models.

Noncustomers were chiefly concerned with the prominence of the computer firm, the size of its technical support staff, and the various marketing services it could offer. Performance/cost ratios, which were quite favorable for the models marketed by the sponsor of the study, meant relatively little to its noncustomers. Not surprisingly, the firm's noncustomers tended to be less technically sophisticated data processors—ones who would be attracted to a large, well-established (albeit higher-priced) computer supplier.

High-Nutrition Cereals

A marketer of a high-nutrition brand of cereal was becoming increasingly concerned over the relevance of its advertising toward promoting a cereal that both tasted good and had high nutritional value. Discussions with advertising agency personnel led to a new campaign that humorously stressed qualities of good taste and high nutrition. The firm's marketing personnel wondered if this new message was getting across to the consumer.

A study of housewife perceptions of the firm's brand in comparison to other cereals was undertaken. The study indicated that the advertising goals *were* being achieved: while perceived as a high-nutrition cereal the firm's brand plotted closer in "perceptual space" to good-tasting cereals than did any of the other high nutrition brands. That is, consumers were perceiving the hybrid advertising appeal in ways desired by the company. In this case, perceptions were measured for the purpose of monitoring the results of a basic change in advertising appeal.

A New Drug Product

A well-known pharmaceutical manufacturer had developed a new over-the-counter item that would be more effective but higher priced than existing items. Marketing management's problem was to determine the copy points to utilize in the introductory phase of commercialization. Since the product was one whose initial acceptance was assumed to be heavily influenced by physicians' recommendations, the perceptual study was directed to this "specifier" group first.

Five sets of copy appeals were examined. Contrary to the supposition of the firm's marketing personnel, the most popular appeal stressed one simple, prominent copy point—an appeal that the firm thought would be too "soft sell." The firm's favorite appeal (before the study) was perceived by the physicians as being more relevant to the current leading (competitor's) product than it was to the firm's new entrant.

A DETAILED ILLUSTRATION OF MARKET POSITION ANALYSIS

The preceding capsule descriptions, while illustrating the nature of market position analysis, are too brief to give the reader a feel for the nature of the methodology. In this section of the chapter, we describe a more detailed example—one dealing with the selection of promotional appeals for fabric softeners.

The sponsor of this study was one of several manufacturers of fabric softeners. The firm's marketing research personnel were becoming increasingly concerned with two basic strategic questions regarding the market positioning of their product: (1) How can the total market for fabric softeners be expanded and (2) How can their share of this expanded market be increased? At the time the study was initiated, all fabric softener manufacturers were using promotional appeals that emphasized the tactual or feel-like benefits associated with the use of the product.

Given the rather experimental nature of multidimensional scaling methodology, the firm's marketing research personnel elected to launch a small pilot study whose purpose was to see how fabric softener users (of any brand) differed in their perceptions from nonusers of fabric softeners.

Method

The first step in the pilot study was to develop a list of activities that a housewife would view as naturally associated with her daily world. From a much larger initial list, the 43 activities shown in Exhibit 1 were finally selected. Note that two items of interest here are activities 12 ("Using a fabric softener in your wash") and 38 ("Wearing soft clothes").

Two small samples (60 respondents) of fabric softener users and nonusers were recruited by a screening-type telephone interview. Each sample was matched roughly with regard to demographics, according to data assembled by the firm's personnel. Since the respondents were asked a varied series of product usage questions in the screening phase, they did not know the specific purpose of the follow-up interview. In the follow-up interview all respondents—identified from the screening interview as users or nonusers—were shown a set of cards on each of which appeared the name of one of the activities shown in Exhibit 1.

After looking through the cards (spread out randomly on a table in front of her), the respondent was asked to group the activities into clusters that represented activities that seemed to "go together" or be related to each other. The respondent was asked to make up ten such groups (with no need to equalize the number of items per cluster) that represented activities that seem to be highly similiar within the cluster.

EXHIBIT 1. List of Activities (Stimuli)

Number

1   Sunbathing
2   Baking a cake for the family
3   Sewing buttons on husband's shirt
4   Receiving an admiring glance from a man
5   Relaxing in a warm bath with bath oil
6   Receiving help from dinner guests with the dishes
7   Smoothing on hand lotion
8   Going to church
9   Drinking a cool drink on a hot day
10 Sleeping on freshly ironed sheets
11 Cooking a fancy dinner for guests
12 Using a fabric softener in your wash
13 Peeling potatoes
14 Saving up some "mad money"
15 Going to the beauty parlor
16 Using a cream rinse after shampoo
17 Moisturizing your face with special cream
18 Doing volunteer charity work
19 Shopping for new clothes for yourself
20 Putting fresh flowers on the table
21 Using a room freshener spray
22 Putting on perfume or cologne
23 Buying a new plant for living room
24 Cleaning out the closets
25 Letting your husband pick the movie to see
26 Hanging freshly cleaned curtains
27 Burning incense
28 Opening windows to air out the room
29 Receiving praise from your family
30 Feeling like a good mother
31 Knowing you are an excellent housewife
32 Serving a special treat to the family
33 Receiving an affectionate kiss from your husband
34 Getting someone else to do your work
35 Sleeping late in the morning
36 Reclining in a soft chair
37 Smelling flowers in a garden
38 Wearing soft clothes
39 Wearing an attractive outfit (new)
40 Receiving an achievement award
41 Powdering the baby
42 Healing a diaper rash
43 Making love

Analyzing the Data

A rather simple measure of perceived interactivity similarity can be developed by merely counting, across respondents, the number of times any pair of activities are grouped together. These frequency counts were made separately for users and nonusers. The resulting tables showed the incidence (across respondents) with which any pair of activities were grouped together.

Two (complementary) methods were used to analyze these frequency data. First, for users and nonusers separately, the data were scaled multidimensionally, leading to the two geometric patterns shown in Exhibits 2 and 3.

Second, the same incidence tables were submitted to a numerical clustering program that groups highly similar activities together in a hierarchical fashion—that is, one in which small clusters of highly related items are progressively grouped into larger and larger clusters, containing less similar items, until all items are merged into one large cluster. The results of this step appear in Exhibits 4 and 5.

Scaling Results

Looking first at the *gross* patterns of activity grouping, we note in both Exhibits 2 and 3 that some evidence for a dimensional interpretation is apparent. Insofar as the horizontal axis is concerned, we note that family-connected activities tend to plot on the left of the origin, while personal activities tend to plot on the right.

Insofar as the vertical axis is concerned, we see that outside activities ("Going to church," "Doing volunteer work") tend to plot above the origin, while inside activities ("Buying a new plant for the living room") tend to plot below the origin. We tentatively conclude that the horizontal axis might be labeled "family-personal" while the vertical axis might be labeled "outside-inside" in terms of the major characteristics of the activities.

It seems clear at this point that between-group differences must be sought at a finer level of structure. That intergroup differences do exist is brought out by examining selected activities. For example, we first focus our attention on activity 12, "Using a fabric softener in your wash."

If we look at the activities in Exhibit 2 (user group) that are near activity 12, we see activities like (1) "Using a room freshener spray," (2) "Opening windows to air out the room," (3) "Putting fresh flowers on the table," and (4) "Hanging freshly cleaned curtains." Thus, for users the activity of "Using fabric softener in your wash" appears to exhibit a cleanliness and freshness theme in terms of the activities perceived to be similar to it. Note that activity 38, "Wearing soft clothes," plots rather distantly from activity 12, suggesting that these activities were not highly associated with each other.

EXHIBIT 2. Two-Dimensional Activity Configuration—Users*

```
                        Outside-Oriented
                   8              18
              25             40
           31                 4
        6     29
           30          33
                  43        39
      32          34     35   17
                             15
  Family  11    2        14          Personal
      13   3        27      19      1
                24              22
           42  12          5
                        9   36   7
                21    10
           28    20      37
       41   26      23              16
                        38
                   Home-Centered
```

*See Exhibit 1 for legend.

EXHIBIT 3. Two-Dimensional Activity Configuration—Nonusers*

```
                        Outside-Oriented
                   8      18
                      25    40
           30             4
       31                        35
          32  27  29    33
              29
          42             39
                  11          15
  Family        6     43   14
                                22   Personal
         26        41        5
                           36      7
     24   21    2        38
                      9   37
           3                  19
                    20  10      17
       12              34      16
              23            1
                   Home-Centered
```

*See Exhibit 1 for legend.

EXHIBIT 4. Hierarchical Clustering of 43 Activities by User Group*

Activities

```
0 3 3 1 3 1 0 0 1 1 2 0 3 1 1 3 2 2 2 2 2 1 2 2 4 4 2 3 3 0 1 0 3 0 3 0 1 4 0 2 3 4
9 6 7 0 8 5 5 7 6 7 2 1 5 4 9 9 0 3 7 4 6 2 1 8 1 2 9 0 1 3 1 2 2 6 4 8 8 0 4 5 3 3

○ ○ ○ ○ ○ ○ ○ ○ ○ ○ ○ ○ ○ ○ ○ ○ ○ ○ ○ ○ ○ ○ ○ ○ XXX ○ ○ ○ ○ ○ ○ ○ ○ ○ ○ ○ ○ ○ ○ ○ XXX
○ ○ ○ ○ ○ ○ ○ ○ XXX ○ ○ ○ ○ ○ ○ ○ ○ ○ ○ ○ ○ ○ ○ XXX ○ ○ ○ ○ ○ ○ XXX ○ ○ ○ ○ ○ ○ ○ XXX
○ ○ ○ ○ ○ ○ ○ ○ XXX ○ ○ ○ ○ ○ ○ ○ ○ ○ ○ ○ ○ XXX XXX ○ ○ ○ ○ ○ ○ XXX ○ ○ ○ ○ ○ ○ ○ XXX
○ ○ ○ ○ ○ ○ ○ ○ XXX ○ ○ ○ ○ XXX ○ ○ ○ ○ ○ ○ XXX XXX ○ ○ ○ ○ ○ ○ XXX ○ ○ ○ ○ ○ ○ ○ XXX
○ ○ ○ ○ ○ ○ XXX XXXXX ○ ○ ○ XXX ○ ○ ○ ○ ○ ○ XXX XXX ○ ○ ○ ○ ○ ○ XXX ○ ○ XXX ○ ○ ○ XXX
XXX ○ ○ ○ ○ XXX XXXXX ○ ○ ○ XXX ○ ○ ○ XXX ○ XXX XXX ○ ○ ○ ○ ○ ○ XXX ○ ○ XXX ○ ○ ○ XXX
XXX ○ ○ ○ ○ XXXXXXXXX ○ ○ ○ XXX ○ ○ ○ XXX ○ XXX XXX ○ ○ ○ ○ ○ ○ XXX ○ ○ XXX ○ ○ ○ XXX
XXX ○ ○ ○ ○ XXXXXXXXX ○ ○ ○ XXX XXX ○ XXX XXXXX XXX ○ ○ ○ XXX ○ XXX ○ ○ XXX ○ ○ ○ XXX
XXX ○ ○ ○ ○ XXXXXXXXX XXX ○ XXX XXX ○ XXX XXXXX XXX ○ ○ ○ XXX ○ XXX ○ ○ XXX ○ ○ XXXXX
XXX ○ ○ ○ XXXXXXXXXXX XXX ○ XXX XXX ○ XXX XXXXX XXX ○ ○ ○ XXX ○ XXX XXX XXX ○ ○ XXXXX
XXX ○ XXX XXXXXXXXXXX XXX ○ XXX XXX ○ XXX XXXXX XXX ○ XXX XXX XXXXX XXX XXX ○ ○ XXXXX
XXXXX XXX XXXXXXXXXXX XXX ○ XXX XXX ○ XXX XXXXX XXX ○ XXX XXX XXXXX XXX XXX ○ ○ XXXXX
XXXXX XXX XXXXXXXXXXX XXX ○ XXX XXX ○ XXX XXXXX XXX XXXXX XXX XXXXX XXX XXX ○ ○ XXXXX
XXXXX XXX XXXXXXXXXXXXXXX ○ XXX XXX ○ XXX XXXXX XXX XXXXX XXX XXXXX XXX XXXXX ○ XXXXX
XXXXX XXX XXXXXXXXXXXXXXX XXXXX XXX ○ XXXXXXXXX XXX XXXXX XXX XXXXX XXX XXXXX ○ XXXXX
XXXXXXXXX XXXXXXXXXXXXXXX XXXXX XXX ○ XXXXXXXXX XXX XXXXX XXX XXXXX XXX XXXXX ○ XXXXX
XXXXXXXXX XXXXXXXXXXXXXXX XXXXX XXXXX XXXXXXXXX XXX XXXXX XXXXXXXXX XXX XXXXX XXXXXXX
XXXXXXXXX XXXXXXXXXXXXXXX XXXXX XXXXX XXXXXXXXXXXXX XXXXXXXXXXXXXXX XXX XXXXX XXXXXXX
XXXXXXXXX XXXXXXXXXXXXXXXXXXXXX XXXXX XXXXXXXXXXXXX XXXXXXXXXXXXXXX XXX XXXXX XXXXXXX
XXXXXXXXXXXXXXXXXXXXXXXXXXXXXXX XXXXX XXXXXXXXXXXXX XXXXXXXXXXXXXXXXXXXXX XXXXX XXXXXXX
XXXXXXXXXXXXXXXXXXXXXXXXXXXXXXX XXXXXXXXXXXXXXXXXXX XXXXXXXXXXXXXXXXXXXXXXXXXXXXXXXXX
XXXXXXXXXXXXXXXXXXXXXXXXXXXXXXXXXXXXXXXXXXXXXXXXXXXXXXXXXXXXXXXXXXXXXXXXXXXXXXXXXXXXX
```

EXHIBIT 5. Hierarchical Clustering of 43 Activities by Nonuser Group*

Activities

```
0 3 2 2 2 3 0 0 3 3 1 0 1 1 0 2 3 1 1 3 0 1 1 2 2 1 2 2 1 0 3 2 3 3 4 4 0 1 4 2 0 3 4
6 4 7 0 3 7 1 9 5 6 5 7 6 7 5 2 8 4 9 9 3 3 2 4 6 0 1 8 1 2 2 9 0 1 1 2 8 8 0 5 4 3 3
o o o o o o o o o o o o XXX o o o o o o o o o o o o o o o o o o o o o o o o o o o o o
o o o o o o o o o o o o XXX o o o o o o o o o o o o o o o o o o o o XXX o o o o o o o
o o o o o o o o o o o XXXXX o o o o o o o o o o o o o o o o o o o o XXX o o o o o XXX
o o o o o o o o o o XXXXXXX XXX o o o o o o o o o o o o o o o o o o XXX o o o o o XXX
o o o o o o o o o o XXXXXXX XXX o o o o o o o o o o o o o XXX o o o XXX o o o o o XXX
o o o o o o o o o o XXXXXXX XXX o o XXX o o o o o o XXX o XXX o o o XXX o o o o o XXX
o o o o o o o o o o XXXXXXX XXX o o XXX o o o o o o XXX o XXX XXX o XXX o o o o o XXX
o o o o o o o o o o XXXXXXX XXX o o XXX o o o XXX o XXX o XXX XXXXX XXX o o o o o XXX
o o o o o o o o o o XXXXXXX XXX o o XXX o o o XXX o XXX o XXX XXXXX XXX o o o o XXXXX
o o o o o o XXX o o XXXXXXX XXX o o XXX o o o XXX o XXX o XXX XXXXX XXX o o o o XXXXX
o o o XXX o XXX XXX XXXXXXX XXX o o XXX XXX o XXX o XXX o XXX XXXXX XXX o XXX o XXXXX
o o o XXX o XXX XXX XXXXXXX XXX o XXXXX XXX o XXX o XXX o XXX XXXXX XXX o XXX o XXXXX
o o o XXX o XXX XXX XXXXXXX XXX o XXXXX XXX o XXX o XXX XXXXX XXXXX XXX o XXX o XXXXX
o o o XXX o XXXXXXX XXXXXXXXXXX o XXXXX XXX XXXXX o XXX XXXXX XXXXX XXX o XXX o XXXXX
o o o XXX o XXXXXXX XXXXXXXXXXX o XXXXX XXX XXXXX o XXX XXXXX XXXXX XXX o XXX XXXXXXX
XXX o XXXXX XXXXXXX XXXXXXXXXXX o XXXXX XXXXXXXXX XXXXX XXXXX XXXXX XXX XXXXX XXXXXXX
XXX o XXXXX XXXXXXX XXXXXXXXXXXXXXXXXXX XXXXXXXXX XXXXX XXXXX XXXXXXXXX XXXXX XXXXXXX
XXX o XXXXX XXXXXXX XXXXXXXXXXXXXXXXXXX XXXXXXXXXXXXXXX XXXXX XXXXXXXXX XXXXX XXXXXXX
XXX XXXXXXX XXXXXXXXXXXXXXXXXXXXXXXXXXX XXXXXXXXXXXXXXX XXXXXXXXXXXXXXX XXXXX XXXXXXX
XXX XXXXXXX XXXXXXXXXXXXXXXXXXXXXXXXXXX XXXXXXXXXXXXXXXXXXXXXXXXXXXXXXX XXXXX XXXXXXX
XXX XXXXXXX XXXXXXXXXXXXXXXXXXXXXXXXXXX XXXXXXXXXXXXXXXXXXXXXXXXXXXXXXX XXXXXXXXXXXXX
XXXXXXXXXXXXXXXXXXXXXXXXXXXXXXXXXXXXXXXXXXXXXXXXXXXXXXXXXXXXXXXXXXXXXXXXXXXXXXXXXXXXX
```

We now turn to Exhibit 3, which shows the activity configuration for nonusers. This time we note that the activities plotted near activity 12 are: (1) "Peeling potatoes," (2) Sewing buttons on husband's shirt," and (3) "Cleaning out the closets." While some of the same activities noted in Exhibit 2 also plot fairly near activity 12 in Exhibit 3, it seems evident that nonusers also associate chore-like activities with the activity of "Using a fabric softener in your wash."

Clustering Results

As another means for comparing activity groupings between users and nonusers, the original similarity table for each group was clustered by means of a hierarchial clustering program. In this way, we are able to check the visually obtained clusterings observed in Exhibits 2 and 3 with a procedure that works directly with the original frequency tables. We note from these clustering results that insofar as users (Exhibit 4) are concerned, activity 12 first groups with activities 21 ("Using a room freshener spray") and 28 ("Opening up windows to air out the room"). This cluster is then joined by activities 24 ("Cleaning out the closets") and 26 ("Hanging freshly cleaned curtains").

In the case of nonusers (Exhibit 5), activities 3 ("Sewing buttons on husband's shirt") and 13 ("Peeling potatoes")—in addition to activities 24 and 26—are most highly associated with activity 12. Again we note the combination of olfactory and chore-like activities in the clustering developed from the nonuser group. Interestingly enough, tactile items like "Wearing soft clothes" do not seem to be highly associated with activity 12.

IMPLICATIONS

The preceding pilot study—coupled with the results of a series of focus-group interviews—essentially indicated that

1. Both users and nonusers associate olfactory-like (rather than tactual) activities with fabric softeners.
2. The nonuser group also associates chore-like activities with fabric softener usage.

From the standpoint of the sponsoring firm's promotional strategy, the pilot study suggested that "softening clothes" was no longer newsworthy and that other benefits—freshness, brightness, clean smell—would appear more interesting to promote. Moreover, in the case of nonusers some means of convincing housewives that (1) their efforts would be appreciated by other family members (prinicipally the husband) and (2) fabric softeners could be conveniently used appeared to be needed. The implications for promotional strategy and/or new product development are apparent, given this information. *And* promotional appeals were changed by the study's sponsors.

In the last decade or so, U.S. marketing researchers have become very interested in a new technique for multidimensional scaling called *correspondence analysis*. This tool had long been popular in Europe, particularly in France.

Correspondence analysis works with two-way (or multi-way) cross tabulations of categorical data—for example, buyers' favorite brands cross-classified by age categories. Typically, such data have been used by marketing researchers to look for associations between two or more categorical variables.

When the cross-tables have many rows and columns, it is difficult to discern patterns from the numbers alone. Correspondence analysis provides a way to portray cross-tabulations in pictorial form. Cells in the table that have differentially high freqencies are represented by row and column points that are relatively close together on the map.

Conversely, a row and column whose cell exhibits a low frequency tends to show the associated points relatively far apart. Assuming that the rows and columns are associated (that is, the joint frequency is not simply proportional to the product of the row and column's marginal frequencies), correspondence analysis tries to find compromise locations of all row and column points that best agree with the table's overall association. As such, it provides explanatory power beyond that of a simple statistical test of row and column independence.

A Numerical Example

As an example, we consider the cross-tabulation shown in Exhibit 6. The input data consist of a 10 x 11 frequencies table obtained by a sample of 404 physicians. A respondent was asked to select those promotional activities (newsletter, clinical reports, etc.) that he/she would most prefer a drug firm to implement in introducing a new antihypertensive drug. A total of 1,375 responses (an average of 3.4 selections per respondent) were obtained. Physicians were also classified by specialty (cardiologist, general practitioner, nephrologist, internist, and family physician) and by proneness to innovate (high versus low), based on their first principal component score developed from responses to five psychographic statements.

Exhibit 6 represents a conventional cross-tabulation of frequencies that can be analyzed by simple correspondence analysis. Exhibit 7 shows the two-dimensional joint space plot of physician segments and promotional activities. As noted, along the horizontal axis the specialty physicians (nephrologists, cardiologists, and internists) are separated from the generalists (general practioners and family physicians). We also observe that the effect of a high versus low "innovativeness" is seen to vary by physician specialty.

EXHIBIT 6. Input Data for Two-Way Correspondence Analysis

	News-letter	Clinical Reports	Use Trials	Ex-hibits	Detail-ing	Dinner Meetings	Direct Mail	Journal Cards	Samp-ling	Sym-posia	Audio/Visual	Total
Cardiologist												
- Innovative CRD-1	14	43	43	27	25	26	11	8	17	41	16	271
- Noninnovative CRD-2	9	30	29	17	31	17	5	3	6	34	22	203
General Practitioner												
- Innovative GP-1	13	23	23	18	52	34	7	15	15	19	25	244
- Noninnovative GP-2	13	26	25	21	56	29	8	14	17	16	29	254
Nephrologist												
- Innovative NEP-1	2	15	12	10	9	10	3	7	6	14	8	96
- Noninnovative NEP-2	1	5	9	5	6	3	1	3	6	6	4	49
Internist												
- Innovative IM-1	2	8	8	6	3	3	0	2	4	9	3	48
- Noninnovative IM-2	6	11	11	7	6	3	2	5	3	7	1	62
Family Physician												
-Innovative FP-1	2	5	9	3	11	9	2	4	0	3	3	51
- Non-innovative FP-2	8	10	10	4	21	11	6	3	5	8	11	97
Total	70	176	179	118	220	145	45	64	79	157	122	1,375

Attitudinal Statements
1. I like to try new and different things.
2. I often prescribe new medications
3. I go to more medical conventions than most of my colleagues.
4. I spend more of my time keeping up with new medical developments than most doctors.
5. I spend more time reading medical journals than most doctors.

Cluster Analysis of Joint-Space Coordinates

While the two-dimensional map of Exhibit 7 provides some help in interpreting the space, one wonders whether a cluster analysis of higher-dimensional coordinates might provide enhanced interpretive value. To that end, the coordinates of the four-dimensional correspondence analysis solution were clustered via a hierarchical linkage program. Exhibit 8 shows the results.

As observed from Exhibit 8, the higher-dimensional solution provides useful ancillary information, beyond that provided by the map. For example, we observe that innovative cardiologists and nephrologists cluster together, along with the more "scientific" information sources: clinical reports, clinical trials, and exhibits. This cluster is later joined by innovative internists and symposia.

Both innovative and noninnovative general practioners cluster tightly, along with the less "prestigious" information sources of detailing and audiovisual. This cluster is then joined by noninnovative family physicians and direct mail promotion. Rather, isolated clusters are noted in the case of (1) innovative family physicians and dinners; (2) noninnovative nephrologists and samples; and (3) noninnovative internists and newsletters.

EXHIBIT 7. Joint Space Obtained from Correspondence Analysis

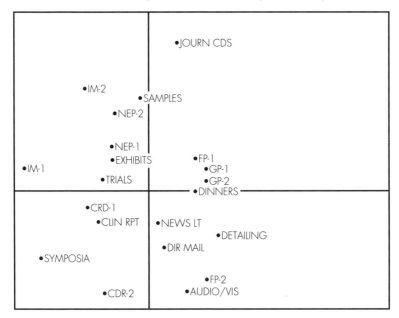

EXHIBIT 8. Cluster Analysis Diagram Based on Four-Dimensional Solution

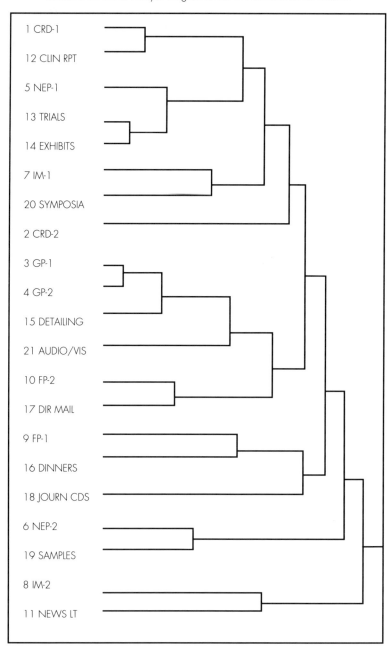

In general, the associated cluster analysis brings out relationships between specialty/innovativeness and preferred promotional activities. At the high end of the prestige scale are clinical reports, clinical trials, exhibits, and symposia; these are typically associated with specialist physicians. General practioners favor detailing and family physicians appear to favor direct mail and dinner meetings. Since the cluster solution entailed four-dimensional coordinates (rather than the two-dimensional coordinates utilized in Exhibit 7), more of the original information was preserved in the cluster solution of Exhibit 8.

Extensions to Higher-Way Data

Correspondence analysis can also be applied to higher-way classification tables such as promotional activities by physician specialty, or by physician's most-used antihypertensive brand. The resulting map would show all three sets of points, rather than the two sets illustrated in Exhibits 7 and 8.

Correspondence analysis has gained enough proponents that many computer program packages are now available for implementing the technique. It has now become routine to supplement numerical cross-tables with the pictorial output of correspondence analysis.

CONCLUSION

From a somewhat more general viewpoint, market position analysis—using multidimensional scaling, correspondence analysis, and clustering techniques—provides help in understanding one's place in the market, as perceived and evaluated by actual or potential customers. In addition, one can assess the position of competitive products. These positions can be monitored over time as a firm changes its product offerings or promotional strategy.

As a diagnostic tool, this methodology can also provide some insights regarding the wisdom of changing the perceptions of buyers' brands, the saliences of customers' perceptual dimensions, and the relevance of the dimensions themselves.

From a strategic viewpoint, both traditional multidimensional scaling and correspondence analysis show how a market (or submarket) perceives brands or services as similar or different. Respondent preferences can also be accomodated. Managers often use the resulting maps to find "gaps" in the market where a new product could be located near a group of consumers who would be attracted to its specific features. As such, perceptual and preference mapping plays a role in product line development.

By the same token, perceptual and preference differences are often noted within the larger market. In this case, niche marketing strategies can be followed to appeal to the needs of different submarkets.

REFERENCES

Carroll, J. Douglas, Paul E. Green, and Catherine M. Schaffer, "Comparing Interpoint Distances in Correspondence Analysis: A Clarification," *Journal of Marketing Research*, Vol. 24 (November 1987), pp. 445–450.

Greenacre, Michael J., *Theory and Application of Correspondence Analyses* (London: Academic Press, 1984).

Lebart, L., A. Morineau, and Kenneth M. Warwick, *Multivariate Descriptive Statistical Analysis: Correspondence Analysis and Related Techniques for Large Matrices* (New York: John Wiley, 1984).

Nishisato, S. and I. Nishisato, *An Introduction to Dual Scaling* (Islington, Ontario: MicroStats, 1983).

Punj, G. and D.W. Stewart, "Cluster Analysis in Marketing Research: Review and Suggestions for Applications," *Journal of Marketing Research*, Vol. 20 (May), pp. 134–148.

Srivastava, R.K., R.P. Leone, and A.D. Shocker, "Market Structure Analysis: Hierarchical Clustering of Products Based on Substitution-in-Use," *Journal of Marketing*, Vol. 45 (Summer), pp. 38–48.

William Lazer
Professor Emeritus
Michigan State University
Principal, William Lazer Associates International
East Lansing, Michigan

M. Bixby Cooper
Associate Professor
Marketing and Logistics
Michigan State University
East Lansing, Michigan

CHAPTER 6

DEVELOPING THE ORGANIZATION'S MARKETING MIX

The concept of the marketing mix, which is less than 50 years old, has gained considerable acceptance as a managerial framework for marketing strategies and decisions. The development of the concept is generally credited to two Harvard professors, James W. Culliton and Neil H. Borden. In 1948, Professor Culliton described the business executive as, "A 'decider,' an 'artist,' a 'mixer of ingredients,' who sometimes follows a recipe prepared by others, sometimes prepares his own recipes; he goes along, sometimes adapts a recipe to the ingredients immediately available, and sometimes experiments with or develops ingredients no one else has yet tried."[1]

This characterization of an executive as a mixer appealed to Professor Borden as a way of describing the actions and results of marketing executive decisions. He soon began to use the term "marketing mix" as a way of describing the end results of executive decisions in marketing.[2] The concept filled a void because it not only characterizes critical marketing management activities, but leads to methods of increasing overall marketing efficiency and productivity as well. The marketing mix as a key concept remains firmly embedded in modern marketing management approaches.

Over the years, the marketing mix has been substantially developed and refined. McCarthy offered a simple four-factor classification of marketing mix ingredients or tools that has popularly been described as the *Four P's: product, price, place,* and *promotion.*[3] Sometimes the mix ingredients are listed under different names or are broken down into finer subclassifications. As a general concept, the marketing mix refers to the totality of a company's offering to the marketplace. It is the mix of controllable marketing variables that firms use to pursue the desired level of sales in target markets.

While the concept of the marketing mix is simple to state, the challenge of developing an effective mix is a complex and difficult task. It requires considerable analysis, planning, and creativity. Both those marketing variables controlled by the organization and those influential external forces that are outside of an organization's direct control must be considered.

In this chapter, we will first consider different levels of the marketing mix. Then, attention will be focused on the process of developing the mix. Following this, the challenges offered by today's global competitive environment, marketing mix extension, and nonbusiness marketing mixes are discussed.

LEVELS OF THE MARKETING MIX

Conceptually, the marketing mix exists at several levels of an organization. It varies in connotation depending on whether it is applied to a single business or to a conglomerate, to one product or service, or to several. Basically, the marketing mix may refer to three different organizational levels: the total corporation, the strategic business unit, and the specific product/service level. While the latter often receives primary attention, it must be remembered that for the greatest effectiveness, specific product/service level marketing decisions should only be made within the context of business unit and corporate mix decisions.

Exhibit 1 depicts the character of marketing mix decisions at the three different organization levels: corporate, SBU, and product levels. From the total corporate perspective, the mix may include a host of diverse offerings consisting of a variety of ingredients that make up an extensive array of business, government, and consumer products and services of multi-nation, multi-product conglomerates. Included are strategic decisions concerning fundamental product or service/market opportunities, pricing, promotional, and distribution strategies.

Product strategies—at the corporate level—deal with such matters as the selection and development of product portfolios, research and development, product scope, product design, and quality. Pricing strategies refer to issues such as overall price level choices, price/value decisions, total product-line price relationships, credit, and terms of sale strategies. Promotion focuses on the planning, implementation, and control of persuasive communications with customers, positioning, and image strategies. Included are the total promotional budget as well as guidelines for allocation of the promotional effort among personal selling, advertising, merchandising, sales promotion, and publicity. Distribution strategies at the corporate level are concerned with which distribution functions to perform internally, distribution scope, degree of vertical and horizontal integration, and control over channel activities. The totality of the above—and related decisions—comprise the organization's total marketing mix.

From a strategic business unit, or other divisional or unit perspective, the marketing mix deals with those marketing inputs that collectively comprise the market offerings of that organizational unit. Consider, for example, the small appliance division of a large, diverse manufacturer of electrical appliances. Product decisions must be made that include such factors as policies related to depth and breadth of product line, individual versus family brand policies, market segments and niches, warranty, guarantee, and repair service policies.

Divisional pricing and credit policies must be established to guide more specific decisions for the family of products offered, including new product pricing, price guarantees, skimming and penetration policies, and price flexibility. Promotional policies relate to the

EXHIBIT 1. Examples of the Marketing Mix at Different Levels of the Organization

Organizational Level	Product	Price	Promotion	Place
Corporate	• Product portfolio • Research and development • Quality • Scope • Design	• Price strategy • Price/value • Product line • Price relationships • Credit and terms strategy	• Total budget • Allocation guidelines • Institutional strategy	• Distribution • Strategy • Scope • Vertical integration
Strategic Business Unit	• Product line depth/breadth • Branding policy • Service policies	• Overall price policy • New product price policy • Price flexibility • Credit and terms policies	• Push versus pull • Promotion themes • Sales organization • Trade promotion policy	• Direct/indirect channels • Locations • Stocking policies
Individual Product	• Specific features Color Size Shape • Brand name • Package design • Warranty • Accessories	• List price • Discounts • Allowances • Terms	• Advertising Media Theme • Trade promotion terms • Personal selling effort	• Specific outlets • Inventory level • Carriers • Locations

extent of pull versus push promotional themes for the division, and sales and sales management activities. The business unit level must address distribution policies concerning direct versus indirect distribution, strategic alliances with suppliers and customers, and logistics concerns such as full-line versus limited-line distribution centers. Together, such divisional policies are among those guiding the development of the marketing mix for specific products.

The marketing mix is often addressed at the level of specific product offerings. Product decisions consist of such concerns as product features, color, size, brand name, packages, label, warranty and guarantee terms, and servicing of each individual product. The pricing mix pertains to decisions such as list prices, discounts and allowances, trade margins, and terms of credit for each offering. The promotion mix comprises decisions related to advertising media, message content, message timing, personal selling and sales practices, and sales promotion tactics for specific offerings. The distribution mix consists of channel decisions such as which outlets and intermediaries to use as well as such physical distribution concerns as specific transportation modes and carriers, inventory levels, and facility locations. Thus the marketing mix—as applied to the product level—refers to decisions about that unique set of ingredients that comprises a single product or service.

The marketing mix, in a very real sense, is the mechanism by which an organization links itself to its selected target market(s). The alteration of ingredients of the mix is the manner in which the organization adjusts to the marketplace. Developing an effective mix is complex and challenging. It focuses on the most fundamental responsibilities of marketing executives such as the formulation of marketing strategies, the development of marketing plans, and key decision making about marketing activities. The basic challenge is to produce, adjust, adapt, and offer a unique and differentiated product/service that satisfies customer and consumer wants and needs in a superior fashion. The mix links organizations to the market and focuses on adjustments to market change. Dynamic market environments place a premium on marketing management flexibility and its ability to respond by continuously altering the mix in a timely and effective manner.

THE MARKETING MIX AND SYSTEMS THINKING

Fundamental to the development of an effective marketing mix is the application of systems thinking by marketing managers. This mix is not rooted in the consideration of individual marketing ingredients such as the advertising media to employ, prices to establish, or product and packaging features. Rather, it deals with total system performance, with the whole marketing mix, with the effectiveness and profitability of that mix as a totality, rather than with the profitability of individual ingredients or submixes.

As described previously, the marketing mix is often considered in terms of four interrelated subsystems or submixes: the product and service mix; the pricing mix; the promotion mix; and the place or distribution mix. The impacts of each of these submixes must be arranged to be supportive and complementary to each other and the whole system, engendering integration and coordination of the submixes, maximizing the total marketing thrust.

In designing a marketing mix, therefore, two perspectives come into play: each of the individual submixes, and the total overall market mix. Conflicts and tradeoffs are involved at both levels. For example, within the promotional mix, tradeoffs may exist between expenditures for advertising versus personal selling. A higher level of tradeoff may exist between the submixes such as spending more on promotional efforts versus lowering prices. The overriding objective is to design tradeoffs that result in the most effective total mix, often at the expense of a particular component(s). The marketing manager's challenge is the effective application of system thinking to avoid suboptimization—whether at the SBU or specific product level—at the expense of the total system.

In any given industry, competing firms may simultaneously attempt to gain market advantage by adopting quite different marketing mix approaches. However, each must reflect systems thinking to coordinate the mix elements effectively. A typical example is in television sets. General Electric (GE) markets a broad line of relatively low-priced television sets that are distributed nationally through multiple distribution channels, including traditional electronics retailers, mass merchandisers, selected supermarkets, and drugstores. GE compliments this strategy with broad-based mass advertising appeals. Sony, on the other hand, markets a somewhat more limited line of higher-priced television sets with a focus on quality. They are distributed primarily through specialty electronics retailers and upscale department stores. Curtis Mathes emphasizes a very limited line of high-quality products backed by a six-year product guarantee. Curtis Mathes televisions are relatively high priced and are distributed through a limited network of dealers that sell only Curtis Mathes electronics.

This example demonstrates how three successful firms—operating in the same industry—differentiate themselves and link to the marketplace with different combinations of marketing mix elements. They have each employed different strategies successfully, based on different products and services, price, channel, and promotional decisions. Each has achieved significant market share and profitability. Close examination of each firm's strategies reveals the application of systems thinking. Consider, for example, the difficulty Curtis Mathes would encounter with its approach to product and pricing if it chose to distribute through the multiple channels employed by General Electric.

Prior to the explicit recognition and acceptance of systems concepts and systems thinking by marketing managers, marketing decisions were often made on a piecemeal basis. Attention was directed to specific ingredients such as pricing, advertising, merchandising, product development, distribution, or personal selling. Marketing situations were approached as independent entities, as separate pieces, rather than as interrelated components of an integrated whole. Marketing specialists saw their tasks as maximizing the output of particular tasks or functions. The result was less than optimum use of marketing inputs with some being overutilized and others underutilized. Some activities thrived at the expense of overall marketing performance. The marketing mix, by contrast, emphasizes total profitability, investigates returns from alternative commitment of marketing resources, and places the emphasis where it should be—on the performance of the total marketing effort.

THE MARKETING MIX PROCESS

Three components of the marketing mix process are analysis, decision making, and monitoring and adjustment. Analysis begins with the development of an environmental information system that provides critical data relating to the uncontrollable macroenvironment. It extends to competitive analysis, market/customer analysis, and internal analysis. The decision-making process includes decisions related to choices of target market segments and niches, and the formulation of specific mix elements that uniquely appeal to chosen customer needs and wants. Monitoring and adjusting activities—the third component—relate to maintaining the relevance of the mix to its dynamic target markets.

Develop Environmental Information System and Evaluate Macro-environments

Fundamental to analysis is development of an environmental information system. This system scans the macroenvironmental forces—sociocultural, lifestyle, technological, economic, international, political, legal—that are beyond the control of managers but nevertheless exert a powerful influence on their decisions. They are critical to developing an effective marketing mix because they influence customer needs and wants, competitor's strategies, and the firm itself. The information system extracts key trends and environmental changes that represent new opportunities for marketing success or threats to effective marketing performance.

The sociocultural environment, perhaps more than any other, is directly involved with shaping the nature of consumer needs and preferences. Factors such as changing cultural values and norms, mores, lifestyles, social class structure, and important demographic trends have a major impact on consumer demand for products and services and the way they are promoted, distributed, and priced.

Consider, for example, lifestyle trends that result in greater demand for convenience. These lifestyle changes have manifested themselves in numerous ways across a broad range of industries. In the food industry, an increasing share of the consumer's food dollar has shifted to away-from-home eating establishments, especially fast-food restaurants. Supermarkets have responded by introducing more convenience through frozen prepared meals, in-store salad bars, and deli-prepared food sections. The packaging industry has developed heat and serve packages. The electronic industry created microwave ovens. And there are a host of ready-to-eat single serving items. In other industries, convenience has had similar impacts. Other sociocultural trends such as the aging and greying of the population, single parents, smaller and more mobile families, non-family households, desire for immediate gratification, concerns for health and physical fitness, and changes in family structure all have their implications for marketing mix strategies.

The technological explosion of the post–World War II period is increasing in intensity. The translation of technological developments into new products and services means new means of promotion and distribution. Portable in-home computers, cellular telephones, fax machines, and satellite television once seemed far-fetched—today, they are a reality. Electronic Data Interchange, video shopping, and information technology are changing the basic nature of business relations with customers and consumers.

The economic environment shapes consumers' ability to pay for goods and services. Employment/unemployment, inflation, industry growth/decline, investment, or other economic trends represent major threats/opportunities to industries, products, and services as consumers delay purchases or trade up or down. Economic changes raise opportunities for businesses to adjust their marketing mix elements to respond more effectively to consumer needs.

The political/legal environment impacts the marketing mix decisions from both basic perspectives as regulation and limitation and industry control. Specifically, this may mean packaging and labeling requirements, advertising and pricing regulations, environmental standards, product safety requirements, and the like. Legal parameters vary by industry, product, and market conditions. Marketing managers must remain ever aware of how these parameters affect mix decisions in their specific realm of responsibility.

Identify and Analyze Competition and Competitors

The second major analytic process in developing marketing mix strategies is competitive analysis. No two organizations can compete effectively in the same marketplace for the same consumer dollar utilizing identical strategies. Competitive analysis enables the marketing manager to identify *who* their competitors are and *how* they compete in the marketplace.

Primary competitors are usually easily identified. For example, John Deere Company competes directly in the lawn tractor business with such well known brands as Toro, Lawn Boy, Murrey, Roper, and Cub. However, it is useful to look more closely and broadly at related competitors who fulfill the same generic customer need. John Deere could define its competitors to include all lawn mowers or even lawn maintenance services.

Once the set of competitors is identified, four generic questions must be answered about how each competes in the marketplace:

1. What are their objectives?
2. What are their current strategies?
3. What are their capabilities?
4. What are their likely future strategies?

The challenges of global competition, and an ever-expanding competitive environment, put competitive analysis at the forefront of marketing management concerns in developing a mix that will uniquely satisfy target customer needs and wants.

Internal Analysis

To a very large extent, a company's marketing mix is shaped and influenced by its internal resources: its financial, human, and physical capabilities, both tangible and intangible. The first step is a critical assessment of company capabilities, which can be a demanding and painful process. It forces managers to identify things they have done and can continue to do well and furnishes a realistic assessment of weaknesses and limitations. Without such an assessment, it is not possible to identify objectively an actionable marketing mix strategy. Internal analysis begins with an examination of organizational performance.

The second step is an assessment of strengths and weaknesses in each functional area. For example, the company's reputation and image, market share, financial condition, production capability, and managerial talent must each be assessed in terms of impact on the firm's ability to implement a marketing mix strategy. To be effective, an internal analysis should not ignore any significant aspects of a firm's overall performance.

The internal organization is particularly relevant to the development and implementation of the marketing mix because cross-functional responsibility pervades. Marketing executives are not the only ones whose decisions impact on the mix. This is particularly true of the myriad of decisions regarding product and pricing components.

The product mix is the joint result of decisions made in manufacturing, research and development, engineering, as well as marketing. While marketers may specify product requirements in terms of consumer wants and needs, the design aspect also depends on factors not exclusively in the marketing realm. The technical problems of manufacturing, the ability to service and repair products, the capacity to respond to product changes, and the need to invest in new facilities are not solely within the scope of a marketing manager's authority. They are, however, critical to the development of the marketing mix.

Similarly, price involves executives from fields other than marketing. Even where marketing executives know the "right" price from a marketing standpoint, they consult with other executives whose thinking may be driven by cost or financial considerations.

These above examples serve only to illustrate that marketing mix decisions must be consonant with the framework of overall corporate capabilities. Even in the face of incredible market opportunities, marketing executives must also consider what the firm is able to implement and coordinate realistically with other corporate functions to formulate an effective marketing mix.

Perform Market and Customer Analysis
The fourth—and most critical—analytical process in developing an effective marketing mix is performing effective market and customer analysis—actual and potential. To establish a strategic edge over its competition, management must:

1. identify the broad market it intends to serve;
2. identify segments and niches within that market and understand customer needs, wants, preferences, and behaviors in each segment and niche;
3. assess the macroenvironment, competitive and internal analysis, and their impacts on each segment; and
4. move from analysis to decision making by choosing target segment(s) and formulating specific marketing mix strategy(ies).

Proper market definition is critical to the success of strategies and effective marketing mix specifications. It is a difficult task for markets, and may be defined in many ways. Included are products or product classes such as the "soft drink market" or "the automobile market"; geographic areas such as the West Coast or European market; institutions such as the retail or wholesale market, and so on. The underlying factor in any market definition is customer and consumer needs. Given broad market definitions, the process is to refine and subdivide each market into finer homogeneous segments. Since various buyer segments seek different benefits—in terms of specific product features and in terms of availability, purchasing convenience, service, and price—specific marketing mixes can be developed for them. The mixes must be responsive to the demands of specific customer demand segments.

The wants, needs, and preferences of market segments are the fulcrum on which the development of an appropriate market mix rests. Understanding customer buying behavior in each market segment is critical because customer behavior is the ultimate driving force behind proper mix decisions. Of particular importance are answers to such questions as: who specifically are the customers in each segment; and how, when, where, and why do they buy. Equally important are answers to questions about the *unmet* needs in each segment. They can be most valuable in the creative design of the marketing mix.

Target Marketing Selection and Formulation of the Mix

Ultimately, the analytical processes described above—the analysis of macroenvironments, competitors, internal resources, and customer analysis—leads to two related decisions: Selection of target market(s) and marketing mixes must be formulated. As difficult as it is to gather the data for the aforementioned analysis, the actual decision process may be even more difficult. It is here that managerial creativity, intuition, and insight is brought to bear—the art of designing the marketing mix. Macroenvironmental analysis may reveal trends and opportunities; competitive analysis can furnish information about current and future competitive strategies; internal analysis highlights the firm's capabilities for capitalizing on trends and opportunities and customer analysis reveals needs, wants, behavior, and unmet needs. But matching the output of these analytical processes provides the basis for the creative definition of target markets and leads to the development of a mix to satisfy those markets.

It is in this sense that Professor Culliton referred to the marketing executive as an "artist." While the analytical processes described may result from scientific inquiry and quantification, the decision-making process requires judgment, intuition, and creativity—the touch of an artist.

Over the years, numerous tools have been developed as either guidelines or conceptual frameworks to aid in decision making. Examples include simulations, a variety of multivariate statistical techniques, and sales response functions that attempt to measure how target markets respond to different levels of expenditure for each of the variables. However, such approaches frequently ignore complex interactions among submix variables and fail to recognize that market response varies *between* markets and *within* markets over time.

A number of conceptual marketing frameworks also yield insights. Some examples are product lifecycle models, classification of motives, consumer purchase behavior paradigms, and classification of goods. A danger is that heavy reliance on such broad generalizations may ultimately result in a plethora of non-distinctive, "me too" market offerings that fail to achieve the unique differentiation so fundamental for success.

Consider, for example, the classic case of Hanes and L'eggs hosiery. It is highly unlikely that any existing response function research or frameworks such as the lifecycle concept would have suggested that a one-size-fits-all product, packaged in an egg-shaped container, distributed through (at one time) a totally new distribution channel, and at a price about one-half that of competing products would have any realistic probability of success. Yet, Hanes marketing executives had the creativity and foresight to blend these elements, and consequently reaped the benefits of a remarkably creative new strategy. Similarly, Xerox management put aside the advice of consultants on the limited market for its copiers, and instead created a mix based on the idea that customers would learn to use the service.

Continuous Monitoring and Adjustment

The above examples do not imply that effective marketing mix development is the result of chance or luck. Rather, a premium is placed on proper monitoring and analysis of the externalities and the adjustment of controllable variables to fit the opportunities that exist. It suggests that continuous evaluation of the effectiveness of existing mix components is important. As environments change, competitors enter and exit, customer needs and wants evolve, and organizational capabilities change. They imply that adjustments and reformulations are needed on a continuing basis to be competitive.

We have entered an era in which environmental and marketplace variables are in a state of flux. Market dynamics are forcing marketing managers to remain ever vigilant. Continuously adjusting and improving marketing mix ingredients to meet market changes is a way of business life—a prerequisite of a marketing orientation. Marketing is a change agent for the organization and the marketing mix is the instrument for change. It permits alignment of company offerings with changing customers and consumer needs and wants. And, as companies vie globally for competitive advantage, constant attention to the ever-changing global marketplace and to continuous adaptation of the marketing mix is critical to achieving effective marketing performance.

Current Marketing Mix Challenges

The current overall business climate is changing in ways that raise special challenges for developing an effective marketing mix. Included are:

1. *Emphasis on value enhancement.* To a major extent, customers now expect to take product quality for granted—it is part of the admission price to the marketplace. The 1980s clearly showed that consumers demand quality, and that quality does not necessarily come at higher costs to sellers or to consumers. The Japanese automobile

industry and the phenomenal success of Wal-Mart are but two examples of the value-enhancement approach.

2. *Service quality concerns.* Historically, service was considered to be part of the "augmented" product. Service offered extra benefits to customers but was not perceived as pivotal or central to fulfilling customers' objectives. However, in recent years innovative marketers have realized that providing quality service may be among the most powerful marketing tools available. Companies are realizing that service provides the impetus for generating and maintaining customer loyalty. This is particularly true because physical product quality has improved to meet "the price of admission to the marketplace." Quality service systems then become prime differentiating factors among competitors. Warranties, guarantees, customer assistance in obtaining information, ordering, and resolving problems are all service elements that aid customers in achieving their objectives. When markets are characterized by an overchoice of similar products, quality service systems enhance the firm's competitive edge.

3. *Social and environmental concerns.* While environmental analysis has long been recognized as a critical process in developing the marketing mix, these factors have been more influential in recent years. Such factors as resource and energy conservation and air, water, and noise pollution, for example, present opportunities to rethink existing mix strategies. They focus attention on such elements as packaging, energy consumption, disposability, waste, biodegradability, and the like. Such concerns will continue to have far-reaching effects, ranging from minor modification such as McDonald's reduction in plastic packages to threats to entire product lines such as Procter & Gamble's and Kimberly Clark's disposable diapers.

4. *Impact of an information society.* Pertinent and timely information is available in such quantity and detail as to potentially overwhelm marketing executives. The information age raises numerous marketing mix challenges and opportunities. On one hand, greater understanding of customers' and consumers' needs and wants is more possible today than ever before. Consider the wealth of information concerning consumer preferences and reaction to marketing mix efforts contained in daily retail store scanning data. Detailed, up-to-the minute information makes possible rapid evaluation and continuous adjustment to consumer demand. On the other hand, the information age has been accompanied by shorter product life cycles, more rapid response by competitors to successful strategies, and enhanced customer knowledge of alternative mix choices. The challenge for marketing executives is to find ways to benefit from the information society by being more responsive to customers

through more effective mix adjustment. There is also a privacy issue of protecting consumer privacy while using detailed information about consumers for their benefit.

5. *Market fragmentation.* Market segmentation implies that not all consumers want or need the same products, but that customer needs can be aggregated for efficient production and distribution. Currently, some markets are being fragmented into increasingly smaller and smaller segments. While this provides opportunities for niche products and niche competitors, fragmentation also stretches the ability of businesses to meet marketplace demand effectively and efficiently. The challenge is to temper fragmentation with efficient marketing and manufacturing capabilities.

Extending the Market Mix

The marketing mix was described earlier as a linking mechanism, one that links the company to market segment(s). This relationship might be portrayed simply as:

$$Company \rightarrow Marketing\ Mix \rightarrow Market\ Segment$$

Realistically, however, firms do not stand alone in their efforts to link to the consumer marketplace to accomplish the desired linkage. They rely on suppliers, channel members, marketing agency specialists, and others. Thus institutions participating in the linkage must be coordinated somehow, or at least receptive and cooperative to an organization's marketing mix efforts. Two examples illustrate the point:

1. A manufacturer may select a particular chain of retail outlets as an ideal mechanism for reaching target customers. However, the retail chain, as an independent entity, has its own mix strategies to consider. The manufacturer is not assured of obtaining distribution through any given retail store. To gain support, the manufacturer's product must be appealing to both channel members and targeted consumers. Pricing strategies must allow for appropriate retail margins, promotional efforts must be consonant with retail buyer strategies, and retail support must be gained. Target Stores, for example, do not simply accept any product from any manufacturer. Rather, as with most major retail firms, they utilize explicit guidelines for product selection and highly sophisticated processes for designating preferred suppliers.

2. Wholesale and retail intermediaries likewise cannot implement their own mix without explicit recognition of their interface with suppliers' marketing mix strategies. Manufacturers are not required to sell products to any retail firm desiring to distribute them. Manufacturer mix strategies of exclusive or selective distribution may restrict the

products available to a given intermediary. Supplier pricing and promotional policies may cause wholesalers and retailers to adjust their programs.

This explicit recognition of the extended linkage among firms has been the driving force in recent years to the development of strategic alliances, partnerships, coalitions, and other networks that multiply the strengths of the participating companies. The basic principle of the extended linkage concept is to coordinate the mix decisions of all parties involved in the value-added process for a given consumer segment—for the benefit of all. The result can be increased consumer satisfaction accompanied by superior financial performance for those involved. The concept of the marketing mix in such situations must then be extended across independent organizations with individual marketing mix decision authority. The resulting marketing mix becomes an overarching concept—one that crosses legal organizational boundaries.

NONBUSINESS MARKETING MIX

The marketing mix as a concept is relevant to nonbusiness applications. It pertains to social causes and ideas, government agencies, symphony orchestras, museums, hospitals, colleges and universities, social welfare institutions, and other nonprofit organizations. Although the organizational objectives of non-profit and profit-motivated entities differ, the principles of developing the marketing mix are similar. Nonbusiness marketers engage in similar analytic and decision-making processes. However, the combination of marketing mix elements differs.

In non-profit settings, the product and service mix relates to the benefits that are delivered to patrons, clients, suppliers, and recipients. The benefits include alleviating hunger, suffering, and pain; generating jobs; uplifting tastes; increasing happiness and well being; advancing educational levels and increasing understanding; absorbing leisure time; and adding to community enjoyment. Nonbusiness marketers may face great difficulty in adjusting their product/service offerings. They often face pressure in pursuing greater segmentation; to do so can mean ignoring some segments. The best product position for the nonbusiness marketer may be unclear since each position may have positive appeals for certain segments but negative appeals for others. Consider, for example, the difficulty faced by the AIDS Foundation in target market selection and product positioning for its campaign promoting "safe sex."

Price in nonbusiness marketing contexts has a variety of meanings. It not only refers to monetary concerns such as donations and contributions, gifts, grants, and other economic values, but also may include psychic, energy, and time costs incurred by patrons, clients, and consumers. The nonbusiness marketer may encounter great difficulty in raising prices. The challenge frequently is to convince target markets that benefits received outweigh added costs.

The nonbusiness promotional mix encompasses a variety of communication tools—both personal and non-personal—to inform, influence, and gain support. Options are usually more limited than those of profit-seeking organizations. Paid advertising may not be feasible due to the high cost of time and space or because social pressures dictate against advertising expenses or particular promotional messages. Some message appeals—such as hard sell—or fear approaches may be prohibited because of the attitudes of target audiences or the nature of the subject itself. (The reaction of some against the Jerry Lewis muscular dystrophy telethons is a case in point.)

Place in the nonbusiness marketing mix refers to the channels used to deliver the benefits to patrons, clients, and customers. Channels are often direct as is the case with museum showings, symphony, opera and ballet performances, hospital services, and charity dispensed by various social welfare agencies. Nonbusiness marketers have difficulty in utilizing and gaining cooperation from intermediaries such as musicians, opera singers, ballet performers, physicians, the media, civic organizations, and other potential facilitators. They normally do not have the funds to build their own distribution channels, are unable to offer the usual monetary incentives, and must rely on appeals to goodwill and social responsibility to gain cooperation. They are at the mercy of the effectiveness of their appeals and the goodwill of channel members to carry out their programs.

Monitoring program effectiveness in a nonbusiness setting can be a trying task. Quantifiable measures such as market share and units sold have limited use in measuring effectiveness of educational, cultural, health, and welfare settings. Frequently, the goals of nonbusiness marketers are long-range and the immediate progress made is imperceptible so that developing measures of ongoing progress is an elusive proposition.

Elements of nonbusiness marketing mix development pose special—but not insurmountable—challenges. They require the same general approach, careful analysis, creativity, and ingenuity necessary in the for-profit sector of the economy. With sound planning and recognition of the challenges, the principles of marketing can be effectively applied in this increasingly important arena.

CONCLUSION

Important marketplace changes are forcing marketing managers to be more attuned than ever to market dynamics. The concept of the marketing mix is an apt framework for reminding executives that ultimately, customers and consumers determine what products and services are to be produced, and how they are to be promoted, distributed, and priced. The marketing mix is a change agent that—properly implemented—establishes and maintains the linkage between an organization and its markets. While the process for developing the marketing mix does not specify the answers to many challenging decisions facing marketing executives, it does, nevertheless, provide a framework for understanding changes in the marketplace and making appropriate adjustments in an organization's offerings.

NOTES

1. James W. Culliton, *The Management of Marketing Costs*, Boston: Division of Research, Graduate School of Business Administration, Harvard University, 1948.

2. Neil H. Borden, "Note on Concept of the Marketing Mix," Boston: Intercollegiate Case Clearing House, Harvard University, 1957.

3. E. Jerome McCarthy, *Basic Marketing*, Homewood, IL: Richard D. Irwin, 1960.

William F. O'Dell
Founder
Market Facts, Inc.
Arlington Heights, Illinois

David K. Hardin
Chairman of the Board
Market Facts, Inc.
Arlington Heights, Illinois

CHAPTER 7

THE MARKETING DECISION

As everyone knows, everyone makes decisions. Some of these decisions are unimportant; others have disastrous consequences when made incorrectly.

So commonplace are decisions that many people make the assumption that the process is largely intuitive in nature, finally resolved by someone pounding a fist on the desk, pronouncing "Go to it!" True, some decisions may be made in this manner, but when the profit or personal consequences are great, the business person must understand the various aspects of the decision-making process.

The development of the right decision criteria may be somewhat more systematic. The company may employ marketing research to uncover data that may prompt new product ideas. Or, the growth of a particular segment of the market revealed by research might lead to the consideration of a reallocation of the total marketing dollar.

The recognition of a significant situation requiring some adjustment is the beginning of the marketing decision. Recognizing significant information may help the marketer recognize a marketing problem.

For example, let us assume that a major breakfast cereal company discovers that its competitor is successfully test marketing an instant breakfast powder. A problem now exists. Should marketing counter with a similar product or, by changing the product concept, seek out a separate market segment? Or, should he or she ignore the product class being created? In any event, a "problem" exists. The question now is: What should be done . . . what adjustment should be made?

MARKETING ALTERNATIVES

It is essential that a complete set of alternative courses of action be developed. The marketing person must first identify the most basic issue. Is the question one of how to allocate the marketing dollar, or how to spend the advertising dollar? The former is more basic. The advertising decision would follow a determination of how large the advertising appropriation is to be.

Often the decision process involves a success in one area and transferring this knowledge to other areas. For example, a successful domestic branch office opening can suggest undertaking overseas expansion. This "discovery" can be termed "environmental."

One marketing environment can result in a multiplicity of separate decision structures—each calling for a different decision. Let's assume that Company A drops the price on a brand in a given product class in which Company B is the leading seller. The apparent tactic of

Company A is to garner a greater share of that product class, hoping that Company B's costs will not permit the latter to drop its price for any extended period of time. Here is a *problem* to which Company B must now adjust. The next step is the formation of alternative courses of action. These possibilities are almost without end. Company B could:

1. Maintain its present price level
   Meet the competitive price
2. Add some agreed upon feature to its brand
   Not add the feature to the brand
3. Increase the advertising budget on behalf of this brand
   Not increase the advertising budget
   Decrease the advertising budget in support of this brand
4. Take the brand off the market
   Not take the brand off the market

There are, of course, other possibilities, but the point here is that items one through four represent separate decision structures. Each one has its own set of alternatives. Each one will result in a different decision choice. The profit consequences of each decision structure are quite different; for example, taking the product off the market has greater profit consequences than adding, say, 15 percent to the brand's advertising budget.

Thus, each and every decision structure must have its own set of alternatives, and *one of the stated options must end up as the final decision.* It is vital that the most basic issue be attacked and resolved before attempting to decide on subissues.

CRITERION FOR DECISION

Every business decision is a prediction. If a marketing manager decides to commercialize a new product, he or she is predicting that a sufficient number of units will be sold to produce the required contribution to profit. If the advertising budget is decreased, he or she is predicting that any loss in sales due to fewer advertising dollars will not be as great as the savings resulting from the advertising reduction. If he or she lowers the unit price of one of the products, he or she is predicting that the increase in sales over the long run will more than offset smaller profit per unit.

It is, of course, essential that marketing people know the specifics of their predictions. When a new product is introduced, someone is predicting a given unit sales level or higher. These predictions are in reality criteria for decisions. They are employing what logicians over the years have called syllogisms. Most usable in today's world is the "hypothetical" or "conditional" syllogism, the "if ... then" approach, which is an essential part of the conditional syllogism.

Simply stated, the conditional syllogism states that "*if* 500,000 unit sales a year can be achieved through the commercialization of this new item, *then* that item will be introduced." The "if" side of the syllogism represents the prediction; the "then" phrase is the course of action under consideration. The "if" side is called the antecedent; the "then" phrase the consequent. The antecedent represents that unknown . . . the uncertainty: "*If* the new product will sell 500,000 units . . .."

It is not always essential that the criterion be reduced to a syllogistic pattern; however, it is most helpful when it is done. It forces one to think along logical lines. The basis for the decision is set forth *in advance.* The marketing person announces what is expected before the final decision is made.

In today's world, profit, *within the appropriate social context,* is the basic criterion. A new product is introduced, or the advertising effort is altered in some way; those responsible for such actions are really saying that they expect their company's profits to increase as a result of the decisions. If the organization is not-for-profit, of course some other benefit would be substituted.

In making many decisions, one cannot obtain a direct measure of profit. For example, advertising expectations virtually defy measurement of profit. Moreover, in many instances the objective of the marketing effort is not immediate profits. Thus the criterion for the decision would be some other measure.

Monetary Measures

A criterion calling for a monetary measure relates to the outcomes of various alternatives *in terms of dollars.* Let's say that the introduction of a new product is being considered. The alternatives are to introduce the product or not to introduce the product. A sales level that this product is to reach at a given point in time must be stated if the item is to be marketed. If the item will not reach that required level, the product will not be marketed.

A predicted sales figure is used if the organization equates sales with predicted revenue, and ultimately with return on investment. The sales prediction is needed to determine or predict revenue. Product costs are known. The scope of marketing effort has been established. The sales level required if the item is to be profitable is known. So, the criterion is sales. Knowing other costs means that once the uncertain figure (sales to be produced) is agreed on, then it becomes "go or no-go."

Monetary measures are usually required for those decisions having alternative courses of action where the marketing alternatives have diverse costs. Whether to introduce a new product is a diverse cost decision because the cost of entering the item on the market (one alternative) costs more than not marketing the product (the other alternative). Thus, a monetary measure becomes the criterion because a revenue prediction must be made. And a sales prediction is essential because sales are the revenue producer.

Let's assume that increasing the advertising appropriation by 100 percent is under consideration. A total of $1 million is now being spent and the marketing management is suggesting the possibility of doubling that figure for the forthcoming year—at the expense of reducing the sales force in rural areas. In order to make the decision as to which route to follow, a sales-revenue prediction must be made. The criterion, then, is sales (revenue).

Many decisions are more complicated. Perhaps a new product is about to be commercialized, but there is uncertainty as to its price. Assume four alternatives: to market the product at price A, B, or C or not to market the product. Figure 1 illustrates how ten options come into being when three prices and three advertising levels are the alternative courses of action. The criterion would be sales-revenue. It is necessary to predict what the sales would be under each of the ten possible situations posed.

Diverse cost decisions that call for a prediction of sales and revenue are often viewed within some companies as finance decisions. Certainly finance people would participate inasmuch as diverse cost decisions involve alternative uses of funds. For example, in most companies, the alternative of marketing a new product includes discussion by both finance and marketing personnel.

The increasing of an advertising budget is a decision rarely made by the advertising manager alone. He or she may participate in the discussion, but the final decision would be made by those responsible for allocating funds. It is normally desirable to have both the finance and marketing people provide inputs to the decision process, especially in view of the fact that the marketing person will be charged with the task of making the sales and revenue prediction.

FIGURE 1.

Advertising Level	Price		
	A	B	C
X	a	b	c
Y	d	e	f
Z	g	h	i

Nine marketing options (a–i) are presented when this combination of price and advertising level is under consideration. A tenth alternative would be not to market the product.

FIGURE 2.

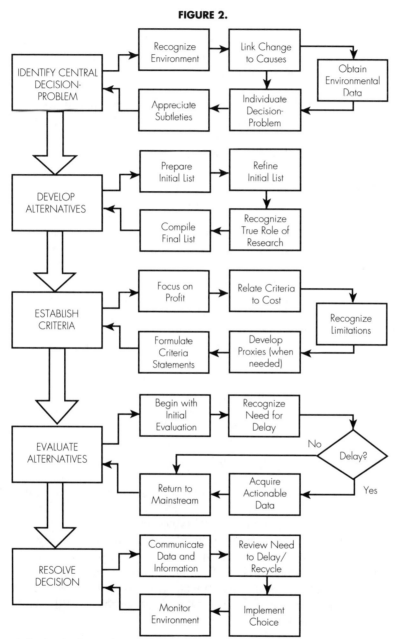

This flowchart of each step in the marketing decision can prove to be invaluable. Reprinted by courtesy of the South-Western Publishing Company from O'Dell, Ruppel, and Trent's *Marketing Decision Making*, 1979.

Nonmonetary Measures

Many contemplated decisions do not seek advance measures of sales and revenue as a basis for determining which alternative will be selected. For example, much advertising is geared to changing the consumers' attitudes toward a given brand, or toward creating greater awareness. To inform the consumer about a given feature or to correct a particular misconception can sometimes be the goal of an advertising campaign.

It is assumed that greater awareness or improved attitudes will ultimately enhance profits. The short-run assignment given to advertising is something short of profits. Much automobile advertising, for example, strives to create a more favorable attitude toward a given make to encourage the prospective buyer to consider that make when in the market for a new car. Automobile advertisers do not urge the consuming public to lunge out of their Sunday night armchairs and rush down to locate a dealer that might be open. On the other hand, a substantial portion of grocery product advertising is aimed at stimulating the shopper to buy a particular brand the next time he or she is in a store.

Therefore, the criterion for identical cost decisions is stated in terms of the objective of the marketing effort: brand awareness, attitude change, awareness of a given feature, etc. Thus, the criterion is stated after the alternatives have been formulated. For many decisions, the nonmonetary criteria are not only acceptable but are preferred over the sales-revenue criteria.

One need only give assurance that one formula will sell better than the other. The criterion can be consumer preference, or stated consumer intention to buy one over the other, or some such nonmonetary measure. It is necessary to know only which of the two is better, not how much better. Assuming that agreement has been reached on two alternatives, it then becomes a matter of determining which of the two is better.

Another example is the decision process when selecting an advertising theme. It costs the same to employ Theme A as Theme B. Thus a nonmonetary measure is desired to determine which of the two themes should be used. The criterion used would depend largely on the objective of the advertising: attitude, awareness, number of people entering a given store, number of people changing their desire to own a given brand, or some other nonmonetary measure. It is not necessary to predict sales for decisions that have identical costs for the various alternatives in question.

DECISION DELAY

Having traveled down the decision path from environment to criteria, it is now appropriate to examine when one should make a decision: without delay or with delay. The extent of the delay before selecting one of the actions being considered is a function of the level of the managerial disagreement and the level of profit consequences of a wrong decision.

If the decision makers quickly decide on which course of action to choose, there is high agreement. When this takes place, the decision makers are saying that they feel there is little question about the criterion being satisfied. Thus there is little disagreement and action is taken; a decision is made easily and quickly.

On other decisions, agreement may not always come readily. The profit consequences of a wrong decision are serious enough that some members of the management group do not agree on whether the criterion figure can be met. Management is saying that it should seek additional information before making the decision. This means a delay until such data can be gathered and analyzed. Such delays are not without cost: opportunity costs as well as costs related to data collection and analysis. In agreeing on a decision delay, management is saying that the decision is too important to make without some reduction in the uncertainty that surrounds the outcome.

In marketing, this information-seeking process is called marketing research. The nature of the research centers around the criterion for the decision. If a diverse cost decision is in the making, the criterion is likely to be sales and revenue. So, the research study would be designed to measure and predict *sales* for the various alternatives in question—in advance of the decision.

How such data would be gathered, what the scope of the research effort should be, and how much time should be allocated to the study would be determined by the marketing researchers and decision makers. But gathering data through marketing research without first knowing how the information is to be used is not only wasteful but it can be extremely costly when the wrong marketing decision is made. Thus it is good to understand the decision-making process—the specific decision structure—from a recognition of the marketing environment, through the alternative courses of action, the criteria for decision, and a recognition of when marketing research is needed. This will ultimately result in better and more profitable marketing decisions.

IMPLICATIONS

Marketing research information can be maximized considerably when the need for the data is fully understood. Many marketing managers and marketing research people seek data without fully understanding why such data are being sought.

Marketing managers should be prepared to answer the basic question: What would I do with the information if I had it? Until this is answered correctly, there are great chances that inadequate data will be obtained. Or, the data will be overly accurate or not accurate enough.

Often business people will discuss at great lengths the possible courses of action that might be taken, only to realize suddenly that they do not have the power to make the decision; it must be made by someone or some group at a higher level within the company. Or, time is taken to discuss decision possibilities that normally should be handled by a person at a lower level. The marketing vice president, for example, does not participate in the creation of advertising copy. Thus it is a waste of time for the marketing manager to permit a discussion of a review of advertising theme choices. Much time is lost in committee meetings by not recognizing this simple fact.

Real world decisions are often more affected by management personnel changes rather than by logic or systematic analysis. Top management too often blindly focuses on a given decision course that fits its prejudices and does not allow new inputs, new information, or new decisions to alter its decision. For example, some managements in industrial goods are really fearful of committing the front-end money to build a consumer products decision. Consequently, they make decisions based on low front-end investment and patient development—and rationalize out of launching consumer products.

An understanding of the decision structure aids considerably in the resolving of the marketing research issues.

Robert A. Lynn
Lecturer in Business Administration
University of Illinois at Springfield
Marketing Consultant
Springfield, Illinois

CHAPTER 8

MARKETING STRATEGY

Marketing strategy is the framework on which all marketing actions rest. It guides the whole marketing program.

MAIN CONCEPTS

Marketing strategy is the use of marketing tools to achieve major marketing objectives. Strategy usually considers the long-term situation, although overcoming an immediate crisis can also become a matter of strategic significance.

The Market and the Competition

The two most basic factors for the marketing strategist to consider are the market and the competition. Much of the marketing effort centers on finding and delivering what members of the target market segment want.

If several competitors, however, all have information about buyers' needs and wants and also have adequate resources to meet the needs and wants, coping with competition becomes the major strategic concern.

Marketing strategy in an active competitive environment takes either an offensive or defensive stand. The established market leader usually practices a defensive strategy, while healthy but lower share marketers use offensive strategies.

Marketing and Overall Strategies

Marketing strategy operates under overall corporate strategy, which may include nonmarketing objectives such as maximizing the aggregate long-term value of all the firm's shares or attaining a target rate of return on shareholders' equity. In many cases, marketing strategy goals, are essential means of achieving corporate strategic goals. If marketing strategy does not succeed, corporate strategy may resort to nonmarketing actions, such as plant closings, to preserve financial soundness.

Tactics and Implementation

Tactics are applications of particular marketing techniques to specific marketing projects. The right advertising of a new product properly timed and placed is a tactic. From the viewpoint of a lower-level manager, such tactics are often thought of as their strategies. For example, a marketing strategy might seek a 5 percent sales increase and might raise the sales budget six percent to accomplish this. Or it might consider a "sales strategy" that would achieve the increased goal through bonuses to salespeople.

Implementation is the execution of both strategy and tactics. A strategy based on expanding the sales force rests on the performance ability of the new salespersons to sell as expected; this in turn requires proper selection and training. A potential strategy that cannot be implemented should not be used no matter how attractive it seems.

ORGANIZATION

Marketing strategy is generally conceived by marketing managers with responsibility for attaining marketing goals. In large organizations, marketing vice presidents or senior division executives have obvious strategic responsibility in firms that practice relatively decentralized management. Mid-level personnel may be encouraged to do strategic planning and execution. In other organizations, product managers and store managers may function mainly as skilled implementors of tactics that support overall strategy.

Strategy and Organization Levels

Top management strategy should drive the marketing strategy. In a firm that markets food through supermarkets and operates restaurants, top management may decide to phase out or sell off the restaurants. The marketing strategist for the restaurants would need to know this to avoid the frustration of pursuing a marketing strategy at variance with top management's corporate strategy. In addition, organizational realities affect marketing strategy. The amount of resources available is one of apparent constraint. The level of skill in the production and sales groups will also affect what can be done.

Types of Strategists

Another consideration is various managerial styles or approaches each of which can work especially well under various circumstances. These strategists can be defined as "explorers," "defenders," and "analyzers." Explorers like to try something new. Defenders prefer holding on to the gains made. Analyzers enjoy carefully deliberated moves more than bold intuitive ones.[1]

Good strategy stands on the match between the environmental realities of the marketplace and the organization's capability. Wal-Mart, for example, developed a strategy of exploring smaller markets with weak competitors. Success made growth possible, and growth was made in low-cost locations that would allow low-price strategy to be profitable. The rate of growth was not so fast as to alert longer established retailers to the new competitor's real threat until Wal-Mart had gained a strong market position.

STRATEGIC OBJECTIVES

The terms *objectives* and *goals* are used interchangeably here. The time horizon of objectives can vary. An early leader in a food product may seek a sustained 40 percent market share after 10 years when the product has matured and competitors have found market niches. A motor vehicles marketer who lags behind a competitor with an improved design might consider strategic price cuts or interest subsidies to hold sales losses at a minimum until the marketer's own improved design comes out.

Marketing Goals

Most marketing strategy objectives can and should be expressed in specific quantitative terms. Here are examples:

• Sales: Raise pet food tonnage by 10 percent over last year.
• Share: Raise brand's category market share from 14 to 16 percent.
• Attitude: Make the brand most aspired to by 50 percent of consumers from 30 to 40 years of age in the over $50,000 per year bracket.

These are often the means to attaining corporate objectives. In some cases, profit can be a marketing strategy objective. A new product might be priced for maximum sales volume consistent with profit of $10 million over the first three years of sales.

Setting marketing objectives involves consideration of the marketer's resources, competitor's resources and expected actions, and the environment faced by buyers. If competitors are all financially ailing during an economic upturn, a strong airline might consider a 20 percent passenger-mile increase attainably ambitious. If a flood of well-designed sport utility vehicles hits a recession market, a financially weak firm might base strategy on a goal of holding market share loss to three percentage points. Over a longer time period, this firm might pursue a "niche" strategy of gaining sales and brand loyalty among members of a very narrow market segment, such as buyers from 22 to 29 years of age in the $20,000 to $25,000 income bracket.

Objectives should be attainable and demand the marketing organization's best efforts. Unattainable objectives can demoralize organization members and call forth less than the best use of marketing resources.

Optimal and Incremental Goals

Optimal or maximum levels in goals demand a desired amount of improvement. These are usually applied to profit goals. There is some combination of price and advertising that would yield the most profit.

Most marketing strategists have long-run goals that are attained incrementally. For example, a firm with 10 percent share may seek 15 percent. In each of the next five years, the goal might be to raise share by 1 percent.

STRATEGY CATEGORIES AND APPROACHES

There are various strategy categories that can be used as guidelines.

Marketing Mix Approaches

Some effective strategies are merely based on use of one or more factors in the marketing mix. Successful new products are examples of attaining objective strategies. A powder-plus-skim-milk diet beverage may get a good start in the marketplace. As competitors predictably appear, the innovating strategist can enhance the product by selling precanned liquid, fruit-juice based products, and solid snack foods. This is a product-based strategy. Most marketing strategy is product and brand based. Line extensions (new flavors and forms) and brand leveraging (the use of an established brand name on new products that have a plausible relation to the brand's positioning) are widely effective. "Flanker" brands are brands or models that extend a product to a higher or lower price class or to customers of a younger or older age group. If there is a movement up the price scale, an unprotected upper "flank" is a strategic danger.

Strategists can face a dilemma. Suppose a "high end" flanker would protect against a competitor's future incursion into an upwardly moving market. In the short run, however, the higher end flanker would not be profitable. If such a flanker is a defensive strategy, it could be a wise expenditure.

A margarine may remain the same product but achieve strategic success through advertising of health-related customer benefits. A company can also increase the volume of advertising, which is also a strategic move.

A soft drink may gain sales through intensified efforts to place it in additional fast food outlets. This is a distribution strategy.

It is seldom feasible to pursue all strategic action alternatives. Affordability, skill availability, and estimated comparative effectiveness can guide the strategist's choice. While most marketing mix-based strategies are mainly oriented toward the market, the choice can also be guided by competitive factors.

A good marketing mix member may be one competitors cannot easily match. Competitors without good R&D budgets may not be able to match new line extensions; those with financial problems may not be able to match a price cut.

There is great marketing power in the effective strategic use of marketing mix elements, either used alone or in combination. The following are examples:

• Product (Barbie doll)
• Advertising (Marlboro cigarettes)
• Price and place (Wal-Mart)

A single marketing mix's strength cannot compensate for major perceived weaknesses elsewhere. Yugo entered the United States market in the 1980s with a low price strategy in the tradition of the Model T Ford and the Volkswagen. Weakness in product quality, however, prevented the low price from being an effective tool.

Broad Groups

Among the earliest marketing strategy classification approaches was that of Igor Ansoff in 1957.[2] The variables affected the changes in the product and the market:

- New product, same market: *product* strategy
- New market, same product: *market* strategy
- Same product, same market: *market penetration* strategy
- New product, new market: *diversification* strategy

Another grouping of strategies is build, hold, and pull back. An attractive market environment and weak competitors could encourage a "build" strategy. An already strong position with rising competitors suggests "hold." High uncertainty without much hope to control the situation can make "pull back" advisable.[3] This should usually be accompanied by product innovations or other marketing mix improvements to be effective over the long run.

Competitor-Based Approaches

In the 1980s and 1990s, marketing strategy often centered on actions against competitors which produced "marketing warfare."[4] Such conditions are encouraged when there is slow market growth and when attractive categories are entered by groups of well-financed marketers, often supported by diversified corporations with "cash cow" products.

In a warfare-analogy environment, it is important to know several things:

1. Are you on the defensive posture when an offensive posture is more appropriate? Usually, leaders must defend against attacks while maintaining a willingness to improve their own market offering.
2. How will your strategy affect competitors? If an aggressive strategy sets off a war by a formerly "friendly" or "good" competitor, perhaps it will do more long-run harm than good.
3. What are competitors doing? Careful study of the trade and local press may give clues. The sales force can be used to help monitor and report on competitors' plans (as they may be revealed by customers).

If a competitor is found to be planning a major move, before it actually occurs, the chance for a bold short-run strategy exists. A two-for-the-price-of-one offer may be promoted to help load the trade with inventory and blunt the launch. Trade deals, price cuts, and ad blitzes might also work.

EVALUATION

Since strategy deals with major matters, it must receive careful evaluation. The process is complicated since in a dynamic marketplace things rarely go exactly as planned.

Results

The most obvious way to judge strategy is by the extent to which it achieves its objectives. If you wanted to sell 40,000 of the new car model the first year and you sold 43,000, most marketers would rate the enterprise as a strategic success. If it only sold 10,000, this would indicate something went seriously wrong, even if the market conditions were less than robust.

A long-term measure of strategic success is the extent to which "brand building" occurs. This is the attainment of high share, high brand loyalty, and favorable buyer attitudes. Strong brands can raise the resale value of an entire firm far beyond the value of the equity shown on the balance sheet.

Process

An unpredictable competitive entry or a surprise recession, may affect results and are not necessarily a reflection on strategy. Similarly a competitor's bankruptcy or a shortage of a competitor's product may make a mediocre strategy perform strongly. Strategy can also be judged by its own internal process:

- Did the strategy make a realistic match of the marketer's capability and the whole marketing environment's features?
- Did the marketing organization function effectively to implement the strategy that was planned?
- Did the strategy make use of a systematic monitoring of competitors' actions?
- Did the strategy combine reasonable careful advance planning with changes that "emergent" factors in a dynamic marketplace thrust on managers after the strategic plan was set?[5]

An effective marketing strategy thus should achieve its results, but it also should deserve to achieve them.

REFERENCES

H. Igor Ansoff, "Strategies for Diversification," *Harvard Business Review* (September–October, 1957): 113–124.

Marian C. Burke, "Strategic Choice and Marketing Managers: An Examination of Business Level Marketing Objectives," *Journal of Marketing Research* 21 (November, 1984): 345–359.

Michael D. Hutt, Peter H. Reingen, and John R. Ronchetto, Jr., "Tracing Emergent Processes in Marketing Strategy Formation," *Journal of Marketing* 52 (January, 1988): 4–19.

Stephen W. McDaniel and James W. Kolari, "Marketing Strategy Implications of the Miles and Snow Strategic Typology," *Journal of Marketing* 51 (October, 1987): 19–30.

Al Ries and Jack Trout, *Marketing Warfare* (New York: McGraw-Hill Book Co., 1986).

H. Keith Hunt
Professor of Business Management
Graduate School of Management
Brigham Young University
Provo, Utah

CHAPTER 9

GOVERNMENT REGULATION AND THE MARKETING MANAGER: DEVELOPING A PERSPECTIVE

Once upon a time, a long time ago, in the narrow strip of land between the edge of the water and the tall dark forest near where the river flowed into the sea, there lived four families, each with several family members and each being located some distance from each of the others. They subsisted on food they grew and on fish and meat they caught. Intermarriage kept the families linked emotionally. All exchange of goods was through a simple barter process. There was no money. No trade credits existed. Occasional violations of what seemed right were handled as family matters, with an occasional battle to assure that each family knew its relative status. Wrongs were quickly taken care of, through some combination of actions ranging from peace gifts to warfare, between parties who knew each other very well. Given the wrong, in most cases the parties knew what was the appropriate combination of actions to restore equilibrium to the simple system. While the system was often brutal, it definitely was simple and effective.

Life has become much more complicated than our "Once upon a time" world. In most cases, we have no idea who makes the products we purchase and consume. We exchange money for products, and we store or borrow money as conditions fluctuate. Many products are so complex that we do not have the capability to evaluate their effectiveness or safety. None of us is an individual life sustainer but rather we are linked for our very survival to most of us doing our own thing well and then exchanging with each other to satisfy needs. Some of our products are so technologically and mechanically complex that it takes whole cities of workers working in concert to efficiently produce the product. This system can be just as brutal as the simple "Once upon a time" system, but instead of simplicity, we have complexity multiplied upon itself. Not only can't individuals directly rectify wrongs, in many cases they are not even aware of the wrong, and in most cases they have no idea how to correct it. The social system is so complex that few people in the society have even a rudimentary understanding of how it operates. Yet all the people, as either consumers or producers or both, try to function within the system to provide an acceptable level of life satisfaction for themselves and their immediate family unit.

As society has become so much more complex, it has gradually invented prescriptions and proscriptions intended to enable the system to work. Which shalt's and shalt not's are in use in a particular society are a reflection of the relative power of the various individuals or associations of individuals existent in the society. Each of the do's and don'ts was specifically introduced into the set of rules to benefit some person or association of persons. Where one person's benefit was another person's detriment, social power and compromise usually determined which rules would hold sway for the current time.

As a marketing manager, you have to operate within this vast, highly-complex set of rules telling you what you must, can, might, cannot, and must not do. If you work a lifetime as a marketing manager in one industry you might not even then understand all the prescriptive and proscriptive regulations that impact on you and on your probability of success. Some things you will do because they seem right to you, never realizing that you are actually required to do them. Other things you will avoid doing because they seem wrong, never realizing there is a rule that you cannot do them.

In still other cases, you will become aware of and come to understand the general and specific rules telling you what you can and cannot do. In each of these cases, whether because you understand the rule or because you are merely doing what seems correct or proper and unbeknownst to you it agrees with the rules, you are behaving in accordance with the standards declared and enforced by society. On the other hand, there will be decisions that to you seem right but that violate some societal rule. If you are aware of the rule and knowingly violate it, you then deliberately risk punishment to gain profit or competitive advantage or whatever your objective might be. Where you are most open to making a serious error is in those decision areas where you are not aware of the societal rules and do not know that you are unaware, not realizing that such a rule might exist.

To the extent that the preceding paragraph is true, as a marketing manager you can get hurt by government rules in only two situations: (1) where you misperceive the risk of violating a rule you are aware of and (2) when you are ignorant of a rule.

The solution to these two situations is the same—it is your responsibility to become fully aware of all the marketing regulations affecting your decision area. You need to know not only the rule, but also the reasoning and history behind the rule so you can correctly judge when and where the rule applies and when and where it does not. You gain this awareness, insight, and understanding through an active, intelligent involvement in professional reading and attending professional meetings. Your competitors, your clients or consumers, and government units will be most willing to point out your mistakes to you.

If you want to avoid those mistakes, or at least know when you are making them and the risk function associated with them, you have to continually add to your knowledge in this area. As you first become aware of a rule or set of rules, you might need some explanation from your legal advisor so you can understand all the ramifications of the rule. Part of becoming knowledgeable about a rule is understanding how the rule came into being and what interest groups wanted it passed. Sometimes the reasons for a rule are obvious. Other times it takes considerable insight and historical understanding to see a rule in its true light. This all becomes critically important if you ever decide that a rule is wrong and you set out to try to get it changed.

Quite simply, then, for trade to freely flow between unacquainted parties and for commerce to operate to the societal good, a wide variety of rules are passed that all parties can rely on in good faith to be the basis for commercial transactions. It is your responsibility as a marketing manager to understand as many of those rules as possible. Spending your time ranting and raving about all the laws working against you that are antibusiness and antifree-enterprise merely marks you as a fool who is unwilling to learn to operate within the set of rules established by society.

Once a marketing manager has internalized the need for understanding the rule system within which he or she operates, two remaining concepts need to be understood: (1) that each rule important to the success of the business needs to be understood from the points of view of all relevant parties, not just from one individual's, and (2) that most of the people involved in the regulation of commerce, except for the marketing managers, have legal backgrounds and espouse the adversary process for resolving conflicts.

It is often the case that a rule, if viewed from only one point of view, is a serious infringement on the free decision making of the one party, maybe even working a serious disadvantage on that party. This is sometimes the case for the marketing manager. A rule requires that you do or do not do something, causing a serious cost or competitive disadvantage to you. Unless you make the extra effort to see that rule from the points of view of the buyer or consumer, of competitors, or of society in general, you will never understand why in the broad sense the rule is good, even though it works a disadvantage on you.

In the previous paragraph, you were urged to understand as many rules as possible. Now, adding to that, it is your responsibility as a marketing manager to not only understand the rule from your point of view, but to recognize the points of view of all other involved parties so you have a full understanding of why all parties feel about the rule as they do. Only then are you in a position to feel you truly understand the rule and to make correct assessments of the risk function associated with violating the rule.

The rules affecting marketing management are developed, formalized, and enforced as part of our system of law. The primary actors, except for the marketing managers, have legal training and are either practicing lawyers or are at least highly familiar with legal proceedings. Scientists use the scientific method in their search. In religion, spiritual feelings and manifestations provide the base for truth. In athletics, winning is truth. In legal matters, truth is arrived at by two or more parties, advocates for each point of view and adversaries in this proceeding, each arranging evidence so as to promote their own point of advocacy and to discredit or destroy their opponent's points of advocacy. A referee or judge hears the arguments and declares which advocate's position is true.

A recognition that most rules affecting marketing managers are developed in an adversary process should alert the marketing manager to at least a couple of things. First, the marketing manager has not been trained to operate effectively in adversary proceedings (indeed, his training and experience are probably highly nonadversarial, whether it is how to operate within the firm's organization or to secure profitable sales from customers), so that marketing manager has about as much chance of being successful in an adversary proceeding as a pro-tour golfer has if one Sunday he or she decides to be a starter for a favorite NFL team. The lack of experience in adversarial proceedings does not mean that the marketing manager should declare a mismatch and give up. Rather, he should seek help from individuals who do have the experience. Also, if he is going to continue to be involved in such matters, he needs to gain his own experience.

The need for help from someone with adversarial experience raises the second alert. Professionals in adversarial domains earn their income from plying their trade in conflict situations. It is to their advantage to generate conflict, to facilitate conflict, to prolong conflict, and to institutionalize conflict. So, while the marketing manager has to use the services of an adversary specialist, he or she needs to continually keep in mind that the specialist is especially attuned to conflict and to operating in the adversary mode, while the marketing manager may be more interested in a conciliatory mode or accommodation mode just to solve the problem so he or she can get on with his or her own specialty of marketing.

The adversary specialist is well grounded in numerous experiences in which the accommodation mode was tried, resulting not only in the accommodation failing but in the adversary base being so compromised that it also failed. Besides, they are comfortable with the adversary process and know how to be successful operating in that mode, and they are substantially less experienced and thus less comfortable operating in any other mode. So, the marketing manager finds himself or herself in the situation where he or she has to have the advice of the regulation expert. At the same time, he or she recognizes that the expert prefers to operate in an adversary mode which tends to formalize the conflict and increase the likelihood of formal legal proceedings. In this damned-if-you-do/damned-if-you-don't situation, the only protection is for the professional marketing manager to develop his or her own knowledge and experience in adversarial processes so he or she can better decide when to fight and when to capitulate, and compare his or her judgment with that of his or her adviser.

Finally, building from the early comments in this chapter, the marketing manager who recognizes that government regulation is necessary for stability in commerce also recognizes that that regulation can be helpful as well as frustrating. Just as regulation forces a marketing manager to incur expenses that benefit the consumer, other regulation protects the marketing manager from the whims of the consumer. Just as regulation protects competitors from an individual or company, so it also protects them from competitors. The marketing manager has the obligation to the firm and society to recognize and use the benefits of regulation for the firm's advantage.

Where new regulation is pending, the uncertainty associated with the new regulation may make the old more desirable, even though the new has much in favor of it. For example, in the late 1970s and the early 1980s, the Federal Trade Commission attempted to make a rule regarding used car sales that would require each used car be inspected by the seller and the condition of specific parts of the car be classified as needing work, being okay, or being uninspected. This information would supposedly help consumers judge which car was most likely to be the best purchase mechanically. However, it would have required used car marketers to develop a formal inspection process, which was a totally new idea. And, there was no evidence that consumers would use the information effectively, if even correctly. So, given the uncertainty, used car marketer associations successfully fought the rule. Most business managers were opposed to the rule because, while the idea was interesting, it was not interesting enough to offset the uncertainty associated with it. This is often the case. Nor can the manager be faulted. The manager knows how to operate successfully under the current rules. Why change? Only when there is considerable consumer outcry against current business practice, such as was novelized by Upton Sinclair in *The Jungle,* does business recognize that the uncertainty of the *status quo* is greater than the uncertainty of the new.

Also, regulation is often used to stifle competition. Rather than changing one's way of doing business, it is sometimes easier to get special interest legislation passed or special regulations passed which protect the endangered business. For example, when chain stores started developing, it was thought easier by many small retailers to urge their states and the federal government to enact special bills discriminating against chains than to revamp their own mode of operation to successfully compete with the chains. In another example, it may make more sense for the small retailer to support the passage and enforcement of a price maintenance program than to attempt to compete head-on on price with chains and large independent stores. In most cases, anticompetition actions will eventually be overturned. But that may take years, even decades, during which the competitive advantage accrues to the special interest group favored by the regulation.

A more frustrating problem is that often the government regulation does not seem to be accomplishing what it was intended to accomplish. Not only is society imposing on the business, but the intended benefit to consumers is not occurring. For example, in the early 1980s, there was substantial talk and action toward requiring various kinds of labels on alcoholic beverages, especially ingredient labels and warning labels regarding fetal alcohol syndrome birth defects. However, preliminary research showed that at-risk people were affected differently by such information—even were differentially perceptive of such information—and that it was highly unlikely that the information program would have any of the planned effects.

On still another front, sometimes consumers do not want to be protected. Pyramid marketing organizations hurt only those who get involved in them, and they want to get involved very badly. Or so the story goes.

Sometimes regulation is needed because consumers cannot be expected to ever know enough to correctly discern whether a product can do what it claims to do. For example, prescription drugs are understood only by thoroughly trained pharmacists. Even a reasonably-trained medical doctor has only a modest knowledge of pharmacology. Consumers cannot be expected to be able to judge whether a prescription is safe or not. So regulations are imposed to force safety. In providing this safety, individuals wanting unproven drugs and purveyors wanting to sell those people unproven drugs are frustrated.

At a quite different level, a mouthwash product claimed for years that its use reduced the number and the severity of colds and sore throats. Individual consumers had no way to prove or disprove this claim, even with use. Even if one had many bad colds and sore throats, one could only imagine how terribly sick one would have been had one not been a regular user of the mouthwash. If a person had few colds and sore throats, then that was positive evidence that the mouthwash did fulfill its claims, yet most people have few colds and sore throats. When it was found that a large portion of the population believed the product's untrue claims, deceptive advertising law was violated and the advertising was stopped.

And sometimes the regulation exists to protect competitors from each other and from other businesses. Predatory competition is prohibited. Prices must be the same to similar sellers who then resell the goods. Different prices to different wholesalers or retailers must be justified by actual cost differences in servicing the particular accounts. Some anticompetitive actions are punishable by triple damages—that is, the actual damages caused by the illegal action are determined and that amount is tripled, making, in most cases, such actions more expensive than could ever be justified by even the most profitable expected return.

In summary, as life in general, and particularly commerce, has become highly complex, a variety of rules and regulations are needed to keep commerce operating smoothly and fairly. It is the marketing manager's responsibility to be aware of and to understand these rules and regulations, both in facilitating his or her own decisions in a positive sense and in avoiding conflict with the rules and regulations in a negative sense. The rules and regulations can even be used to advantage in some cases. Important rules and regulations need to be understood from the viewpoint of each of the involved parties. Professionals in the world of rules and regulations (often lawyers) are educated and trained in the use of adversary proceedings; most marketing managers are not even aware of how adversary proceedings arrive at truth and thus are unlikely to be able to operate in that mode without the advice of an experienced person. At the same time, such advice is likely to be conservative and may not lead to a quick, simple resolution of a problem. Finally, rules and regulations work for you as well as against you, and the marketing manager needs to recognize how rules and regulations are helpful, learning to use rules and regulations, new or already in place, to better his or her own competitive position.

William L. Trombetta, Esquire
Professor of Marketing and Management
Chairman, Department of Management/Marketing
Fairleigh Dickinson University
Madison, New Jersey

CHAPTER 10

SUBSTANTIVE AND PROCEDURAL CHANGES IN ANTITRUST LAW: IMPLICATIONS FOR MARKETING MANAGEMENT

INTRODUCTION

Most marketers are aware that antitrust law has a significant impact on strategic marketing management and decision making. However, they may be unaware that a number of relatively recent United States Supreme Court decisions have created a new legal environment for trade regulation. Specifically, subtle but significant changes have occurred in the evolution of substantive *per se* or horizontal law; a veritable revolution has occurred in procedural law in general as a result of three extraordinary back to back Supreme Court decisions involving the motion for summary judgment. This chapter is designed to provide an overview of these profound changes for the marketing practitioner.

The Antitrust Laws

There are four federal antitrust statutes: the Sherman Act, the Clayton Act, the Robinson-Patman Act, and the Federal Trade Commission Act. In addition, every state, except Pennsylvania, has its own antitrust legislation ("baby antitrust acts") patterned to a great extent on federal antitrust statutes. For the purpose of this chapter, the focus will be on the Sherman Act.

Section 1 of the Sherman Act prohibits contracts, combinations or conspiracies that unreasonably restrain trade. For example, agreements among independent competitors to fix prices or to allocate markets or customers represent classic violations of Section 1. It is very important to note that a Sherman Section 1 violation requires more than one competing entity (the numerosity requirement).

Section 2 of the Sherman Act prohibits any person from monopolizing, attempting to monopolize, or conspiring to monopolize any part of trade. For example, predatory conduct by one competitor to drive another competitor out of business would violate Sherman Section 2. Although Section 2 has a conspiracy provision, it is primarily aimed at predatory or unreasonable *unitary* conduct. In other words, the predatory conduct of a single competitor can run afoul of Section 2 whereas a Section 1 violation requires two or more independent competitors.

Violation of the antitrust laws can be very costly in a number of respects, including criminal as well as civil sanctions, substantial fines, automatic trebling of damages, injunctive relief, and enormous litigation costs in both money and time.

The Basic Antitrust Standards

There are two basic standards of legality in antitrust law: the *per se* rule and the rule of reason. The Supreme Court has held that there are certain types of commercial conduct that are so inimical to competition and so lacking in any redeeming value they are conclusively presumed to be unreasonable and therefore illegal, *per se*. Under this *per se* standard, it is not necessary to inquire as to the harm caused or any market definitions in which the conduct occurred. The courts will not entertain any proposed excuses or justifications for this kind of inherently illegal conduct. Among the practices deemed to be *per se* unlawful are price-fixing and horizontal (within or at the same level of distribution) allocation of customers or markets (*Northern Pacific Railway Co. v. United States,* 1958).

The rule of reason standard is whether a trade restraint is more procompetitive than anticompetitive in the relevant product and geographic markets (*Chicago Board of Trade v. United States,* 1918). Under this standard, reasons and proposed justifications for the challenged conduct will be allowed for consideration. Additional critical issues in a rule of reason analysis will be the existence of a defendant's market power (usually by examining the extent of the relevant product and geographic markets foreclosed) and whether competition was promoted more than it was suppressed.

Recently, a middle ground between the *per se* rule and the rule of reason has arisen, sometimes referred to as the "truncated" approach. Under certain circumstances, courts have refrained from applying the *per se* standard; rather, the challenged conduct has been condemned as unreasonable, but without resorting to a full-blown rule of reason analysis (Proger 1991). This approach encompasses the complementary features of the *per se* and rule of reason approaches. Hence, for our purpose, the focus will be on the two traditional standards: *per se* and rule of reason.

The distinction between the *per se* and rule of reason standards is critical to understanding the change in traditional analysis of the so-called "hard core" *per se* violations, such as price fixing. Depending on the standard being applied, the challenged conduct will receive very different treatment under the law. A plaintiff under the rule of reason will have to prove that the defendant has market power (typically, a surrogate for market power in antitrust cases is high market share) in the relevant product and geographic markets and that the conduct at issue is more anticompetitive than procompetitive. This is very time-consuming and expensive litigation which the plaintiff rarely wins. Hence, it is in the plaintiff's interest to position his case in the *per se* category (Jorde and Lemley 1991). To the extent that the traditional *per se* types of conduct can receive more favorable treatment, from the defendant's perspective, the implications for strategic planning and marketing management are profound. We now turn to the first momentous change in substantive antitrust law.

THE SUBSTANTIVE EROSION IN
THE PER SE STANDARD: PRICE-FIXING AND
JOINT, COLLABORATIVE BEHAVIOR

The BMI Case

The first Supreme Court decision to retreat from the formal categorization of *per se* conduct is *Broadcast Music, Inc. v. Columbia Broadcasting System* ("BMI") (*Broadcast Music, Inc. v. Broadcasting System* 1979). *BMI* involved a classic *per se* violation; yet, for the first time in nearly ninety years of antitrust law, the Supreme Court accorded *per se* conduct the more lenient (from the defendant's perspective) rule of reason treatment.

BMI involved a challenge to a blanket licensing system by which BMI and American Society of Composers, Authors, and Publishers ("ASCAP") negotiated fees to copyrighted musical compositions on behalf of thousands of authors and composers. Columbia Broadcasting System ("CBS") alleged that this arrangement was illegal price fixing.

Blanket licenses give the licensees the right to perform any and all of the compositions owned by the authors, etc., as often as the licensees desire for a stated period. Fees for blanket licenses are ordinarily a percentage of total revenues or a flat dollar amount, and do not directly depend on the amount or type of music used.

After a trial, the District Court dismissed the complaint holding, among other things, that the blanket license arrangement was not price fixing and, consequently, not a *per se* violation of the Sherman Act. The Court of Appeals reversed holding that the challenged conduct was a form of price fixing illegal *per se.* The Supreme Court held that the issuance of blanket licenses by BMI and ASCAP was not *per se* unlawful price fixing.

SUPREME COURT REASONING

The Court essentially characterized ASCAP and BMI as clearinghouses that made sure if a composition was used, the artist received a royalty. The blanket license system controlled unauthorized use of compositions and negotiated licenses to use the music. Because of the nature of the blanket licensing arrangement, prices for all compositions were necessarily fixed.

The Court rephrased the issue in this case: not, is this price fixing; rather, is the conduct at issue here *per se* price fixing! Prior to *BMI,* any and all agreements on price had no redeeming value and could never be justified (see *United States v. Trenton Potteries Co.* 1927 and *United States v. Socony-Vacuum Oil Co.* 1940).

In *BMI,* the Court made a number of precedent-shattering statements that turned away from formalistic, simplistic labeling of competitive conduct. Now, conduct that does or could affect price will be evaluated according to a new standard: is the conduct such that it "is 'plainly anticompetitive' and very likely without 'redeeming virtue'" (*BMI* 1979). The new threshold inquiry into collaborative behavior, including price fixing (other than overt, naked price fixing where the sole purpose is to eliminate price competition) focuses on "whether the effect and . . . purpose of the practice are to threaten the proper operation of our predominantly free market economy; that is, whether the practice facially appears to be one that would always or almost always tend to restrict competition and decrease output" (*BMI* 1979).

The Court used as an example two partners in a firm who agree to set the prices of their goods or services. While this is literally "price fixing," it is not the kind of conduct that is *per se* illegal price fixing (*BMI* 1979).

The Court held that the blanket license was reasonably necessary to make this market work because of the practical difficulties in negotiating with each individual composer. Another critical factor in the *BMI* Court's reasoning was that a "new product" was created here:

> *Here, the whole is truly greater than the sum of its parts; it is, to some extent, a different product. . . . Thus, to the extent the blanket license is a different product, [BMI] is not really a joint sales agency offering the goods of many sellers, but is a separate seller offering its blanket license, of which the individual compositions are raw material. [BMI and ASCAP], in short, made a market in which individual composers are inherently unable to compete fully effectively* (BMI 1979).

The Court also analogized the practice at issue to a joint venture that is typically analyzed under the rule of reason:

> *Not all arrangements among actual or potential competitors that have an impact on price are per se violations . . . or even unreasonable restraints. ... Joint ventures and other cooperative arrangements are also not usually unlawful, at least not as price fixing schemes, where the agreement on price is necessary to market the product at all* (BMI 1979).

Implications for Marketing Management

BMI puts aside mere labeling and indicates that courts will examine collaborative conduct to determine if procompetitive effects can be demonstrated. The blanket license arrangement resulted in lower costs to licensees of the music by eliminating separate negotiations with thousands of individual composers.

A new product was created through the joint licensing. Finally, the Court analogized the BMI situation to a joint venture: a lawful collaborative undertaking among competitors to achieve a legitimate, superordinate objective beyond the reasonable means of any one joint venturer.

More than ever before, marketing managers will have an opportunity to attempt to justify and demonstrate procompetitive collaborative efforts. Marketing plans will become ever more important as documentary evidence to established legitimate business objectives and the strategies and tactics necessary to achieve them.

For example, the General Motors-Toyota joint venture resulted in a new product that required two competitors to agree on the price of the new car. In health care, networks of competing hospitals and physicians have formed into independent practice associations and preferred provider organizations in response to managed care: systemic alliances among insurers, corporations, and third party payers to manage the delivery of health care by controlling what and when medical services are appropriate and the prices of these services through negotiating price discounts and contracts with health care providers that cap professional fees.

These health care provider formations are fraught with antitrust exposure due to the risk that fee discussions may arise among the competing health care providers. Nonetheless, *BMI* signals, and the antitrust enforcement authorities agree, that the procompetitive benefits associated with competitors coming together to develop a "new product," one that each doctor or hospital acting alone could not offer, a managed care network, outweighs the anticompetitive aspects—independent, competing doctors setting fees among themselves for the convenience of third party payers, insurers and corporations (Trombetta 1987).

In sum, *BMI* suggests that the courts will look to the purpose of the restraint. If the objective is legitimate—lower prices; enhanced quality; improved service; increased consumer satisfaction; or some combination of these procompetitive features—the courts will suffer some ancillary restraints (price fixing or market allowances, e.g.). Hence, the overriding objective and net effect of collaborative efforts among competitors must be procompetitive; any trade restraints must be secondary to the legitimate objective. For the first time in antitrust history, the Supreme Court's message is that it will consider the economic realities of the marketplace in evaluating the legality of heretofore *verboten* practices.

NCAA

National Collegiate Athletic Association v. Board of Regents of the University of Oklahoma ("NCAA") was the second Supreme Court decision that dealt with heretofore strictly forbidden *per se* conduct in a rule of reason fashion (*NCAA* 1984). *NCAA* involved a complaint by certain colleges over the NCAA's football television regulations. The NCAA contracts specified the total number of games televised in a season, and the maximum number of games that a university could televise.

The NCAA claimed that its controls and contracts were reasonable. They protected gate attendance that might otherwise be adversely affected or destroyed by television. The NCAA claimed that its restraints were not anticompetitive; rather, they enhanced the variety and quality of college football programming.

As in *BMI, NCAA* involved a classic *per se* situation: the restraints raised price and reduced output. Yet, although the Supreme Court found the NCAA program unlawful in the end, that decision resulted after the Court examined the NCAA's preferred procompetitive justifications, typically only allowed in a rule of reason context.

Supreme Court Reasoning. As in *BMI*, despite the classic *per se* conduct, the Court characterized this industry as one in which horizontal restraints on competition are essential if the product is to be available at all (*NCAA* 1984).

Implications for Marketing Management. Along with *BMI*, *NCAA* continued the trend away from simplistic pigeon-holing toward more sophisticated analysis of horizontal agreements that may have procompetitive effects.

Indiana Federation of Dentists

Federal Trade Commission v. Indiana Federation of Dentists ("Indiana Federation") involved a group boycott among dentists to refuse to submit x-rays to dental insurers for use in benefits determinations (*Federal Trade Commission v. Indiana Federation of Dentists* 1986). As a result of cost containment pressures in health care, dental health insurers attempted to limit the payment of benefits to the least expensive, yet adequate treatment for patients. Hence, dentists, along with claims forms seeking reimbursement from insurers, were required to submit any dental x-rays in examining patients to assist the reviewers in evaluating questions as to whether a dentist's recommended course of treatment was in fact necessary. The dentists agreed among themselves to withhold the x-rays under the guise that merely sending the x-rays would not provide enough information and could even mislead the reviewers.

Supreme Court Reasoning. Even though the Court characterized the dentists' collective refusal as a group boycott, another classic *per se* violation category, it declined to apply the *per se* rule: "We decline to resolve this case by forcing the Federation's policy into the 'boycott' pigeonhole and invoking the *per se* rule" (*Indiana Federation* 1986).

Even under the more lenient rule of reason, the dentists' collaborative conduct was condemned:

> *Application of the Rule of Reason to these facts is not a matter of any great difficulty. The Federation's policy takes the form of horizontal agreement among the participating dentists to withhold from their customers a particular service that they desire—the forwarding of x-rays to insurance companies along with claim forms. . . . Absent some countervailing procompetitive virtue—such as for example, the creation of efficiencies in the operation of a market or the provision of goods and services . . .—such an agreement limiting consumer choice by impeding the 'ordinary give and take of the market place' cannot be sustained under the Rule of Reason* (Indiana Federation 1986).

Implications for Marketing Management

The progression from *BMI* through *Indiana Federation* at the Supreme Court level continues at the lower court levels as well as courts factor into their decisions strategic planning, marketing analysis, and economic realities in *per se* contexts. The substantive erosion in the *per se* standard will allow marketers to demonstrate and support legitimate goals in previously foreclosed practices such as agreements on price among competitors in particular.

THE REVOLUTION IN PROCEDURE: THE MOTION FOR SUMMARY JUDGMENT

If the erosion in the *per se* standard was evolutionary, the aggressive use in the procedural motion for summary judgment was revolutionary with perhaps even more profound implications for marketing management.

Definition and Purpose of Summary Judgment

The purpose of the motion for summary judgment is to save courts and litigants from the burden of litigating cases where no genuine dispute exists (Friedenthal 1988). Its purpose is to dispose of useless lawsuits (Levine 1988).

The Old and New Approaches to the Motion

Rule 56(c) of the Federal Rules of Civil Procedure provides that summary judgment may be granted, prior to trial, through affidavits, depositions, and other materials showing that there is no genuine issue as to any material fact and that the moving party is entitled to relief as a matter of law (Rogers III 1979).

In the "old days," as recently as 1985, the Supreme Court disdained the use of summary judgment in antitrust litigation. Trial judges maintained a rigorous belief of the right of a party to confront and cross-examine witnesses at trial and to have his "day in court."

This thinking is personified in the then landmark *Poller v. CBS* case (*Poller v. CBS* 1962). In this antitrust case, after a certain amount of discovery, the defendant moved for summary judgment. The Supreme Court reversed the trial court's granting of the motion with language that would last for almost twenty-five years: "summary procedures should be used sparingly in complex antitrust litigation" (*Poller v. CBS* 1962). The Court held that:

> *motive and intent play leading roles, the proof is largely in the hands of the alleged conspirators, and hostile witnesses thicken the plot. It is only when the witnesses are present and subject to cross-examination that their credibility and the weight to be given their testimony can be appraised* (Poller v. CBS 1962).

The *Poller* standard is sometimes referred to as "the slightest doubt" standard: when an antitrust claim contains issues of motive or intent, summary judgment is inappropriate whenever the slightest doubt exists whether the motion for summary judgment should be granted (Henninger 1987).

Before we turn to the new era of summary judgment (post-1985), a discussion of one of the most powerful antitrust cases is in order—the *Monsanto* decision.

THE SIGNIFICANCE OF MONSANTO

In 1984, the Supreme Court decided a case with monumental implications for marketing management: *Monsanto v. Spray-Rite* ("*Monsanto*") (*Monsanto Co. v. Spray-Rite Service Corp.* 1984). *Monsanto* was relied on by the Supreme Court in its precedent-shattering 1986 trilogy of decisions revolutionizing the use of summary judgment.

Ironically, *Monsanto* was not a summary judgment case. The case was fully litigated going to trial and decided on its merits. Adding further irony, *Monsanto* was a *vertical* price fixing, dealer termination case, not a horizontal agreement case. Vertical restraints involve agreements between or among different levels of distribution. For example, if a manufacturer terminates a price cutting distributor at the behest of one or more of the discounter's distributor competitors, a vertical price fixing agreement could be alleged. Nonetheless, the language and reasoning in *Monsanto* are critical to the Court's 1986 *Matsushita* decision dealing with summary judgment (*Matsushita Electric Industrial Co. v. Zenith Radio Corp.* 1986) ("*Matsushita*").

Spray-Rite, a Monsanto distributor, began to price discount chemical herbicides. Monsanto terminated Spray-Rite allegedly for failing to comply with a newly instituted distributor policy that required increased push promotions and training salespeople (*Monsanto* 1984). Spray-Rite claimed that it was terminated as a result of complaints about its price discounting from other Monsanto dealers (*Monsanto* 1984).

Vertical price fixing is also a *per se* category of conduct, yet the *Monsanto* Court entertained business reasons for terminating a dealer. For example, the Court was concerned that a manufacturer could unilaterally and independently terminate a distributor for legitimate business reasons and still be liable for alleged vertical price fixing simply for receiving complaints from its other dealers about a price-cutter.

The Court stressed that a manufacturer has the right to deal or refuse to deal with any distributor on a unilateral and independent basis. The Court reasoned that it was natural for dealers to complain to the manufacturer and for the manufacturer to legitimately entertain those communications. Then the Court expressed a new evidentiary standard for evaluating conspiracy allegations that has become precedent-setting not just for substantive antitrust law but for the procedural motion for summary judgment as well:

> *The correct standard is that there must be evidence that tends to exclude the possibility of independent action by the manufacturers and distributor. That is, there must be direct or circumstantial evidence that reasonably tends to prove that the manufacturer and others had a conscious commitment to a common scheme designed to achieve an unlawful objective* (Monsanto 1984).

Again, even though this language has to do with a fully litigated trial decision on the merits and notwithstanding that *Monsanto* had to do with a vertical price restraint, not horizontal, we will see the power of this language as incorporated into the "new" summary judgment.

THE PROCEDURAL REVOLUTION OF 1986: THE TRILOGY

In 1986, three major, precedent shattering summary judgment cases were decided by the Supreme Court, two of them back to back on the same day! Taken together, these three decisions will have a truly profound impact on marketing strategy, planning, and management.

Celotex

In *Celotex Corp. v. Catrett,* the plaintiff sued on behalf of her deceased husband for wrongful death claiming that he died as a result of exposure to Celotex's *asbestos products* (*Celotex Corp. v. Catrett* 1986) ("*Celotex*"). After a certain amount of discovery had taken place, defendant Celotex moved for summary judgment to dismiss the case on the basis of evidence that the deceased was a heavy smoker. Hence,

Celotex argued that it was as probable that the deceased died from smoking as from asbestosis. The Court ruled that the non-moving party (here, the plaintiff), with the burden now shifted to her, had to go beyond her complaint and pleadings with new evidence to show that there was indeed a genuine issue for trial. This the plaintiff failed to do and summary judgment was granted for the defendant, Celotex Corp.

Anderson v. Liberty Lobby

Celotex was a product liability case; *Anderson v. Liberty Lobby* was a libel/defamation case (*Anderson v. Liberty Lobby, Inc.* 1986). Columnist Jack Anderson allegedly published statements about a lobbying organization describing it as racist, anti-Semitic, and neo-Nazi.

In a defamation case involving a public figure such as Liberty Lobby, the plaintiff had to prove with clear and convincing evidence that Anderson and his magazine made the statements with actual malice. After a certain amount of discovery, defendants relied on an affidavit of one of the defendant magazine employees who had written two of the allegedly defamatory articles. The employee testified that he got information about Liberty Lobby from numerous sources believing the information to be accurate.

In ruling in a motion for summary judgment by defendant Anderson, the Court discarded the old summary judgment precedent of "slightest doubt." In deciding what constitutes sufficient evidence to create a genuine issue as to a material fact, the Court held:

> *The question here is whether a jury could reasonably find* either *that the plaintiff proved his case by the quality and quantity of evidence required by the governing law* or *that he did not* (Anderson v. Liberty Lobby *1986*).

Matsushita

The plaintiffs in *Matsushita* were American television manufacturers, including Zenith. The defendants were twenty-one Japanese firms and their American subsidiaries of consumer electronic products. The plaintiffs ("Zenith") claimed that the Japanese firms engaged in a conspiracy to eliminate plaintiffs from the American consumer electronics market by keeping prices artificially high in Japan and artificially low in the United States—in essence, a predatory pricing *conspiracy,* which brought the case within the ambit of Sherman Section 1.

Matsushita was one of the most complex antitrust cases ever, both procedurally and substantively. The case involved massive discovery and time: over one million documents in discovery and ten years in litigation.

The trial court granted the Japanese defendants' motion for summary judgment. The Third Circuit Court of Appeals reversed, holding that it was reasonable that a conspiracy to price predatorily could be found. In a 5-4 decision, the Supreme Court reversed the Court of Appeals.

The Supreme Court reasoned that if there were in fact a conspiracy by the Japanese, it came up woefully short over twenty years. In other words, the Court reasoned that the alleged conspiracy simply made no economic sense and that the evidence was as consistent with independent behavior as with conspiracy.

Relying on *Monsanto,* the *Matsushita* majority held that "antitrust law limits the range of permissible inferences form *ambiguous* evidence in a [Sherman] Section 1 case." (*Matsushita* 1986, emphasis added). Further, "conduct as consistent with permissible competition as with illegal conspiracy does not, standing alone, support an inference of antitrust conspiracy." (*Matsushita* 1986). Again, relying on *Monsanto* for what it takes to survive a motion for summary judgment, the Court held:

> *To survive a motion for summary judgment ..., a plaintiff ... must present evidence that tends to exclude the possibility that the alleged conspirators acted independently ... [Plaintiffs] ... must show that the inference of conspiracy is reasonable in light of the competing inferences of independent action or collusive action that could not have harmed [plaintiffs].* (Matsushita 1986).

Emphasizing that the alleged conspiracy made no economic sense, the Court went on to hold:

> *The absence of any plausible motive to engage in the conduct charged is highly relevant to whether a 'genuine issue for trial' exists. ... Lack of motive bears on the range of permissible conclusions that might be drawn from ambiguous evidence: if petitioners [Japanese defendants] had no rational economic motive to conspire, and if their conduct is consistent with other, equally plausible explanations, the conduct does not give rise to an inference of conspiracy* (Matsushita 1986).

The upshot of *Matsushita,* along with *Celotex, Anderson v. Liberty,* and *Mansanto* is that it will be increasingly important for marketers to establish that trade restraints are the result of legitimate business reasons. For marketers, the procedural change in summary judgment means that a marketer will have an opportunity after a certain amount of discovery has transpired to move that a lawsuit is useless or frivolous, that there is no genuine issue to be tried on the merits before the court. The way to do this is to be in a position to offer evidence supporting legitimate business behavior. The other side will then have to come forward with evidence that disproves or excludes the possibility of independent action. If the other side cannot come up with the additional evidence to establish a genuine issue for trial, the suit will be dismissed. We now turn to a more detailed analysis of *Matsushita*'s elements.

The "Standing Alone" Element. The decisions just cited, particularly the *Monsanto* and *Matsushita* decisions, make much of the "standing alone" element: i.e., conduct, in and of itself, is not sufficiently conclusive to prove unlawful behavior (*Scott* 1992). For example, the termination of a dealer along with other dealer complaints about price-cutting, standing alone, does not give rise to an inference of conspiracy. It would be a foolish business that did not consider its distributors' concerns.

On the other hand, if the terminated dealer could show by direct evidence beyond the coincidental timing of complaints by his competitors and his termination (circumstantial evidence) that the manufacturer met with the complaining dealers and assured them that the price-cutter would be persuaded not to discount, the manufacturer's motion for summary judgment should be denied; the additional evidence, the "something more," creates a genuine issue as to whether in fact there was a conspiracy among the manufacturer and the complaining dealers to unlawfully fix prices vertically.

As a practical matter, the defendant, (the manufacturer here) would be wise to be in a position to offer independent business reasons for the termination to demonstrate that the plaintiff's circumstantial evidence (assuming that the terminated dealer could not come up with direct evidence of a vertical price fixing conspiracy) is subject to more than one interpretation, and therefore ambiguous (*DeSanti and Kovacic* 1990). The manufacturer should be able to *document* that the dealer was not terminated for discounting but for poor service, inferior warranty work, not meeting minimum hours, and any array of typical, legitimate requirements that might be put on a distributor that is related to offering consumers value and satisfaction.

The Economic Plausibility Element. Recall that a key element in *Matsushita* was that the claim had to be economically plausible; i.e., it had to make economic sense. Among other facts, this inference of economic implausibility was supported by the fact that Zenith had not lost any significant market share for over twenty years even though the supposed predatory price conspiracy was in effect since 1953 (*Matsushita* 1986). Hence, it would behoove a defendant in an antitrust action to offer evidence that the conduct complained of makes no economic sense.

This may be easier said than done. In *Matsushita,* the evidence was so extreme in challenging the credulity of the scheme that the economic implausibility aspect was devastating to Zenith. The "standing alone" element is easier to establish through evidence supporting legitimate business objectives and conduct.

Is the "New" Summary Judgment Working?

Any assessment of the "new" summary judgment is to be found at the lower federal court level; and to date, the courts have not been shy about granting the motion, primarily for defendants, particularly in antitrust cases (Note 1989). As of March 1990, a computer search has revealed over 3,000 citations to the Supreme Court's *Celotex* decision in state and federal court opinions (*Yamamoto, et al.* 1990). One appellate court even stated: "Meet these affidavit facts or judicially die" (*Southern Rambler Sales, Inc. v. American Motors Corp.* 1967).

In *Richards v. Nielsen Freight Lines ("Richards")*, each of the defendant long haul trucking companies were able to establish a legitimate business reason for terminating their interline agreements with the plaintiff trucking company. As in *Monsanto* and *Matsushita,* the *Richards* Court held that each defendant was as likely to have acted independently as pursuant to a boycott conspiracy.

Anderson v. Liberty can be used in an antitrust case to obtain summary judgment where a plaintiff's case is weak. (*Soma and McCallin* 1991). For example, in *Argus v. Eastman Kodak,* Kodak was granted summary judgment. Using the "implausible claim" language of *Matsushita,* the court also analyzed the sad financial shape Argus was in before Kodak allegedly engaged in predatory pricing conduct to drive Argus out of business. Hence, Argus' poor management could have been equally responsible for its demise as Kodak's "aggressive" pricing. Argus could not offer more evidence and lost on summary judgment as the court relied on *Matsushita* (*Soma and McCallin* 1991).

In sum, the courts are encouraging the filing of summary judgment motions (Issacharoff and Loewenstein 1990). Even more telling, courts are not reviewing the sufficiency of the defendants' motions. In a sample of 140 contested summary judgment motions in 1988, in the 98 decisions for the defendant, 60 percent of these were entered without any discussion of the sufficiency of the defendant's production in support of the motion; and in twelve of these cases, the courts granted summary judgment for the defendants based solely on the insufficiency of the plaintiffs' efforts early in the cases (*Issacharoff and Loewenstein* 1990).

CONCLUSION: IMPLICATIONS FOR MARKETING MANAGEMENT

The dramatic changes in substantive antitrust law and procedural law have profound implications for marketing management. For the first time in nearly 100 years of antitrust law, marketers can do things in heretofore strictly prohibited areas such as price fixing and market/customer allocations. Overt, naked attempts not to compete must be avoided, but legitimate, procompetitive undertakings need not necessarily fear simplistic labeling of the conduct. If price fixing and/or market allocations are integral to legitimate efforts to lower prices, improve quality, and increase consumer satisfaction, marketers now have the opportunity to document the procompetitive purposes and effects through strategic planning and marketing research.

The increased availability of summary judgment changes the balance of power between parties in a lawsuit by raising both the cost and risk to the plaintiff and making it easier for a defendant to get out of a sham lawsuit early (Issacharoff and Loewenstein 1990). For the first time, courts can evaluate competing inferences from conduct in the light of legitimate business reasons for the conduct (Henninger 1987).

Matsushita is support to establish through marketing planning and marketing research that claims are economically implausible. Furthermore, a party can document legitimate objectives and business reasons underlying challenged behavior. The burden is then on the party challenging the conduct to come up with evidence "that tends to exclude the possibility that defendants acted independently" (*Matsushita* 1986). Therefore, marketing planning and marketing research will become increasingly important, in addition to their inherent value as marketing tools, to minimize the risk of becoming mired in time consuming and extremely costly litigation.

REFERENCES

Anderson v. Liberty Lobby, Inc., 477 U.S. 242 (1986).

Argus v. Eastman Kodak, 801 F.2d 38 (2d Cir. 1986), *cert. denied,* 479 U.S. 1088 (1987).

Broadcast Music, Inc. v. Columbia Broadcasting System, 441 U.S. 1 (1979).

Celotex Corp. v. Catrett, 477 U.S. 317 (1986).

Chicago Board of Trade v. United States, 246 U.S. 231 (1918).

De Santi, Susan and Kovacic, William. 1990. *Matsushita:* Its Construction and Application by the Lower Courts. *Antitrust Law Journal* 59 (August): 609–49.

Federal Trade Commission v. Indiana Federation of Dentists, 435 U.S. 684 (1986).

Friedenthal, Scott. 1988. Cases on Summary Judgment: Has There Been a Material Change? *Notre Dame Law Review* 63: 770–804.

Henninger, John. 1987. The Evolving Summary Judgment Standard For Antitrust Conspiracy Cases. *The Journal of Corporation Law* 12 (Spring): 503–34.

Issacharoff, Samuel and Loewenstein, George. 1990. Second Thoughts About Summary Judgment. *Yale Law Journal* 100 (October): 73–114.

Jorde, Thomas M. and Lemley, Mark. 1991. Summary Judgment in Antitrust Cases: Understanding *Monsanto* and *Matsushita. Antitrust Bulletin* 36 (Summer): 271–92.

Levine, Marcy J. 1988. Summary Judgment: The Majority View Undergoes a Complete Reversal in the 1986 Supreme Court. *Emory Law Journal* 37 (Winter): 171–215.

Matsushita Electric Industrial Co. v. Zenith Radio Corp., 475 U.S. 574 (1986).

Monsanto Co. v. Spray-Rite Service Corp., 465 U.S. 752 (1984).

National Collegiate Athletic Association v. Board of Regents of the University of Oklahoma, 468 U.S. 85 (1984).

Northern Pacific Railway Co. v. United States, 356 U.S. 1 (1958).

Note. 1989. Summary Judgment in Federal Court: New Maxims For a Federal Rule. *New York Law School Law Review* 34: 201–24.

Poller v. CBS, 368 U.S. 464 (1962).

Proger, Phillip. 1991. A Primer on Antitrust Law in the Healthcare Field. Paper presented at the Annual Antitrust in the Healthcare Field Conference of the National Health Lawyers Association, Washington, D.C., February 13, 1991.

Richards v. Neilsen Freight Lines, 810 F.2d 898 (9th Cir. 1987).

Rogers III, C. Paul. 1979. Summary Judgment in Antitrust Conspiracy Litigation. *Loyola University Law Journal* 10: 667–712.

Scott, Charity. 1992 Medical Peer Review Litigation and the Healthcare Quality Improvement Act. Paper presented at the Annual Antitrust in the Healthcare Field Conference of the National Health Lawyers Association, Washington, D.C., January 30, 1992.

Soma, John and McCallin, Andrew. 1991. Summary Judgment and Discovery Strategies in Antitrust and RICO Actions After *Matsushita*. *Antitrust Bulletin* 36 (Summer): 325–39.

Southern Rambler Sales, Inc. v. American Motors Corp., 375 F.2d 932 (5th Cir. 1967), *cert. denied*, 389 U.S. 832 (1967).

Trombetta, William. 1987. Is This The Best Thing Yet in Three-Letter Medicine? *Medical Economics* 64 (August 10): 127–31.

United States v. Socony-Vacuum Oil Co., 310 U.S. 150 (1940).

United States v. Trenton Potteries Co., 273 U.S. 392 (1927).

Yamamoto, Eric; Leonard, Katherine; and Sodersten, Shawna. 1990. Summary Judgment at the Crossroads: Impact of the *Celotex* Trilogy. *University of Hawaii Law Review* 12: 1–45.

Nigel F. Piercy
Chair in Strategic Management
Aston Business School
Aston University
United Kingdom
Visiting Professor
M.J. Neeley School of Business
Texas Christian University
Fort Worth, Texas

William D. Giles
Director
Strategic Management Resource Centre Ltd.
United Kingdom

CHAPTER 11

MANAGING THE MARKET PLANNING PROCESS: THE SEARCH FOR CONTINUOUS COMPETITIVE RENEWAL

INTRODUCTION

The goal of this chapter is to review briefly the conventional model of strategic market planning and to identify some of the shortcomings in providing a basis for managing the planning process. The management agenda identified has as its goal the creation of a culture of continuous competitive renewal, that is the permanent and ongoing search for new advantage and better position in the marketplace.

There are two underlying contentions here. The first of our foundations is that the market planning process is no more than a means to an end—where that end is achieving competitive advantage, not simply producing plans. We start with some cynicism about the value of sophisticated planning, the output of which is disregarded by executives, which changes little of substance in the running of the company or in how it deals with its customers in the marketplace.

The second of our underlying contentions is that while it is only a means to an end, market planning is one of the most powerful means to the end of competitive advantage and the continuous renewal of that advantage, which executives have at their disposal. It is for this reason that what we discuss below is the construction of an agenda for actively and creatively managing the *process* of market planning, rather than the conventional listing and explication of yet more sophisticated analytical techniques.

We will see in this chapter that most authorities and most executive development activity treats the *process* of market planning as an orderly and logical sequence of steps in applying rational-analytical techniques to develop strategies and programs. Their focus is on analysis and modeling sophistication to output carefully constructed strategic and operational plans normally to standardized formats.

Issues like corporate culture, management style, information sharing, organizational structure, influence, participation, and the like, if they are considered at all, are treated as facilitating mechanisms or mere context, to be set aside as trivial compared to the real business of complex analysis and plan writing. This is exactly wrong. These issues are not mere context, they *are* the process.

We will argue that it is success in managing these process issues that determines whether anything useful ever happens as a result of market planning and whether we succeed in tapping the potential for organizational learning and competitive renewal that lies in the planning process.

EXHIBIT 1. The Quality of Output from Market Planning

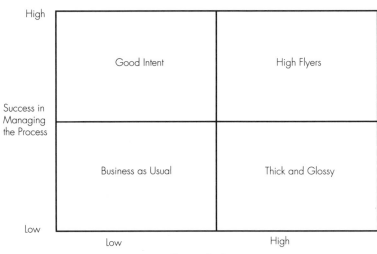

Putting these two contentions together suggests that the real trade-off for management is between planning sophistication and success in managing process issues. This is summarized in Exhibit 1.

The initial question for the managers is whether their market planning avoids the traps of "Business As Usual"—crude plans, but it hardly matters because no one takes much notice of them anyway; "Thick and Glossy"—beautiful plans that everyone ignores; or "Good Intent and Fine Words"—people get excited about planning, but they do not have the tools to put the good intentions into practical effect.

What follows in this chapter focuses on how to manage a way into the "High Flyer" situation, where we achieve both commitment and ownership through the planning process and produce plans that are capable of implementation.

CONVENTIONAL MARKET PLANNING MODELS

It is quite apparent that the marketing literature is replete with widely used prescriptive works that focus on the need for systematic market planning and that describe the procedures, analytical techniques, and format for planning (e.g., Jain 1990; Kerin, et al. 1990). Conventionally these approaches offer flow models of market planning process of the type shown in Exhibit 2. The logic of such models is impeccable.

EXHIBIT 2. A Conventional Model of Market Planning Process

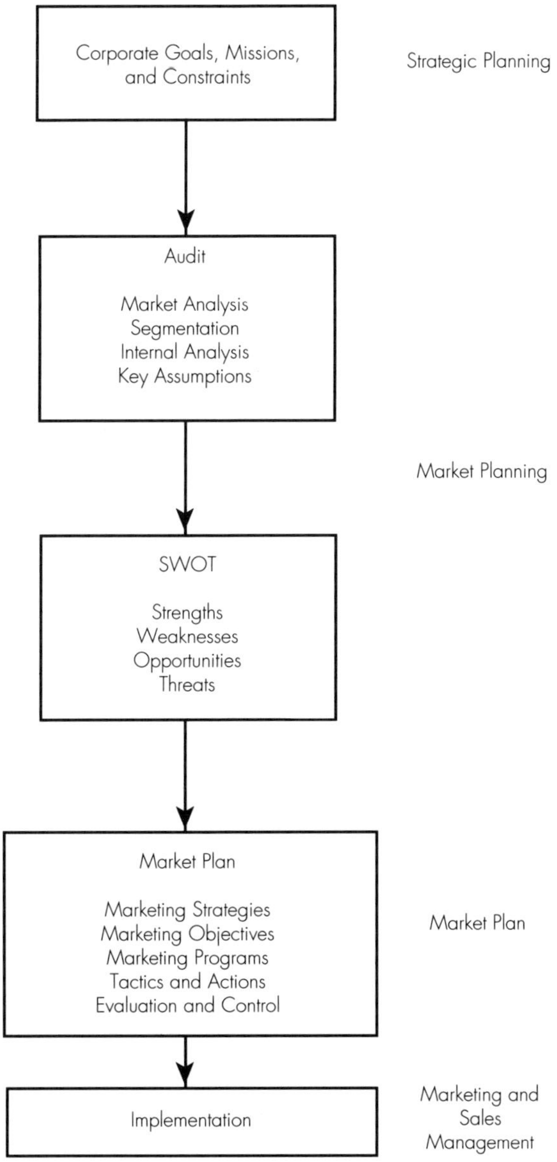

| Corporate Goals, Missions, and Constraints | Strategic Planning |

Audit

Market Analysis
Segmentation
Internal Analysis
Key Assumptions

Market Planning

SWOT

Strengths
Weaknesses
Opportunities
Threats

Market Plan

Marketing Strategies
Marketing Objectives
Marketing Programs
Tactics and Actions
Evaluation and Control

Market Plan

Implementation

Marketing and Sales Management

The assumed starting plan for market planning is with a clear statement of corporate mission and goals with any constraints emerging from the strategic planning process. The core activity for market planners is the analysis of the marketplace and the relative competencies and capabilities of the company to arrive at a statement of corporate strengths and weaknesses in the light of opportunities and threats in the marketplace in question. From this a market plan is generated, identifying market strategies and tactics for the market in question over the time period required. Implementation is then a matter for line executives in marketing and sales.

To a reasonable degree of approximation, this type of model describes the conventional view of market planning as it is described in the literature, taught in business schools, and represented in executive training programs.

As a model of building formal systems, for locating market planning in relation to corporate and other functional planning activities, or for providing a framework to identify the points for application of analytical techniques, there is no problem with this type of representation.

There are, however, some minor problems with this conventional model of market planning:

• It almost wholly ignores the real world
• It is inward looking and myopic
• It does not work

A few words of justification for these assertions are probably in order.

Quite simply, the conventional model of a logical, sequential, and analytical planning process ignores two unavoidable characteristics of real planning processes: They are operated by *people,* and they take place in *organizations.* It is worth considering the evidence about how market planning goes wrong.

WHAT GOES WRONG?

Some may think the previous assertions are somewhat exaggerated. The evidence is that there are substantial problems in making market planning effective. A number of studies throughout the world have suggested various conclusions about the practice of market planning:

• Conventional flow models of planning represent a simplistic concept of market strategy and may be positively harmful to performance (Cousins 1990)
• Conventional models may confuse the issue at stake by presenting legitimate output formats as models of the process required to reach the output (Piercy and Giles 1990)

- The analytical rigor of the planning techniques used may be limited (Wensley 1981, Kiechel 1982)
- Managers report market planning to have failed them and to be inflexible, destructive of initiative, with plans unused in practice, and little more than a meaningless ritual (Greenley 1988, Leppard and McDonald 1987, Verhage and Waartz 1982, Cosse and Swan 1983, Piercy 1992)

These signs that all is not well in market planning as it is practiced are confirmed by some of our own observations and exploratory research.

Much of our current understanding of the real problems of effectively implementing and operating strategic market planning in organizations comes from the responses made by groups of executives in planning workshops and the like to two wholly naive questions that we have asked over a period of several years: "What do you want your market planning process to achieve for your company?" and "What goes wrong with market planning in your company?"

What Do You Want From Market Planning?

Broadly, the answers from managers to this question are as follows.

1. *A Good Market Plan*—A response that generally refers to plans that are achievable, actionable, and capable of being implemented, rather than to technical, analytical sophistication.
2. *Teams and "Ownership" of Output*—A recurring comment that plans that are not "owned" by teams of executives are unlikely to gain implementation, even if they are formally approved and accepted by the company.
3. *A Continuous Process*—While executives typically do not want to spend more time planning, they *do* want planning to operate continuously and not to be a "once-a-year ritual."
4. *A Way to Identify Real Information Needs*—Executives answered that planning is a way of isolating and identifying their *real* information needs.
5. *A Way to Understand Strategy and Shake Dogma*—Executives said they often do not understand their own companys' strategies and suggested that they had what amounts to culturally based "dogma" rather than genuine strategies for the future—they want to find ways of shaking and testing the beliefs and values of their culture.

On the face of things, anyway, managers seem to want quite surprisingly reasonable things from market planning. This leads directly to our second naive question.

Why Don't You Just Do It?

Perhaps the most outstanding characteristic of the responses to our second question about what goes wrong with market planning in practice was that on no occasion that we have recorded did executives complain of the lack of either formal planning techniques, computerized models, or statistical information systems. The perceived gap is not scientific planning methodology. Rather, the planning pitfalls executives perceive appear to be in the following areas.

1. *Analysis Instead of Planning*—Executives have told us frequently that they see planning as bogged down with analytical techniques and models that are far removed from the reality they perceive and that do not lead to actionable plans.

2. *Information Instead of Decision*—In a similar vein, executives have described their planning disintegrating into constant demands for more and better information. Some are cynical enough to suggest that the reason for this is that it is easier than making decisions.

3. *Incrementalism*—At its simplest, executives have described to us many situations where the primary determinant of plan is quite simply the previous plan or at least the previous budget. The planning task then disintegrates into negotiating and arguing about minor departures from the previous year rather than creating new strategies.

4. *Vested Interests Rule*—Executives suggest that the powerful people in the company exert undue influence over plans to protect budgets and head counts, to build resource claims, and so on. Many manifestations of this were cited: refusal by key players to participate in planning followed by a rejection of plans by those same players on the grounds of lack of consultation; blockages in the availability of important internal information to planners; side-tracking disputes about jurisdiction and minor company rules and policies; outright, dogged argument against anything that changes the *status quo*; "politicking," bargaining, and "horse trading" outside planning meetings to divert plans from going in unwelcome directions; and so on.

5. *Organizational Mindset*—Many executives have suggested that conventional planning processes are by definition inward looking and bounded by "the way we do things here." So, they never produce anything new.

6. *Resistance to Marketing Change*—Some executives have suggested that strategic change emanating from the marketing department is seen as threatening—or even unreasonable—and is often successfully resisted by other departments and organizational interest groups.

7. *No Ownership or Commitment*—It seems in many cases that plans are produced (often by staff planners) and accepted, but in the absence of champions determined to make them work, nothing ever happens as a result of the planning effort.

8. *No Resourcing*—Executives have pointed out many resource-related pitfalls: the simple refusal by management to provide resources and, perhaps most threatening, approval and acceptance by management of the plan but rejection of the accompanying resource request.

9. *No Implementation*—We have received bitter complaints about situations where planning absorbed resources and management time and even created excitement and support for change but led to nothing more than a report on a shelf, which was never effectively implemented.

10. *Diminishing Effort and Interest*—Largely as a result of lack of resourcing and implementation, executives point out that if planning is to be no more than an annual ritual, and managers perceive this, then it is hardly surprising that efforts and interest diminish over time. It becomes a self-fulfilling prophesy that planning is a waste of time.

These pitfalls may not be true of how planning works in *your* organization. The point is that if you look at what managers say they *want* from market planning and the reasons why it goes *wrong,* there is almost no mention of wanting more sophisticated planning techniques and systems.

The trouble with this is that what we really know a lot about is the techniques and the systems. If you look at the conventional market planning textbooks, planning manuals, briefcase planning systems, consultancy advice, management training, and all the rest—they are obsessed with model building, computer systems, and analytical techniques. In contrast to this, what managers seem to be telling us is that we are all missing the point about what really matters in making market planning effective as far as they and their companies are concerned.

We need, then, to rethink how we work on market planning with companies and develop an approach that is about *managing* the market planning *process,* not just the techniques of planning.

Dimensions of the Market Planning Process

The way we present the market planning process to companies now is summarized in Exhibit 3. We suggest that there are at least three dimensions of the market planning process, and if we are in any way serious about *managing* market planning, then we have to address all three of these process dimensions.

EXHIBIT 3. A Multidimensional Model of Market Planning

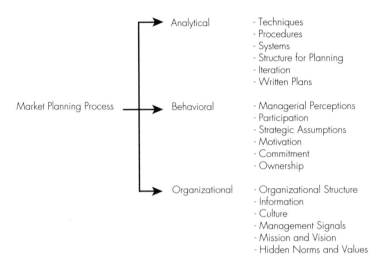

Analytical Planning Dimension

There is no doubt that to produce effective market plans we need the tools for the job—the *techniques* to analyze our problems and opportunities and identify the solutions and strategies; the formal *procedures* and systems to organize our planning and make it part of running the business; a *structure* for our planning to make it comprehensive and manageable; *iteration* to make our planning dynamic and thorough; and a *written plan* as the output capturing our ideas and strategies as a basis for communicating them.

This is an important element of the planning process, but it has two caveats. First, let us not delude ourselves that this is *all* that planning is about, because then we end up believing that if we can just formalize planning enough and train people in more sophisticated techniques of planning (or perhaps hire professional planners who have this expertise already), then we will improve our performance. There is abundant evidence that it is not so. Second, let us be wary of the trap of creating a planning bureaucracy that actually gets in the way of *doing* things.

Behavioral Planning Dimension

Process means *how* we do things as well as *what* we do. How we do things leads us straight to the problems that our people have in building and using market plans.

The type of issues we have to sort out here have very little to do with formal planning techniques: *managerial perceptions* of planning and the uncertainties they are expected to confront in planning; *participation* levels and types in the planning groups and teams and managers' attitudes towards this; and hidden *strategic assumptions* managers make (and believe) about what the company can and should do and what drives the market; the *motivation* (or otherwise) to make planning effective; the *commitment* to strategic change, or the preference for the status quo; and the *ownership* by individuals of the problem of making things happen, without which it is unlikely that too much will ever happen as a result of market planning.

The sad truth is that we know that these things matter, but many of us ignore them when we try to manage our market planning.

Organizational Planning Dimension

Ultimately, all of this has to be seen in the context of the organization itself: the *organizational structure,* with all this means in terms of formal responsibilities, vested interests, and power to get things done or stop things from happening; the *information issue* and the problems of access and control of information, the inadequacies, and the politics; the *culture* of the organization—"the way we do things here," and all the subcultures in different parts of the organization; the *management signals* that tell us about the real attitudes and beliefs of management rather than the lip service; the existence and direction of *mission and vision* in how the organization is run; and the hidden *norms and values* that really determine what people do in the organization.

We may not know too much about managing people in planning, but we know even less about matching formal planning to organizational attributes of this kind.

The conclusion to which we are drawn is that we know *most* about what matters *least* in planning (the analytical techniques and formal systems), and we know *least* about what matters *most* (the behavioral and organizational dimensions) and that we have not even yet recognized the underlying problem of managing these dimensions of planning to formulate a consistent, managed planning process.

Some Research Evidence

Although it is crude, we have done some exploratory research to substantiate the existence and significance of these hidden dimensions of the planning process. The research was conducted among medium and large UK companies—companies where there is some form of market planning (so you would expect them to be above average in getting the planning act together).

A technical note is available elsewhere (Piercy and Morgan 1990), but the basic question we sought to answer was, "What predicts the credibility and utilization of market plans?" The issue is whether we produce plans that people believe in, and use, to run the business. The predictors of plan credibility and utilization that we found in the study were (1) the formalization of planning and learning of planning techniques; (2) a factor called "planning thoroughness"; (3) the avoidance of behavioral planning problems; and (4) positive signals from the organizational environment.

Formalization and Planning Techniques. The degree to which market planning was formally organized and documented, and the more analytical techniques were brought to bear, the higher the credibility and use was of the plan.

Planning Thoroughness. This factor has to do with three things: the degree to which planning drew on experience and knowledge from all parts of the organization; whether the planning activity was seen to be adequately resourced in time and money; and whether people believed that good planning performance was rewarded in the same way that good operational performance was.

Avoidance of Behavioral Planning Problems. We used a large number of attitude and belief measurements to identify a number of behavioral planning problems at the individual level:

- *Planning recalcitrance*—Characterized by people believing that planning was a bore and a ritual and that it was disorganized, with executives mainly picking on the weaknesses in plans and being easily sidetracked into short-term operational issues.
- *Fear of uncertainty in planning*—Executives are seen to resist long-term commitments and to be uncomfortable with long-range forecasting and so emphasize the present, not the future. People resist learning and change and desperately seek a "rational" decision-making technique that will make the decisions for them and take the discomfort away.
- *Political interests*—People see planning as dominated by the vested interests in the company, leading to planning becoming bidding and bargaining for resources, with information sharing precluded and much padding in forecasts and estimates.
- *Planning avoidance*—People are seen to go through the motions in planning and to give compliance, not commitment, so nothing gets challenged because planning is about avoiding responsibility for doing anything.

Organizational Signals. This was a measure of a number of factors to do with the company's attitude toward strategic planning, toward marketing, and the customer philosophy of management (or lack of it), as perceived by the people who do the market planning.

These would seem to be the things that are associated with market plans that are credible and actually used. Where this leads is toward a somewhat different agenda to be addressed in managing market planning—in *all* its dimensions.

MANAGING ALL THE DIMENSIONS OF PLANNING PROCESS

This model of the market planning process with several dimensions provides us with a framework for organizing management efforts to put a handle on market planning.

Managing the Analytical Dimension

This is the most documented element of market planning, and most texts are full of models and sophisticated techniques. However, going back to the basics suggests three areas where we can make a major impact on the real analytical effectiveness of market planning. This may be the starting point in orienting planning to competitive renewal instead of simply producing plans.

Vision. Before we analyze, do we ever communicate and share a clear and existing vision of where we want the business to go? Or do we remain vague and unclear, offering our executives a rehash of last year's goals or impossible wish lists? If our goal is continuous competitive renewal, then sorting out unclear vision is first on the list.

Most senior executives will tell you that they have a mission statement and/or a strategic vision. On the other hand, many middle managers, whose job it is to implement this vision, will tell you that they are working in a vacuum, uncertain about their goals. Oceans of corporate time are spent on word crafting the perfect mission statement to the enormous satisfaction of its authors. The result is a statement that covers every possible eventuality without actually saying anything. Managers scratch their heads and then it is back to business as normal.

It does not have to be like this. Exhibit 4 shows a projection of company performance into the future. The lowest line represents the usual incremental year-on-year approach. The next line represents current expectations based on doing more tomorrow of what we already do today. So within this box lie the expectations of the work force both in terms of how much (performance) and how soon (time). There is nothing very visionary about this, but here is the key.

For a vision to be visionary, it must aim outside both these axes. It should demand both more performance—that gives the organization the stretch it needs—and be further out in time to give people a chance to achieve it. Creating strategy to build this future can now take place in a different environment. The organization sits up here, out in the future, looking back toward the present. The immediate decisions are now very different to the other two conventional approaches.

This is fine in the pictures, but how do we articulate it? The useful vision statement treats hard and soft issues with equal importance. Exhibit 5 shows some sample headings that we can use. Each heading

EXHIBIT 4. Vision

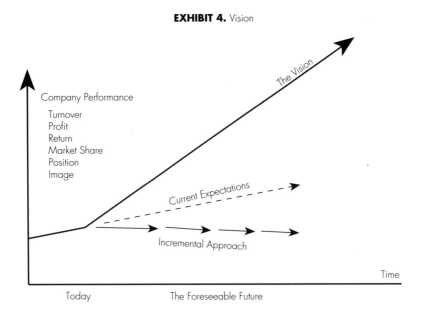

EXHIBIT 5. The "Really Useful Vision" Statement

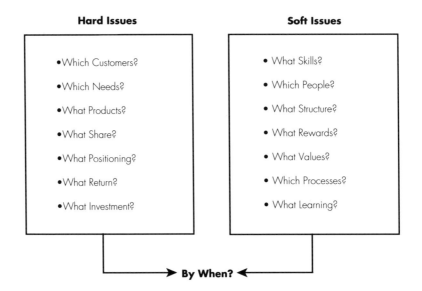

EXHIBIT 6. Developing New Ways of Looking at the World

Effects of Environmental Changes on the Business

	Excellent	Indifferent	Disastrous
High	Utopia		Catastrophe
Medium		Neutral	
Low	Disappointments		To Be Watched

Probability of Events Occurring

only needs at the most two or three key points to explain it.

The useful vision statement contains some hard goals about markets, customers, products, needs, share, and of course financials. It also contains some soft goals about people, organization, learning, skills, and rewards. And of course, it would not be complete unless we answer the question "By when?"

What is important here is breadth, not depth. These are visionary ideas and goals—not conventional objectives and targets. This is the first step in an iterative process for the whole organization. The whole thing fits on two pages. Everyone should know it by heart.

The underlying truth is that clear visions are not about sophisticated analysis or clever presentation. They just have to be simple, memorable, an colloquial.

Developing New Ways of Looking at the World. Corporate culture is not just "the way we do things there." It is also "the way we look at things here." One incredibly simple but very productive analytical technique is to formalize environmental scanning in market planning to produce the type of model shown in Exhibit 6. We can then confront the really big questions.

EXHIBIT 7. Make SWOT Analysis Work

Strengths	Weaknesses
Matching	Conversion —————
Opportunities	Threats
	Conversion —————

Matching Strategies   - Relating our strengths to opportunities in the market

Conversion Strategies - Changing weaknesses and threats into new strengths and opportunities, or at least neutralizing them

- Where in our strategies do we explicitly exploit the events that give us "utopia"?
- Where in our planning do we defend against the events in "catastrophe"?
- Do we try to avoid the "disappointments" observing our thinking?
- Does our information system watch the things that matter, or just the things that are easy to watch?

Make SWOT Work. To work effectively, SWOT analysis just needs new rules:

- It should focus on specific markets or events
- It should encourage sharing of information and opinions
- It should be customer-oriented—Nothing counts as a strength or a weakness unless customers can see it and rate it highly
- It should be environmental—Opportunities and threats exist in the market, not in the company

If we follow these rules, then SWOT analysis can be turned back into an effective strategy generator. The goal is to force us to look at ourselves as the customer does and to confront the logic of the match

EXHIBIT 8. Commitment versus Complexity

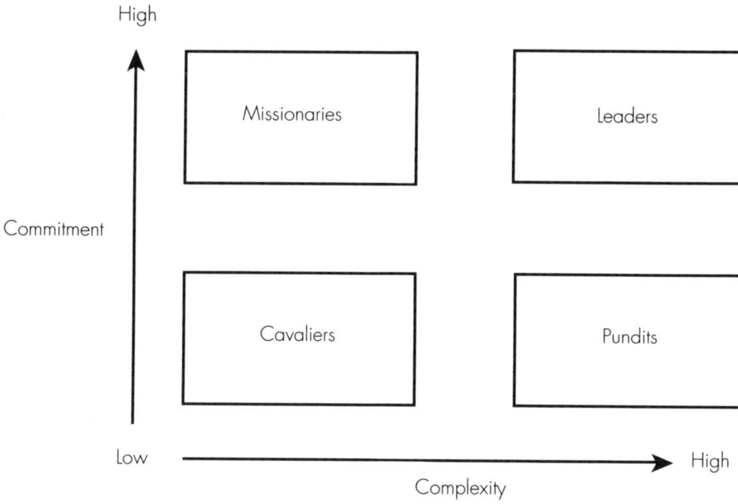

between our capabilities and the marketplace. This is summarized in Exhibit 7.

Managing the Behavioral Dimension

However we deal with the issue of techniques, we cannot avoid the fact that the planning process is about people in terms, for example, of finding the behavioral planning problems discussed above. There is a critical confrontation between analytical technique and formalization (planning sophistication) and people (in terms of the ownership and commitment to implementation we create or destroy in planning).

We can use the matrix in Exhibit 8 to define the position of companies. It enables us to classify either whole companies or individual business units according to their people's level of commitment and ownership versus the complexity and sophistication of the planning process and strategy generation they use.

Companies, organizations, or business units can be grouped into four categories: Cavaliers, Pundits, Missionaries, and Leaders:

- *Cavaliers* have neither the commitment of their people nor any clear business direction. Their planning systems and processes are superfi-

EXHIBIT 9. Theory versus Practice

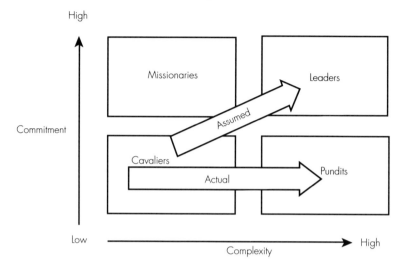

cial. Put another way, no one knows what is going on and nobody cares anyway.

- *Pundits* are typified by large planning departments and ivory tower ideas. Planning is done far away from the operations interface.
- *Missionaries* show great ownership commitment and share values, but as yet their market understanding and business direction have not matured.
- *Leaders,* which is what we would all like to be, have both a high level of commitment and high level of understanding. They exhibit all the hallmarks of sound business direction and effective action.

Applying this model to practice has led us to some interesting conclusions.

As suggested in Exhibit 9, the implicit assumption has always been that as organizations get better at producing plans and learn more sophisticated planning techniques, the level of commitment and ownership by the work force would increase correspondingly.

To the contrary, what we have found in practice is that organizations tend to invest in planning specialty as the tangible evidence of their desire to improve. This takes them further and further into the Pundits box. Typically, corresponding investments were not made on the vertical human axis since this was less tangible and harder to measure. This reflects the grand corporate strategy departments that may

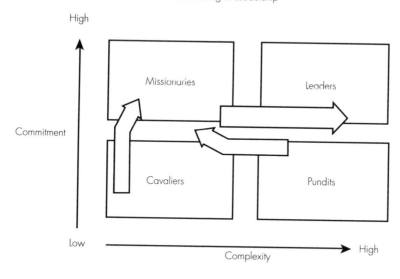

EXHIBIT 10. Moving to Leadership

well have had all the answers but the right people did not understand how to ask the questions.

So just how do we aspire to the Leaders box? Well, there are only a few routes available, as summarized in Exhibit 10.

If we are in the Cavaliers box, we can move into the Missionaries box. But, if we are in the unfortunate position of being in the Pundits box, we may have to backtrack by leaving some of our sophistication behind in order to climb up to the Missionaries box. From the Missionaries box, we can leap into the Leaders box.

What does all this mean? Simply this: In managing the behavioral dimension of market planning, ownership, belief, and commitment all come before sophistication. By investing in this axis first we can get the entire organization pulling in the same direction. Later, we can add the sophistication.

If we go about it the other way, we drift further and further into the ivory tower cul-de-sac. This is all about putting planning back where it belongs: in the hands of the line managers. The role of the manager is changing in the '90s—from doer to facilitator and process designer.

To summarize, if we balance the analytical dimension of planning against the behavioral dimension, we suggest the following:

• *"Better" strategies do not automatically lead to better implementation*—Increasing investment in sophistication without an equal investment in ownership makes planning an ivory-tower activity. The planners become Pundits and implementation fails.

- *Over-sophistication hinders ownership*—Once a Pundit, additional investment in technical expertise is unlikely to turn an organization into a Leader. The behavioral investment that increases ownership is different to the technical expertise that increases sophistication.
- *Ownership can make implementation work regardless of strategy*—An organization can only reach the Missionary stage after a significant human investment in behavior and attitudes of its people. This will be effective if a level of strategy sophistication has not previously been achieved. If it has, it may be necessary to reinvent strategy in order to nurture ownership.

Managing the Organizational Dimension

While it is unavoidable that the planning process is about people, it is also about organization—the real context in which most of us have to operate—with all that this implies about culture, management style, structural inadequacies, information blockages, and so on.

Here the challenge is to evaluate the way the planning activity fits into the organizational context.

The Shape of the Planning Process. One approach to reshaping the planning process to revitalize it amounts to turning it upside down and inside out (Piercy and Giles 1989), as suggested in Exhibit 11. The new model is based on the simple observation that as long as planning is iterative, it matters little where you start in the "logical" sequence. By starting with the marketplace as it is seen and understood by line managers and working backward and forward from this, we may lack sophistication but can gain ownership on the way.

Where Does Planning Fit? Too often we emphasise the ritual of the annual planning pilgrimage. There is too often an assumption that our market planning can be compressed into a month or so each year and the rest of the time is left for us to get on with our "real" jobs.

One of the reasons for this is when we consider who should be doing the planning. Too often planning is given to someone who has neither the authority, responsibility, or experience for the task. Each level of management should be responsible for its own plan and each level, and therefore, requires its own process. Exhibit 12 shows what happens when this goes wrong.

We have here a matrix of management levels on one scale and time scales on the other. This is what happens when senior managers get embroiled in short-term planning when their real responsibility lies in longer-term planning. They lack the detailed knowledge. It is a waste of very expensive time and a poor use of their experience. But most important of all, they rob the implementors of any sense of ownership.

However, the reverse also has its problems when long-term planning is delegated too low down in the organization. The unfortunate

EXHIBIT 11. Turn Planning Process Upside Down and Inside Out

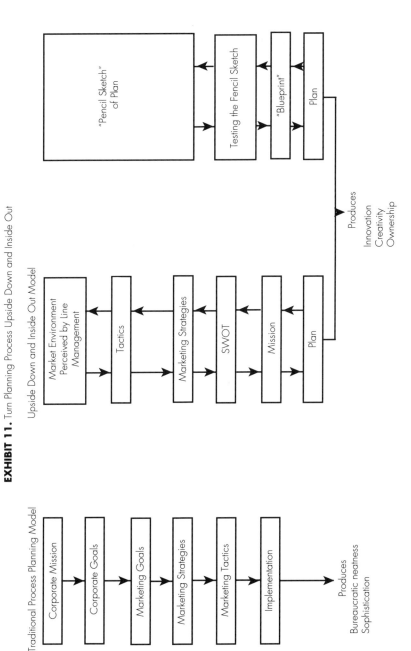

Traditional Process Planning Model

Corporate Mission → Corporate Goals → Marketing Goals → Marketing Strategies → Marketing Tactics → Implementation →

Produces
Bureaucratic neatness
Sophistication

Upside Down and Inside Out Model

Market Environment Perceived by Line Management ⇄ Tactics ⇄ Marketing Strategies ⇄ SWOT ⇄ Mission ⇄ Plan

Produces
Innovation
Creativity
Ownership

"Pencil Sketch" of Plan ⇄ Testing the Fencil Sketch ⇄ "Blueprint" ⇄ Plan

EXHIBIT 12. Confusing Who Does What in Planning

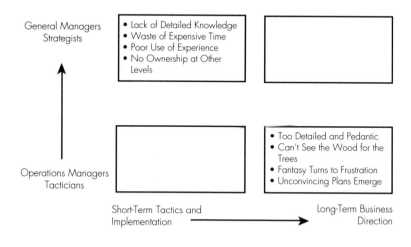

EXHIBIT 13. The Result of Confusing Planning Roles

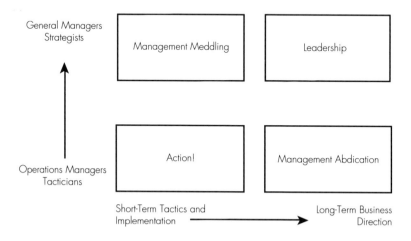

incumbents become over-detailed and pedantic. They cannot see the wood for the trees and become hopelessly lost in unwanted detail while missing the big picture elsewhere. Alternatively, they create fantasy plans that cause frustration when they cannot be delivered. Whatever route is taken, unconvincing plans emerge.

This leads us to the conclusion that different levels of management have different planning roles and each requires its own management process. This is the difference between turning planning upside down and inside out as already discussed, or simply attempting to make planning "bottom up."

Exhibit 13 shows how it should work. Senior managers and the trained strategist concern themselves with the longer term—that is, what leadership is all about.

However, many senior managers feel more comfortable in short-term operational planning. After all, as they have risen through the ranks, that is where they have come from. We call this *management meddling.*

Similarly, when the operations people and the tacticians are left to get on with the detailed implementation planning, we achieve some *real* action. Often these same people get forced into long-term planning to fill the vacuum created by lack of leadership. We call this *management abdication,* not delegation as some managers would like to believe.

EXHIBIT 14. Top Down-Bottom Up Planning

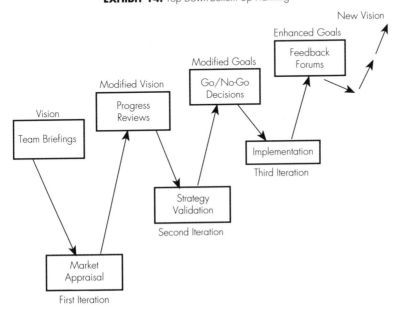

One further point on this subject is that planning is not a game for individuals, nor is it a spectator sport. Creativity is sparked by the interactions within small work groups or teams tasked to tackle specific issues. Asking individuals to prepare plans for others to tear apart belongs to a punishment culture that helps no one.

How Often Should We Plan? Creativity does not come to order. It leaps up suddenly over long periods of time—hence the idea of continuous competitive renewal. So the short answer to this question is "all the time."

Building the understanding to generate new business direction is a way of life, not a one-time activity. It requires constant iteration.

Exhibit 14 shows an approach that is both top down and bottom up. The only proviso is that the starting point for this process must be the vision statement discussed earlier. What we see here is a schedule of planned events—team briefings, progress reviews, go and no-go decisions, and feedback forums. Leadership aspirations are traded against the ability and the capacity of the organization to deliver. Through a series of iterations, the two come closer and closer together.

The ultimate aim is to create a new vision standing on the shoulders of the old one. The elapsed time for this process to be worked through may be several years, only to be restarted again at the beginning with a new vision. Several of these processes can overlap each other. This is the essence of continuous competitive renewal; creation and action take place at the same time, each learning from the other. What we are after is that sudden step change in performance. But it does not come to order and it cannot be planned for. Only by a continuous process of improvement can we put ourselves in a position to spot it before our competitors and take advantage of it when it comes.

This brings us back to the annual planning cycle. It is a snapshot in time of the progress we have made so far. It should not be additional work; it should reflect planning that is going on anyway and work that has already been done.

But Does It Match the Organization? The underlying problem we face in confronting the organizational dimension of market planning is designing and managing the process to make planning productive and to get to implementation. This requires that our planning process be comparable with the reality of the corporate culture. In one organization, for example, the debate with executives came down to the issues in Exhibit 15.

Where the corporate culture is supportive of our goals and we manage the dimensions of planning process consistently, we can achieve an effective planning process. Conversely, faced with resistance from the culture and low planning effectiveness, little changes and probably little damage is done. The company in question should have worried more about how to avoid the destructive planning

EXHIBIT 15. Fitting Planning Process to Corporate Culture

Technical Planning Effectiveness

	High	Low
Supportive Corporate Culture	Effective Planning Process	Destructive Planning Process
Unsupportive	Conflicting Planning Process	Ineffective Planning Process

process, where a supportive culture demands results and planning competencies are inadequate, or how to avoid the trap of a conflictual planning process where the planners become committed to implementation and the culture blocks it.

There are no easy answers to these questions, but they have to be confronted in working for consistency between the real corporate environment in which we have to operate and the changes we make to the planning process.

THE REAL MANAGEMENT AGENDA

If we are serious about putting a handle on the market planning process, so we can use it to unleash our company's potential for competitive renewal, then the research evidence and our observations of practice suggest the real agenda to be addressed has at least four parts: (1) techniques and formalization; (2) behavioral issues in market planning; (3) organizational issues in market planning; and (4) consistency between all these issues.

Techniques and Formalization. It is clear that if we want plans to be credible (the first stage in getting them implemented), then we need to provide a formal system and the appropriate techniques. This seems to be for two reasons: It shows people we are serious about market planning, and it gives executives the tools to do the job. This is necessary but not sufficient, however.

Behavioral Issues. The critical issues here are the *managerial perceptions* of the planning process, with all that this means in terms of their *motivation* to make planning work effectively, and their *commitment* to planning. The variables to be managed here are *training* for the planning job, designing *participation* from a motivational and political viewpoint, and *signals* the organization sends about planning.

Organizational Issues. The critical question is the degree to which the organization is seen to be, and believed to be, *supportive* of the planning effort. Part of the answer is the *example* set by senior management, the resourcing of planning, and the rewards for good performance in planning. Ultimately, these things are important as they have an impact on *planning credibility* in the organization and reflect the surrounding issues of culture, organizational structure, information systems, and so on.

To attack such an agenda, which is an ambitious undertaking after all, we have made the following points:

1. Emphasize *vision* and use it to trigger planning instead of accepting incrementalism and myopia.
2. Use *marketing intelligence* to grow new ways of looking at the world.
3. Use *SWOT analysis* to look at ourselves as the customer does (not how the CEO does) and to face up to the match between our competencies and capabilities and what matters in the market.
4. Actively manage the *people issues* in planning. Choose the trade-off between planning sophistication/complexity and ownership. Work to get to the Leaders box.
5. Adapt for the *culture issue* in the organization. Shape the process to win the hearts and minds of the people who matter, not for bureaucratic neatness and management meddling or abdication. Work for planning as a corporate way of life, not an annual ritual. Match the planning process to the realities of the corporate environment.

To summarize, the *process* of market planning is significant because the way we design and manage the process will have a direct impact on what goes into the market plan, and even more to the point, whether anything useful ever *happens* as the result of planning. Apart from anything else, it is one of the few chances we have to do something constructive to move the company's culture closer to our strategy, rather than *vice versa*. Indeed, it is becoming clear that what a managed planning process offers us is a mechanism to put a handle on organized development because planning process is a form of organizational learning and adaptation. Our goal here is to guide that organizational development and learning toward our market-led goals.

REFERENCES

Cosse, Thomas J. and John E. Swan (1983), "Strategic Marketing Planning by Product Managers—Room for Improvement?" *Journal of Marketing,* 47 (Summer), pp. 92–102.

Cousins, Laura (1990), "The Aims and Process of Marketing Planning," in Proceedings: British Academy of Management, Glasgow.

Greenley, Gordon E. (1988), "Management Perceptions of Marketing Planning," *Journal of Management Studies,* 25 (6), pp. 575–601.

Jain, Subhesh C. (1990), *Marketing Planning and Strategy,* 3rd ed., Cincinnati, Ohio: South-Western.

Kerin, Roger A., Vijay Mahajan and P. Rajan Varadarajan (1990), *Contemporary Perspectives on Strategic Market Planning,* Boston, M.A: Allyn and Bacon.

Kiechel, Walter (1982), "Corporate Strategists," *Fortune,* 27 December.

Leppard, John and Malcolm H.B. McDonald (1987), "A Reappraisal of the Role of Marketing Planning," *Journal of Marketing Management,* 3 (2), pp. 159–171.

Piercy, Nigel (1992), *Market-Led Strategic Change,* Oxford: Butterworth Heinemann.

Piercy, Nigel and William Giles (1990), "The Logic of Being Illogical in Strategic Marketing Planning," *Journal of Services Marketing,* 4 (3), pp. 27–37.

Piercy, Nigel and Neil A. Morgan (1990), "Organizational Context and Behavioral Planning Problems As Determinants of the Effectiveness of the Strategic Marketing Planning Process," *Journal of Marketing Management,* 6 (2), pp. 127–144.

Verhage, Branislow and Eric Waartz (1988), "Marketing Planning for Improved Performance: A Comparative Analysis," *International Marketing Review,* 2 (Summer), pp. 20–30.

Wensley, Robin (1981), "Strategic Marketing: Betas, Boxes, or Basics," *Journal of Marketing,* 45 (Summer), pp. 173–182.

John K. Ryans, Jr.   William L. Shanklin
Professors of Marketing and International Business
Kent State University
Kent, Ohio

CHAPTER 12

MARKETING TO NONEXISTENT MARKETS

... The newer and more innovative a product is the more likely it is that the public might not appreciate it at the beginning. In 1950 our company marketed a tape recorder. Despite the fact that it was a great achievement and a technological innovation for us, at the time it looked like a toy to the general public. Nobody thought about recording speeches or using a tape recorder to learn languages. I believe that in the case of an entirely new product, a market must be created, not surveyed. Another way to say this is that a new product is the creator of a market and a new product cannot survive without the creation of a new market.[1]

— Akio Morita, Chairman and CEO, Sony Corporation

A person perusing most marketing literature, notably academic books on marketing, is told that a company's route to prosperity is the identification and fulfillment of customer needs and desires within the company's strategic competencies or lines of business. In the vast majority of the cases, this is sound advice. A company's commitment to the development and marketing of a product, process or service almost always should be preceded by market demand as identified by marketing research. Yet, there are notable exceptions to this general rule or guideline.

Whenever a product or service is developed in response to perceived market demand, which is normally the case, an appropriate terminology to describe the process is demand-side marketing.[2] In other words, the perceived demand triggers a company's involvement with the product. This sequence is "smart" marketing, because "what profits are there in developing and marketing products for which there is insufficient demand?" Obviously, none.

However, demand-side marketing carried to extreme stifles innovation, entrepreneurship, or intrapreneurship (i.e., entrepreneurship within a going corporation rather than a startup). There are instances when a product, service or process is developed and marketed even though it is highly problematical whether or not market demand is sufficient or can be created. These cases are referred to as supply-side marketing, by which we mean:

Supply-side marketing, then, refers to any instance when a product can create a market ... in other words, a demand ... for itself in lieu of the conventional other-way-around. Or, put another way, the product is responsible for the demand, rather than the demand being responsible for the product.[3]

Supply-side marketing is fraught with risk; the two go hand-in-hand. But supply-side marketing—and those entrepreneurs with the tolerance for risk and courage to see their ideas through—is responsible for the technological innovations throughout industrial history. If assorted individuals and companies had waited for customer demand to justify the need for developing and marketing a new product, many technological innovations would have been a longer time coming.

Albeit supply-side marketing is inherently high risk, there are ways to mitigate the risk. Our extensive research among high-technology companies, which resulted in our book *Marketing High Technology*, enables us to make some suggestions along these lines.[4]

FRONTIER MARKETS

One could argue that what appear to be nonexistent markets are really situations of latent demand. However, semantical debates miss this essential point: At the time the revolutionary product or service is being conceptualized and developed, there is no market for it. The existence of a market is contingent upon *both* a demand and a way (an applied technology) to fulfill it.

Obviously, a comprehensive cancer or AIDS cure would have tremendous market demand, but the market for most technological breakthroughs is not so manifest. Consider several supposedly expert opinions regarding the practicality and commercial possibilities of the then-new technologies:

"What can be more palpably absurd than the prospect held out of locomotives traveling twice as fast as stagecoaches?" —The Quarterly Review, 1825.

"I must confess that my imagination, in spite even of spurring, refuses to see any sort of submarine doing anything but suffocating its crew and floundering at sea." —H. G. Wells, 1901.

"The ordinary 'horseless carriage' is at present a luxury for the wealthy; and although its price will probably fall in the future, it will never, of course, come into as common use as the bicycle." —The Literary Digest, 1889.

"While theoretically and technically television may be feasible, commercially and financially, I consider it an impossibility, a development of which we need waste little time dreaming." —Lee DeForest (American inventor and pioneer in radio and TV), 1926.

"There is not the slightest indication that (nuclear) energy will ever be obtainable. It would mean that the atom would have to be shattered at will." —Albert Einstein, 1932.

"This is the biggest fool thing we have ever done . . . The bomb will never go off, and I speak as an expert in explosives." —Admiral William Leahy, advising President Harry Truman, 1945.

Imagine a corporate CEO assessing whether or not to proceed with Research and Development (R&D) and commercialization of a new product or process based upon the *negative* recommendation of a Lee DeForest or an Albert Einstein. A CEO might well have said, for instance, "DeForest says the commercial and financial possibilities for this television concept are remote at best. That's good enough for me." Fortunately, for the sake of technological progress and mankind, it was not "good enough" for RCA.

RESEARCHING PIONEER MARKETS

For purposes of market research and planning, we have found it useful, indeed essential, to distinguish between market-driven companies that operate on the demand-side and innovation-driven companies that operate on the supply-side. We have explained the difference between the two as follows:

> ... in market-driven high technology, the main directions for R&D are from marketing. R&D's reaction comes in the form of guidance on what is technically feasible and ideas from scientific circles. Formal marketing research, typical to consumer and industrial markets, is helping high-tech managers guide R&D ... Innovation-driven high technology offers a marked contrast, as R&D provides the stimulus and marketing officials must find applications or simply sell the product. These efforts can help create new markets by applying lab breakthroughs to largely unperceived buyer needs.[5]

Naturally some companies, especially large ones, simultaneously have R&D projects that are market-driven and others that are innovation-driven.

Market-driven and innovation-driven R&D require different marketing research approaches and techniques. The marketing research techniques most appropriate to commercializing innovation-driven R&D fall mainly in the domain of qualitative rather than quantitative marketing research. Many of the more mathematically-based methods of marketing research used in market-driven ventures (i.e., more mature products and services) require an abundance of data, usually obtained from a random sample of people or firms so that statistical inferences can be made. This requirement is difficult to meet in high-tech industries, for two reasons.

First, whenever markets are being created or obsoleted rapidly by significant product breakthroughs, as they often are in innovation-driven high technology, not much is available in the way of valid historical data. As one executive puts it, "Our company doesn't put much faith in surveys based on what consumers said yesterday."

Second, data obtained from prospective buyers via traditional data collection techniques (telephone interviews, paper-and-pencil mail surveys, and the like) are of dubious value for answering questions about products based on new technologies. Our evidence is overwhelming that in many high-tech markets, consumers are too confused—sometimes even scared or intimidated and not too strong of descriptors—to offer much direction to a company.

The product-education (demonstration) opportunities and indepth probing afforded by qualitative research, such as focus group discussions, temper these kinds of confusion/intimidation problems. Thus, it is not surprising that our research indicates that focus groups and nominal groups, in conjunction with several more sophisticated techniques, are popular means in high-tech companies for generating new product ideas and evaluating potential market demand (see Exhibit 1).

In addition to the marketing research techniques used in innovation-driven ventures, "who to ask" is terribly important in terms of obtaining answers that are truly helpful in making go/no-go decisions and designing "winning" marketing strategies. It is far more desirable to have opinions from 10 buyer-innovator types; opinions, for instance obtained in a two-hour focus group, than to have judgments from a random sample of 1,000 people; most of whom only vaguely can conceive of a new product, its technological benefits and how well it might fit into their work styles or life styles.

Another more accurate indicator is the Delphi technique. As used by a jury of six experts, this method is likely to give more correct estimates of how successful dramatically new products may be in the marketplace next year than are the predictions of the most sophisticated econometric model built that must be fed a plethora of historical or cross-sectional data.

We have found that the techniques which use innovative customers, or industrial users in new product research, and methods which use the Delphi method in forecasting are popular among *successful* high-tech companies. For example, in one of our studies, three-fourths

EXHIBIT 1. Assessment of Qualitative Techniques in Generating New Product Ideas

Rank	Usage %		Not Helpful (%)	Helpful/ Extremely (%)
1	78	Brainstorming	13	87
2	58	Focus group	17	83
3	28	Nominal group	14	86
4	46	Attribute listing	26	74
5	42	Forced relationships	38	62
6	20	Morphological analysis	10	90

of the firms we asked indicated that they have attempted to test new product concepts on innovators; and the vast majority of them reported that their "hit rate" on predicting how successful a new product will be in the marketplace was markedly improved.

Another study we conducted, this one specifically in the robotics industry, offered even more corroboration that indepth discussions with current or potential customers is usually the best way for a company to uncover ideas for new products as well as evaluate the feasibility or market potential of technological breakthroughs. We have found that customer-innovators (those who are typically among the first to buy new products) are an especially wealthy source of useful information about new product or application issues.

CUSTOMERS BUY BENEFITS AND VALUE, NOT TECHNOLOGIES

A common error in innovation-driven ventures is that the firm concerns itself with improved technologies rather than improved customer benefits. The reality is, customers buy benefits, not technologies. The relevant question is *not* whether the new technology is superior to the existing technology. Instead, the salient query is whether the new technology provides a bundle of benefits to customers, such that they are eager to abandon the older technology.

Numerous examples can be cited where a new technology did not catch on because customers were comfortable with the existing technology or were not willing to pay an increased price for something technically better. Emerson was wrong; if you build a better mousetrap, people will not necessarily beat a path to your door. Take Emerson's mousetrap adage literally; from a technological standpoint, a better mousetrap can be built than the wire/wood/cheese technology that has been so enduring. Yet, people like the wire and wood trap and are not likely to abandon it for something technologically better, but *more costly.*

So the key to evaluating technological breakthroughs is to ask objectively whether the new technology provides better *benefits* to the customer at a price he or she is willing to pay. Is the new technology more beneficial and a better value than the old technology it will make obsolete or render less useful? For example, most automobile customers could care less whether their cars start with "points" or electronically, just so they start reliably at an affordable price.

Think about the customer benefits of these pairs of products or services: hand-held calculator vs. slide rule; television vs. radio; VCR's vs. purchasing tapes or going to the movies and horseless carriage vs. horse-drawn carriage. In every case, the replacement technology was obviously superior to the older technology. Still, in no instance did a vast market emerge until the *perceived value* was established in enough potential customers. For instance, it took the original

Henry Ford to develop the assembly line manufacture of automobiles that broke open the market for cars. Robots will replace human labor only in cases where it can be justified from the standpoint of costs vs. benefits. Because of labor costs, Third World countries may find it difficult to justify robotizing their manufacturing unless this technology can provide inordinate production advantages.

Innovation-driven ventures must meet several tests, then, if they are to hope to obsolete existing products and markets and create new ones: Namely, (1) Is the new technology more beneficial to prospective buyers in terms of improving the quality of their life styles or work styles? (2) Will it generally be perceived as such? (3) Will the new technology be seen as a better value (price vs. benefits) than the extant technology? If not, when will it be and what will it take in the way of persuasive marketing to make it so?

Interestingly, at this writing, growth in the in-home personal computer market has slowed considerably. Why? Because the *average* person and household does not see how the benefits of an in-home personal computer are worth the price that must be paid. Obviously, the market will eventually explode, but when? Once the technology yields enough benefits that can be communicated to those in the vast middle-American market so that they are willing to pay the price. And if history repeats itself, the price will be considerably less in inflation-adjusted, real terms than it is today. Color televisions, microwave ovens, autos and other technological innovations followed this pattern.

ESTABLISHING COMMERCIAL PRIORITIES

Opportunity prioritization is—or should be—the high technology company's critical initial step toward commercialization of lab output.[6] By this we mean that, subsequent to indepth marketing research on market potential, the firm must decide which existing or presently nonexistent "future" market(s) it is interested in pursuing. When someone says market potential, market demand or market research, it is assumed that a relevant market has been identified and is firmly in mind. For example, the nomenclatures automobile market, or micro-computer market or soap market conjure up clear pictures to most people. But in innovation-driven high technology, this is often not the case.

Take biotechnology. The potential applications of genetic engineering are countless. A biotech company could very well decide *not* to compete in pharmaceutical/medical markets at all, although these are the applications most people think of for biotechnology R&D. A biotech company might, for instance, "create" markets in agribusiness (e.g., disease-free orchids) or environmental pollution cleanup (e.g., oil spills). Similarly, the fields of lasers, robotics and fiber optics have many possible applications (markets) that do not exist today.

Any R&D breakthrough needs to be evaluated within the context of a formal market opportunity identification analysis. In this regard, future opportunities in known and prospective or developing industries are formally assessed. After completing this stage, a company will have identified several possible applications for its new technology, applications that will likely cut across industries. And the firm will have a sense of the future prospects for these industries. At this point, some applications or industries can be eliminated from further consideration, for various reasons.

After a thorough screening, the industries and related applications that remain all will have some potential. Realistically, however, the company will be unable to exploit fully all the potential applications that have been identified, even if all the industries appear to have exceptional prospects. However, before doing the marketing research needed to better target opportunities, it is vital for the company to do some ordering of, or establishing priorities for, the prospective industries. The cost alone of undertaking extensive marketing research necessitates first designating the industry or industries that look to offer the most profitable long-term opportunities.

Once this priority-setting task is achieved, the company can turn its attention to conducting some of the indepth marketing research, particularly qualitative research among potential customers, that we have mentioned. For example, primary (original) research can be carried out to obtain more specific information on possible demand of lasers in the clothing manufacturing business. (Lasers are used to cut patterns.) With the resulting feedback as guidance, more informed choices can be made in the actual ranking and selection of target markets.[7]

Innovation-driven companies must put the "market" in market research. That is, before market research can be undertaken effectively, it must be determined what existing or future market(s) the company has in mind. Under few circumstances should a marketing researcher be turned loose to find an application for an R&D breakthrough without some firm direction as to what market(s) the company has in mind. Otherwise, the researcher is left to flounder about. But is employing good marketing research techniques and establishing commercial priorities sufficient? No, there is an additional ingredient to consider.

ROLE OF ENTREPRENEURSHIP

Indeed, effective marketing to frontier markets requires far more than establishing commercial priorities and corporate reliance on marketing research and market analysis. It also depends on entrepreneurial spirit, the right corporate culture. Marketing research and market analysis can make supply-side marketing more calculated (informed) risk-taking, but there comes a time when management must rely on intuition and fortitude to go ahead with a project. Former ITT CEO, Harold Geneen, makes the point in his book, *Managing,* that almost all large companies which think they are entrepreneurial are, on closer examination, really not. They may fund highly risky projects, but, even if the projects fail entirely, the amount of assets of risk is so small that the net effect on corporate earnings is virtually imperceptible. Because of their fiduciary responsibility to stockholders, most *Fortune* 1000 CEOs must take mainly trustee roles rather than entrepreneurial ones. In Geneen's view, "Betting the Company" is characteristic of startup ventures, but is inappropriate for large going concerns, unless the company is in big trouble. (Which paves the way for a Lee Iacocca, who does bet the company.) And that is precisely why the net job growth in the United States in recent years has come from small business, not from the *Fortune* 500.

Geneen is right; the entrepreneurial spirit embodied in supply-side marketing is rare in large companies. Even so, exceptions exist. There are companies wherein the culture promotes innovation and entrepreneurship. And we know for sure that corporate culture, whether it be a *Fortune* 500 or a startup venture, is crucial if supply-side marketing is to have a fighting chance to succeed.

EIGHT MASTERS LISTED

Fortune magazine, with the help of respected business executives and academics, has identified what are considered to be eight "corporate masters of innovation." Although these companies (American Airlines, Apple Computer, Campbell Soup, General Electric, Intel, Merck, 3M, and Philip Morris) are all large ones, they have managed to retain a culture conducive to innovation and entrepreneurship. We believe that the basic philosophies which pervade these eight companies are essential to effective supply-side marketing, irrespective of company size.

What are some of these philosophies?

- Strong sense of corporate mission.
- Paranoid about change and competitors.
- Devotion to marketing.
- Decentralization (but not anarchy).
- Unpunished subordinates' failures (except for incompetence).
- Mandatory interdisciplinary communications (e.g., between marketing and R&D).[8]

We do not intend to discuss each of these here but do want to elaborate on one characteristic to point out the managerial adroitness it takes to translate an entrepreneurial corporate culture into a functioning system that truly works. A host of recent articles, books and speeches say that a company has to decentralize to encourage and promote innovation and entrepreneurship, which generally is correct. But it is one thing for a CEO to say, "Let's decentralize to promote an entrepreneurial culture," and quite another to implement it.

Take two contrasting examples. IBM has been eminently successful in separating its microcomputer business unit from the remainder of the company, philosophically and physically. In spite of a few setbacks with the PC Jr., the IBM's Boca Raton decentralization was, and is, a great success story. Another computer company, Atari, decentralized with opposite results. When James Morgan became head of Atari, he found tremendous redundancy in R&D that was sapping the ailing company of what strength it had left. When Morgan asked why one engineer lived in Louisville, Kentucky, where Atari had no R&D facilities, he was told the engineer liked living and working there. So, if not properly managed, decentralized can degenerate into near anarchy.

Moreover, decisions about decentralization necessitate considerable thought and study. It might pay to decentralize marketing, but not R&D. For instance, some years ago, Hewlett-Packard mostly centralized its R&D in order to curb R&D redundancy within its divisions and to promote intracorporate R&D sharing.

The point is, there is a great deal of glibness today about how innovativeness and entrepreneurship must start at the top (with the CEO), then pervade the organization, and finally be stimulated through decentralization. We agree with these precepts, but with the caveat that they are hard to implement in practice. Marketing to pioneer markets (i.e., supply-side marketing) requires an entrepreneurial spirit, the right corporate culture, which, in turn, must be achieved through proper incentives to employees, devotion to marketing, carefully orchestrated decentralization and the rest of the aforementioned characteristics of the "masters of innovation." Which is why only a small percentage of all companies are masters of it.

We want to stress that the need for supply-side marketing should not be used by a company as an *excuse* to develop and commercialize a product, service or process. Too frequently, companies devote time, money and effort to products that *realistically* have little or no chance to succeed commercially. Maybe some engineer is enamored with the technology behind the product, or management lets its hope to recoup the company's investment cloud its judgment.

Supply-side marketing is risky, but it is *calculated* risk-taking. Marketing to frontier markets requires strategy and work. It demands a facilitating corporate culture and organization, a focus on potential customers and customer benefits, a healthy dose of (especially qualitative) marketing research guided by lucid market and industry priorities laid down by top management, thorough analysis based on the market research and . . . intuition and fortitude.

Occasionally in this article, we refer to our prior research. During the period 1982-1984, we conducted an extensive formal study among some 125 leading high technology firms. The techniques employed in the various phases of this study included in-person and telephone interviews, questionnaires, and case studies. Augmenting this formal research were our consulting and conference presentation experiences. Since 1984, our formal and informal research activities in high technology marketing, in multiple industries and companies, has continued, thus creating an expanded data base. The data presented in Exhibit 1, for example, were collected in the earlier phases of the ongoing research project.

NOTES

1. Akio Morita, "Creativity in Modern Industry," *Omni,* March 1981, p. 6. Reprinted by permission.
2. William L. Shanklin, "Supply-Side Marketing Can Restore Yankee Ingenuity," *Research Management,* May–June 1983, pp. 20–25.
3. *Ibid,* p. 20.
4. For a more comprehensive discussion, see William L. Shanklin and John K. Ryans, Jr., *Marketing High Technology* (Lexington, Massachusetts: Lexington Books, D.C. Heath and Company, 1984).
5. William L. Shanklin and John K. Ryans, Jr., "Organizing for High-Tech Marketing," *Harvard Business Review,* November–December, 1984, pp. 164–171.
6. See for elaboration, John K. Ryans, Jr. and William L. Shanklin, "High-Tech Megatenets: 10 Principles of High Technology Market Behavior," *Business Marketing,* September 1984, pp. 100–106; and also, John K. Ryans, Jr. and William L. Shanklin, "Positioning and Selecting Target Markets," *Research Management,* September–October, 1984, pp. 28–32.
7. Shanklin and Ryans, *Marketing High Technology,* pp. 64–69.
8. Stratford P. Sherman, "Eight Big Masters of Innovation," *Fortune,* October 15, 1984, pp. 66—84.

REFERENCES

Alavi Maryani, "A Meta Analysis," *MIS Quarterly*, March 1992.

Rajiv K. Sinha, "A Split Hazard Model," *Journal of Marketing Research*, February 1992.

David Mathe, "Influence of Technology and Demand Factors On Firm Size and Industrial Structure," *Research Policy,* February 1992.

Higgins and Shanklin, "Market Acceptance For High-Technology Consumer Products," *Journal of Consumer Marketing,* Winter 1992.

John C. Totten
Vice President, Analytical and Technical Products
Nielsen Marketing Research
Northbrook, Illinois

Mike Duffy
Director of Forecasting and Planning
Kraft General Foods, Inc.
Glenview, Illinois

Chapter 13

Marketing Technology and Consumer Scanning

Introduction

In this chapter, we will review the uses of data collected from electronic scanning at the point-of-sale (POS). Scanning systems are in place in most major grocery outlets, many drug stores, and major mass merchandisers such as Kmart and Wal-Mart. In addition, a variety of specialty businesses such as video rental outlets use POS systems to capture sales and rental transactions. Our discussion will center on the uses of POS scanning systems by manufacturers and retailers of consumer packaged goods of the type found in grocery or drug stores. However, most of the methods discussed are easily adaptable to any marketing operation able to collect and accumulate transaction data by individual line item in the product line offering.

Information on product sales is collected by manufacturers for a variety of reasons, but there are three major reasons: to assess the level of consumer demand for a product and detect changes in that demand pattern; to assess the strength of competitive products, detect changes in competitive marketing activity, and assess the impact of competitive changes on products of interests; and to provide information that will assist the sales force in obtaining improved treatment of the manufacturer's product by the retailer.

The typical distribution system for consumer goods is a complex network of interrelated activities involving manufacturers, distributors, brokers, wholesalers, and retailers. The manufacturer may not have much control over final retail prices because the costs for the intermediate distribution functions must be absorbed into the final retail price. Fluctuations in inventory levels throughout the system generally lead to patterns of manufacturer shipments that when using only manufacturer shipment data may vary significantly from the pattern of consumer demand for the product. The direct link between competitive marketing actions and shipments of a manufacturer's own product is generally so confounded by the number of competitors and the existence of inventory fluctuations throughout the system that little analysis can be done of the link between competitive activity and brand sales.

For manufacturers of consumer packaged goods, the data collection issues were initially addressed in the 1930s with the establishment of audits of retail sales. Art Nielsen established an audit service that used a sample of stores audited approximately every two months and provided estimates of the pricing and sales levels existing for a brand and its competitors. The results of this sample could be "syndicated," or sold to multiple manufacturers in the category at a considerable savings in cost versus the cost an individual manufacturer would incur in collecting similar data. As time passed, a variety of services became available to measure competitive activity, such as newspaper feature advertising, radio and TV advertising, and in-store display activity. Syndicated data from other points in the distribution system, such as warehouse withdrawal data, became available.

In the 1960s, a coding standard for consumer products was established. The Universal Product Code (UPC) system allowed manufacturers to assign a unique code to each of their products that could be read by retail store scanning systems, and used to look up retail prices and to update retail volume movement records. In the late 1970s, grocery stores began to adopt POS electronic scanning systems to read and process the UPC codes. This allowed electronic accumulation of data. In the mid 1980s, several companies announced syndicated data services based on POS scanner data for price and volume information with supplemental audit data on retailer feature ads and in-store display activity. By 1993, Nielsen Market Research and Information Resources, Inc. were the two largest suppliers of such information in the United States, and both were expanding internationally. Major retailers, such as Kmart and Wal-Mart, provide direct sales information to 50 to 70% of their suppliers, but usually do not provide information on competitive sales.

Data on retail store sales performs a useful function, but does not allow examination of the behavior of individual purchasers of a brand or product category. Many important questions exist that require review of individual buyer behavior. For example, in planning an advertising campaign, an important question is often "What fraction of buyers of the product category have purchased my product in the preceding year?" If the answer is a low fraction, then the objective of the advertising campaign might be to persuade non-buyers to try my brand. However, if the answer is a high fraction, then the campaign objective might be to encourage higher rates of repeat buying of the product. Such information might be collected by a survey of consumers, asking a broad cross-section about their recent purchase and usage of products in the category of interest. To examine the behavior of individual consumer purchasing over time, a number of services have been formed to collect and summarize information from consumers via a written purchase diary that is collected and processed on a periodic basis. Such written diaries are most useful when the distribution system is complex and fragmented, or when little POS data capture exists. The workload on the consumer to maintain the diaries restricts data collection to relatively few product categories per panelist.

POS retail scanning systems gave the ability to capture the complete transaction detail of an individual consumer, and the ability to match this information with the list of competitive products stocked in a store and their pricing levels. For marketing activities aimed directly at individual consumers, such as couponing and media advertising, consumer purchase data is combined with information on the activity, such as coupon distribution, coupon redemption, or media exposure in sales estimation models.

In the sections to follow, we shall review some of the common business problems where analyses of scanner data are used, and explore some of the emerging trends that are changing "traditional" analysis methods. The extreme improvements in computing cost/performance in the past decade make possible the processing of large volumes of detail data, and the application of increasingly complex models for data analysis and exception reporting. The discovery of significant differences in consumer response to manufacturer and retailer marketing activity among brands in a category, and across markets for a brand, is now focusing analysis activity on individual retail accounts in a market, and even on individual stores within the account for a truly "micro-marketing" approach.

INFORMATION ON SALES

The Beer Game

MIT's Sloan School of Management has developed a number of management simulation games to illustrate the difficulties management faces in a complex production-distribution environment. In the "Beer Game" reported on by Professor John Sterman, a distribution system consists of retailer, wholesaler, distributor, and factory. Information is limited to analysis of orders and shipments. Consumer demand is not known in advance, and revealed only to retailers on a week-by-week basis as the game proceeds.

Typical experiments start with a steady level of weekly demand and have a simple step function 100% increase in retail demand after about ⅙ of the game weeks have been played. The results reported are that the games almost always exhibit three key patterns: (1) Oscillation—orders and inventories show large amplitude swings on about a 20-week cycle; (2) Amplification—the further removed from retail sales, the greater the swings in orders, with peak orders at factory level usually more than double the peak order rate at retail; and (3) Phase Lag—the order rates peak later and later as you move from retailer to factory. After the game is complete, participants at levels other than the retailer may exhibit complete disbelief when the simple nature of the demand function is revealed. Professor Sterman reports finding similar oscillation, amplification, and phase lag in the U.S. Industrial Production series for materials, intermediate goods, and final products.

Manufacturer Shipments

Most manufacturers maintain detail files on their own shipments. These files usually originated as a by-product of the accounting system, and are used as a basis for production planning, demand forecasting, and inventory management. Shipment data may be difficult to match to consumer demand at levels of detail finer than all-outlet annual sales. There is usually a complete lack of comparable information on competitive brands, so it is difficult to tell from shipment data alone whether increases or decreases in shipments are due to general changes in category sales patterns, or due to a competitive activity change that yields a more or less favorable competitive positioning for your own brand. Retail trade promotion is an important contributor to fluctuations in manufacturer shipments. In recent years, the allocation of funds among trade and consumer activities has been shifting toward a greater and greater proportion of manufacturers' marketing expenditures directed toward retail support activities (see Exhibit 1). Current estimates are that for many manufacturers, over 50% of their total marketing budget is spent on trade promotion activities.

Trade promotion activities generate significant short-term increases of 2 to 20 times normal retail sales on the promoted item. The variability of actual results from the expected average promotional sales is extremely high, causing the retailer to order extra stock for protection against unexpectedly high demand. If there is extra product left after the promotion, the retailer often reprices this product to normal price, and pockets the manufacturers' promotional allowance on this product as additional profit. The manufacturer sees a significant decline in post-promotion orders as this excess inventory is worked off of retail shelves.

A second practice associated with manufacturer trade promotions is "forward-buying." The promotional discounts offered by the manufacturer are usually sufficiently attractive to make it profitable for the retailer to purchase additional inventory beyond that needed for stock-out protection during the promotion. If planned promotional activities are announced in advance, then retailers may delay ordering and deplete normal inventories in order to restock with lower cost promotional product. This behavior leads to a marked decline in manufacturer orders and shipments just prior to the start of the promotion. It is currently accepted that most retailers buy about 90% of frequently promoted consumer package goods on deal, but sell about 60% at the normal price.

A manufacturer in this situation can obtain almost no information from recent shipments about the probable impact of reducing the number of deals at retail. It is also not uncommon to find that the dollar amount of promotional allowances is significantly larger than the manufacturers' pre-tax profit. Conversely, the promotional allowances offered by the manufacturer are currently estimated to amount to between ⅓ and ½ of the retailers pre-tax profit. Management of this

EXHIBIT 1. Ad Trade Promotion Expenditure Importance

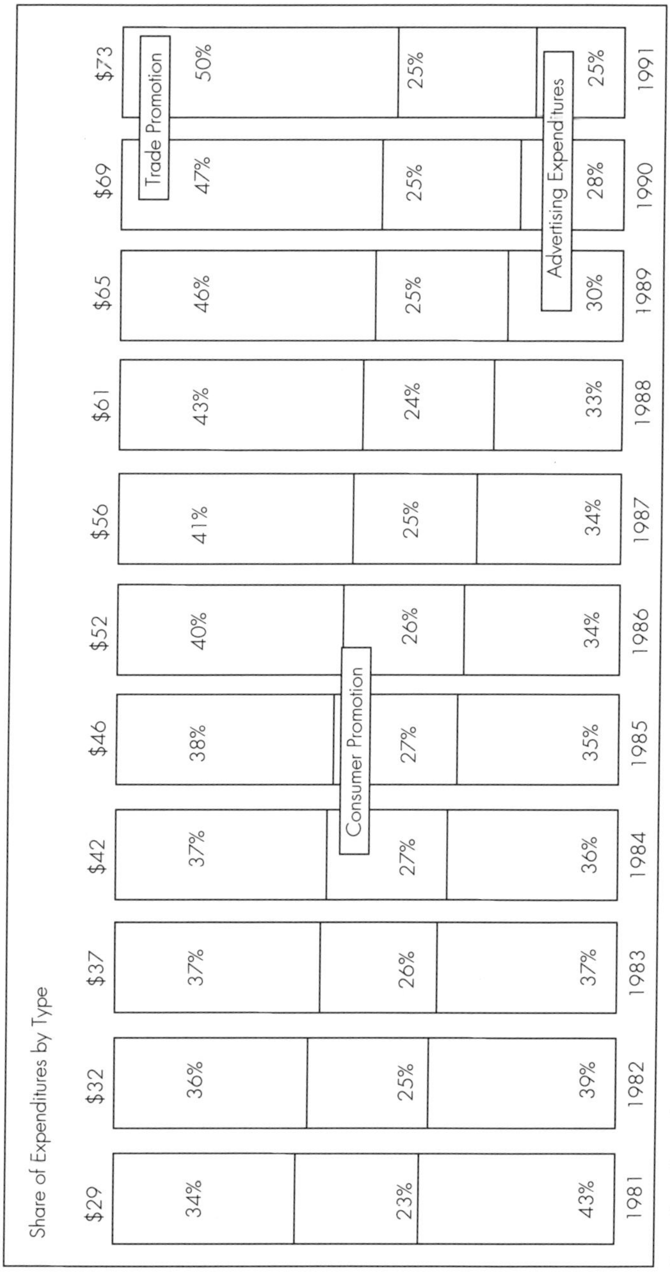

Share of Expenditures by Type

	1981	1982	1983	1984	1985	1986	1987	1988	1989	1990	1991
Total	$29	$32	$37	$42	$46	$52	$56	$61	$65	$69	$73
Trade Promotion	34%	36%	37%	37%	38%	40%	41%	43%	46%	47%	50%
Consumer Promotion	23%	25%	26%	27%	27%	26%	25%	24%	25%	25%	25%
Advertising Expenditures	43%	39%	37%	36%	35%	34%	34%	33%	30%	28%	25%

Source: Donnelley Marketing
Source: Nielsen Marketing Research Estimates

large dollar transfer between manufacturer and retailer requires detailed information on the impact at retail of the various activities that might be supported by promotional dollars.

In summary, manufacturer shipments cover sales from all outlets and account for total movement, but may include promotional volume surges, pre- and post-promotion dips, crowded promotion calendars, and may mask huge inventory stockpiling-depletion swings in the distribution system. Shipment information is difficult to match to consumer demand in geographic subdivisions of total sales area due to diversion, out-of-stocks, and lack of information on competition. Even if these concerns are covered, the oscillation, amplification, and phase-lag relations present in a multilevel distribution system obscures the relation between manufacturer marketing actions and consumer demand.

Retail Sales Data

Retail sales data is close to final demand, but suffers from a number of measurement problems. In the complex distribution system that exists for consumer packaged goods in the United States, products may be sold through many different types of retail outlets including grocery stores, drug stores, convenience stores, and mass-merchandise stores. As population growth has slowed, each outlet type has viewed expansion into products normally handled by other channels as growth opportunities. This channel "blurring" has made it difficult to measure sales across different channels in a consistent and comparable manner.

In order to monitor levels of marketing activities, a number of auxiliary data reporting services are available. These include monitoring of coupon redemption activity, radio, TV, print advertising by the manufacturer, and the feature-ad and in-store display activity by retailers. In most cases, these services provide information on competitive activity in addition to information on the manufacturer's own brand. The increasing popularity of in-store advertising, POS promotional material, and store-specific marketing activity (such as instantly printed coupons or electronic coupons) gives rise to a number of niche opportunities for auditing and syndicating information on new forms of in-store marketing activities.

Syndicated data on store sales available in 1993 combines many of these data collection methods into an extremely comprehensive database. Using POS scanners, data on individual item sales at the store level is captured weekly (or even daily). This data consists of an item code, a count of items moved, and either an item price or total dollar sales amount. To this is added the results of manual audits indicating the presence of retailer ad-features and/or in-store displays. Mathematical models compare current pricing to past pricing to assess whether there is a price reduction from "normal" or "base" price. Other models are employed to estimate the probable level of sales ("baseline" sales) that would have occurred in the absence of any in-store promotion such as price discounts, ads, or displays. Information on the availability of manufacturer supported coupon activity may be supplied from audits of coupon drops, from consumer diary reporting, or increasingly, from POS scanning of the coupons. Media information on TV advertising is measured in gross rating points (GRPs), and may be entered at the product-market-week level from syndicated services that monitor media commercial activity. The product code can be linked to master files containing descriptive information about the product such as brand name, package size, product form, flavor, ingredients, color, and many other attributes. The store identification code can be linked to master files containing descriptive information about the store layout, general pricing policy, and descriptive information about the types of consumers located in the stores trading area (usually based on U.S. census data).

The purchaser of syndicated store data may add additional data, such as shipment and order information for sales to the retailer, the types of promotional incentives and allowances offered to the retailer, and information on marketing activity performed that is not measured by the syndicated data, such as sweepstakes, contests, mail-in offers, product sampling programs, and non-traditional marketing activities, such as in-store television, in-store ads delivered by a variety of different vehicles, production cost or sales margin, and other relevant activity. For the balance of this chapter, we ignore such additions and focus on the data provided in syndicated sales databases, the organizational units of the manufacturer and retailer who might use such data, their issues, and the manner in which the data is reported and analyzed to support decision making on marketing issues.

Consumer Purchase Data

In an electronic consumer panel, data collection on individual purchases is coupled with collection of retail store sales data, with audits of ad features and in-store display data. Usage of coupons is matched with the purchase data. For a subset of households, television viewing is also monitored. The panelist is required to provide demographic information on an annual basis and to show an identification card on each purchase occasion. This low workload leads to lower attrition rates over time among the POS panelists than those experienced in written diary panels.

Databases covering consumer behavior over extended periods of time allow extensive analyses of brand loyalty, and the ability of promotional activity to influence brand switching. Having the store data available allows review of the availability and pricing of brands not chosen when a category purchase was made. The ability of ad-features to shift consumer purchases among competing retailers can be studied.

An important study area is the source of increased volume received by a brand when a retail promotion occurred. Analysis of purchase timing allows decomposition of the increased volume sold during promotional periods into that due to stockpiling by loyal brand buyers, that portion due to brand switching, and that portion due to increased category consumption.

Both Nielsen and IRI offer large scale consumer purchase panels with scanner collected data. Panel product purchase data is not normally used for tracking and control purposes, but is used in understanding the impact of various marketing activities, assessing the degree of competitive interaction among brands, and for understanding the nature of seasonal variations in category sales. When there are puzzling results in the retail store sales data, consumer panel data can be an important resource for diagnostic purchases.

DATABASE CONTENTS

Detail Observations

The typical detail observation in a retail store movement database is for a single store, one UPC item for one week. The detail movement data collected directly from scanners for the UPC is:

1. *Unit sales movement*—A count of the number of items sold in the store over the week.
2. *Dollar sales movement*—This may represent actual dollar movement, possibly at several different prices during the week, or may be the most recent price multiplied by unit movement.
3. *Information on usage of retailer coupons may be included*—Most probably the number of retailer coupons used on purchases of the UPC item. Average value of retail coupons redeemed may also be included.
4. *To the scanned data, causal detail such as information on the presence and type of retail feature ads and in-store displays may be added from store audits.*

Finally, fields based on proprietary models may be added to the detail data. Both IRI and Nielsen provide:

1. *Base price*—This quantity is the output of models designed to estimate the "normal" or "expected" price for the item in the store week. This field is used together with actual price to generate a model-based classification of some prices as "temporary price reduction" (TPR) pricing, and therefore to classify the week as a "TPR" promotional week.

2. *Base volume*—This quantity is the output of models designed to estimate the "normal" or "expected" unit sales for the item in the absence of retail sales promotional activity (ad-feature, in-store display, or TPR). The typical retail grocery store generates about 15,000 to 25,000 observations of detailed movement data a week.

Relational Data

Using relational database methods, a large variety of descriptive information may be merged with the detailed movement data. There are many descriptive elements that can be related to stores. A store is related to its parent organization (chain, independent, etc.), and is related by geography to city, county, market, state, sales regions, and sales divisions. Store format codes may describe the layout of the store, management philosophy (hi-lo versus everyday low price) and stocking policies (full-line stocking versus limited stocking of high-velocity items). Store geodemographics describe the socioeconomic characteristics of consumer households in the store's trading area. Store size is a measure of the relative selling power of a store. Predominant in grocery stores is the all-commodity volume (ACV) measure of store size given by total dollar sales across all items in the store. A related, and easier to generate measure is "scan dollars"—the total dollar sales of all items in the store that are UPC coded. While store ACV or scan dollar actually varies on a week to week basis, an annualized number updated on a quarterly or annual basis is often used.

Related to weeks are a number of items such as assignment to months, quarters, and even to year. Weeks may be flagged as "holiday weeks" or "key pay weeks," which allows retrieval, summary, and contrasts of these weeks versus "regular" weeks. Related to the UPC code are many characteristics—manufacturer, brand, size, flavor, special packaging, color, form, ingredient, and assorted nutritional qualifiers (low-fat, low-salt, low cholesterol, etc.). UPCs are usually assigned to competitive product categories, although the exact definition of the UPCs in a category may vary from manufacturer to manufacturer. "Volume equivalency" conversion factors convert a UPC's item movement into a standard category volume measure (quarts, pounds, cups of coffee, etc.). The unit of standard volume may vary from manufacturer to manufacturer within a category, and reflects the individual manufacturers view of the comparability of the individual UPCs.

Selling Conditions

Store-week-UPC detail is often characterized by "selling conditions." These are represented by true/false variables indicating whether the condition is true for the particular store-week-UPC combination. The most common conditions characterize promotional activities that may generate significantly different sales rates. In this class are "any feature," "any display," and "any TPR". These conditions may be further divided; "any feature" may be true if any of the following conditions are true: large (A-size) feature ad, medium (B-size), or small (line ad or C-ad).

Another class of selling conditions is generated by converting continuous variables into ranges. These conditions are usually specific to a product category. Some examples are: unit price at or below $.99, unit price from $1.00 to $1.49; unit price above $1.49; no price discount; price discount below 10%; discount 10 to 24%; or discount above 25%. More complex definitions may involve comparison across several data records. Ranges of price difference versus competition fall into this class. Even with relatively few ranges defined on price discounts or price differences versus competition, the full list of possible conditions may number in the hundreds.

A short list of possible conditions (under 50) will cover most of the mutually exclusive conditions under which sales are made. A popular list of selling conditions is given by pairing a price discount condition list with a list of feature/display conditions. The feature/display list is:

1. "Major Feature" (A or B ad) with no display
2. "All other Features" with no display
3. "Major Display"
4. "Minor Display"
5. "Major Display with Major Feature"
6. "Major Display with A/O Feature"
7. "Minor Display with Major Feature"
8. "Minor Display with A/O Feature"

The price discount list is:

1. Price discount, if any, less than 5%
2. Price discount in the 5 to 15% range
3. Price discount in the 15 to 25% range
4. Price discount in the 25 to 35% range
5. Price discount over 35%

REPORTING SCHEMES

Reporting of the data is organized into a four- or five-dimensional scheme, where an individual number in the report has the following identifiers or indices: geography, product, time, and either fact-condition combined or fact and condition.

A hierarchial summary scheme is often imposed on the data. The lowest level of detail reported is usually not the store-week-UPC information, but some slightly higher level of summarization. The geography dimension is most commonly summarized, with stores combined to give a total for a common store management unit (such as grocery chain) within a market. Low-level reporting then is usually at chain-week-UPC summary of detail, or even summarized to market-week-UPC. The second most common summarization is to combine like UPCs into a brand size summary. Many consumer products have a number of UPC items that are packaged, priced, and promoted similarly, varying only in flavor and color. For business tracking and gross analysis, similar UPCs are summarized into a brand-size-item, the lowest level reported.

Typical summary schemes are:

Geography: Chain → Market → Region → Country
Time: Week → Month → Quarter → Year, or Week → Bimonth → Year
Product: UPC → Size, Form, Flavor → Major Segment → Brand → Manufacturer → Category
As many as 8 to 9 levels commonly exist in the product hierarchy.
Condition: The following minimal set of mutually exclusive conditions are often used, with summarization to "Total all conditions."
    No promotion,
    TPR with no feature or display,
    Any feature without display,
    Any display without feature, and
    Any feature with display.

FACTS

Auxiliary Facts

To expand the usefulness of the unit and dollar movement data, a number of auxiliary facts may be derived. Some examples are:

1. Discount = base price minus average price
2. % Discount = 100* discount/base price
3. Sales rates = any of the unit or equivalized volume facts may be divided by the outlet coverage fact to give a sales rate fact.
   (e.g.: Unit sales per million ACV, average sales per store selling)
4. Promotion efficiency index (PEI) = 100 x equivalent volume sales ÷ equivalized base volume sales
5. Incremental volume sales = equivalized volume sales – equivalized base volume sales

The imposition of a hierarchy allows calculation of many new facts that relate an individual cell fact to other facts at the same or higher level in the hierarchy. Examples include:
1. Market share
2. Index versus year ago or versus previous period (for any measure)

3. % change versus year ago or previous period (for any measure)
4. Rank (usually on a product of geography or condition dimension)

Addability of Facts

By adding volume and dollar facts across cells, and then recomputing price facts, many subtotals of facts can be computed from summary databases. For example, a brand's volume is simply the sum of the volumes of the individual brand sizes, even at a market level. However, there are many facts that require a return to the most basic store-week-UPC level data to create. These are the "non-addable facts," and are associated with classifying "conditions" when multiple product items are combined in a time period, or when multiple time periods are combined. As an example, suppose that Brand A has two sizes—Size 1 and Size 2. In a four-week period in a retail account, Size 1 is featured for two of the four weeks, and Size 2 is featured for two of the four weeks. If they were the same two weeks (both sizes of Brand A featured together), then Brand A was featured in two of the four weeks. But if Size 1 was featured in the first 2 weeks, and Size 2 was featured in the second two weeks, then Brand A was featured in all four weeks. The possibility of overlap means that the feature activity levels for the brand cannot be obtained by adding the activity levels of the individual brands. Similar problems occur in determining the levels of distribution coverage for a brand with multiple sizes, in determining the brand share in stores selling the brand, and in determining the average number of brand sizes carried per store selling.

Market Level Facts

While sales information at retail is collected at the individual store level, and detailed analysis of store conditions versus store sales rates may yield insights, other marketing activities affect consumer groups within a market, and thus all stores in which these groups shop. TV advertising and couponing are such activities.

Typical Syndicated Facts on TV Media and Couponing

TV	Local versus National
	Day part
	Target audience
	Reach
	Frequency
	Share of voice
Coupon	Face value
	Circulation, delivery (FSI, ROP)
	Redemption
	Household inventory of coupons

PROJECTION ISSUES

Retail Sales Sample Data

It is possible to capture data from all stores of a single retailer even if that retailer has hundreds of individual stores. It is seldom possible to capture data for all retail stores in a market, as many smaller outlets are not yet equipped with POS scanners, and even if so equipped, may not be willing to provide detail sales data. Even if complete POS data were available, the costs of processing it and adding manual audits of in-store conditions could raise costs significantly. In 1993, the syndicated services attempted to cover approximately the largest 10% of outlets in a distribution channel (which often account for over 50% of total channel sales), and use statistical sampling methods to project the data to estimates of total sales in the distribution channel. Even if it is easy to capture all of the POS movement data, any additional data to be provided via manual audits may be so expensive to collect that only a sample of the possible universe is used.

When designing an information system based on sample data, experts on statistical sampling theory should be involved. Provision must be made for the closing of outlets in the sample, merging in data from outlets newly added to the sample, and accounting for trends in the total volume of products handled by the distribution system channel being monitored. For example, a recent trend in the United States consumer packaged goods area is for mass merchandisers to add lines of shelf stable items usually found in grocery stores. The projection system must account for growth due to increasing penetration across channel stores and growth due to the increasing use of the mass merchandiser outlets by product purchasers. Simultaneously, sales of such products may be declining in traditional distribution channels.

One of the findings from analysis of detail POS sales data coupled with causal information on detail marketing activities in a retail account or city is that the same marketing inputs may produce significantly different sales results from one geography to the next. In addition, the translation of a manufacturer's marketing activity may vary significantly from geography to geography, so that identical promotional offers to two different retailers may produce completely different pricing and promotional activities being offered to consumers by the two retailers. This supports the current trend by manufacturers toward "micro-marketing," or tailoring marketing actions and programs specific to local regions rather than using a "one size fits all" national program.

Household Purchase Sample Data

Household purchase data by its very nature poses a number of complex problems in projection and interpretation. The data can be kept at finer levels of detail on time of purchase (even down to the hour), but probably represents only a sample of the purchasing by the household. If the data is captured by POS scanners, the data in stores not equipped with POS scanners may be lost. If scanned in the home, then accurate information on the price and in-store promotional conditions may be lost. Accurate recording of usage of coupons on purchases may be a problem in either case. If multiple members of the household participate in purchasing activity, the levels of coverage may be biased (some members may be more faithful in recording purchases than others).

On the other hand, more detailed causal information may be available at the household level. A broad variety of demographic information may be collected, such as the family income; age, education, occupation, and sex of each family member; and information on the type and quality of major possessions such as house and cars. Current research indicates that some 45 to 65 life-stage/life-style groupings aid significantly in projecting household purchasing to store-level purchasing. With such projection, data from the U.S. census at a zip code level can be used to determine the approximate frequency of the groups among an individual store or chain's shoppers. Data on the media portions of a marketing program may be associated with individual households by monitoring TV viewing, receipt of mailed coupons, magazine readership, and use of radios. Additional classifications may be assigned to households based on their purchase histories. Examples are store loyalty, brand loyalty, and "deal" loyalty indices, classification as light, medium, or heavy buyers of various product categories, classification based on type of TV programs used, and propensity to use coupons.

REPORT DESIGN

General Report Design

There are three general management functions that are supported by database reports and analyses. The first of these is the monitoring of current brand performance in the marketplace, and the preliminary selection of sets of performance measures to monitor in more detail. The second is the evaluation of sales performance under various alternative marketing conditions. The third is the projection of analysis results into estimates of sales performance likely to be realized in non-sampled outlets, or estimates of the probable sales performance likely to be realized by a proposed future marketing plan.

An individual report will be prepared for some level of time-product-location, possibly for several levels. A single set of facts will be selected. A report will almost always have one or more measures of sales performance, and one or more causal measures, where the causal measures reflect the marketing actions affecting sales performance.

The performance and causal measures may be repeated several times for different conditions.

Sales Performance Measures

The two most common measures of sales performance are volume and share. Volume may be measured in terms of unit sales, dollar sales, or equivalized volume sales. Share is obtained by selecting the volume for an individual product or item, dividing by the total volume for some summary across time, product, or geography, and multiplying by 100. Most often, the summary is across all products in the category to give an items share (market share) of category sales. If the summary is across time, such as a year, the result is the particular periods share of the item's total annual sales. If the summary is across geography, then the result might be the share of U.S sales for the product that is sold in Chicago, or the share of product sales in Chicago that is sold in a particular retailer's chain. Sales performance measures may also be indexed versus previous period, or for the same period a year ago.

Instead of total volume, one might use baseline volume, or incremental volume. This might be converted to share of baseline volume or share of incremental volume. For some applications, an important measure of sales performance is sales rate. This is obtained by dividing volume (unit, dollar, or equivalized) by a measure of the size of the stores in the geography. Common size measures are ACV (millions of dollars of annual sales by stores selling the item), percent of stores in the area selling the product or item, or number of stores in the area selling the product. A recent addition to the list (PEI) is used in evaluating the results of sales generated by retailer promotions compared to the expected value of sales with no retailer promotion.

Causal Measures

The causal measures usually represent the result of sales or marketing activity by manufacturer or retailer. For tracking purposes, only an overall result may be given, but for analysis, the causal measures may be reported by mutually exclusive conditions. When trade promotion activity is the basis for the exclusive conditions, some measures of volume performance are also reported by condition. Where available, data on media and coupon activity may be included to round out the picture of marketing and sales activity. Some of the measures used to track and analyze volume results are:

1. To monitor prices available to consumers, measures include weighted average actual price, weighted average base price, and percent price reduction. Prices may be measured on a unit basis, or on an equivalized volume basis.

2. To monitor the extent of physical distribution of the product, measures include outlet coverage measures such as percent of stores selling, percent of ACV selling, or the total ACV of stores in which the product is sold. If there are multiple items in the product (sizes, flavors, colors, etc), then an important measure might be average number of item carried per store that carries the product.

3. To monitor trade promotion coverage by condition, measures might include outlet coverage measures for the condition (e.g., percent of ACV with an A feature), and time coverage measures (e.g., average weeks of display by stores that had in-store display at least once). These might be combined into a weighted weeks measure that multiplies the outlet coverage and time coverage measures. For example, in a four-week period, one might obtain one weighted week of TPR performance by any of the following scenarios: 25% of the stores have a TPR for four weeks, all of the stores have one week of TPR (not necessarily in the same week), or in weeks 1 and 2, 50% of the stores have TPR performance, and in weeks 3 and 4, the remaining 50% perform. When trade promotion measures are reported by condition, one or more measures of sales performance are generally also reported by condition, such as volume, share, sales rate, incremental volume or share, incremental volume sales rate, or PEI indices.

4. Media measures possibly reported might include GRPs, reach, frequency, and share of voice. These might be reported in total, or by daypart (specific parts of the programming schedule). For coupons, measures might include circulation, average face value, redemption, share of redemption, or coupon inventory levels (average number of coupons held per household).

In the sections to follow, examples of the use of these measures in constructing reports will be shown. It is important to select measures that are consistent in their definitions. For example, if the sales performance measure chosen is equivalized volume, then market shares

REPORT 1. Nielsen Scantrack®—Weekly Dollar Share Trend
Category: Bottled Sparkling and Mineral Water
13 Weeks Ending APR2190.1
San Francisco

		Period			
	13 Weeks	JAN2790.1	FEB0390.1	FEB1090.1	FEB1790.1
Total Calistoga	23.0	21.3	21.2	22.4	23.4
Total Vittel	0.5	0.6	0.6	0.7	0.6
Total Perrier	0.5	2.5	2.5	1.6	0.1

Copyright© 1993 A. C. Nielsen Company.

should be calculated on equivalized volumes, and prices should be reported in prices per equivalized volume. Sales rates should be calculated by using equivalized volume in the numerator. PEI calculations and sales indices versus a previous period should also be made using equivalized volume.

MARKET POSITION AND DIAGNOSTIC REPORTS

Trend Reports

One of the most basic reports available on most databases is the trend report, which allows a quick comparison of performance over time. The tabular layout often has time periods as columns, although

REPORT 2. Nielsen Scantrack®—Product Profile Trend
Category: Bottled Sparkling and Mineral Water
13 Weeks Ending APR2190.1
San Francisco

	Period				
	JAN2790.1	**FEB0390.1**	**FEB1090.1**	**FEB1790.1**	**FEB2490.1**
Total Calistoga					
% Store selling	100	100	100	100	100
% Sales rate	177934	170307	173042	186264	186131
Sales rate	1779.3	1703.1	1730.4	1862.6	186.3
$ Sales w/causal	3408	2465	36916	28424	23766
% Promoted	1.9	1.4	21.3	15.3	12.8
$ Share	21.3	21.2	22.4	23.4	22.7
Display	12	7	22	23	33
Feature ads	0	0	35	33	69
Average price	1.55	1.55	1.41	1.34	1.38
Total Vittel					
% Store selling	70	80	80	76	80
$ Sales rate	5029	4963	5246	4679	4823
Sales rate	71.8	62.0	65.6	61.6	60.3
$ Sales w/causal	0	0	0	0	0
% Promoted	0.0	0.0	0.0	0.0	0.0
$ Share	0.6	0.6	0.7	0.6	0.6
Display	0	0	0	0	0
Feature ads	0	0	0	0	0
Average Price	1.45	1.36	1.41	13.9	1.43
Total Perrier					
% Store selling	93	93	88	12	2
$ Sales	21062	20329	12017	402	150
Sales rate	226.5	218.6	136.6	33.5	75.1
$ Sales w/causal	999	735	365	0	0

Copyright© 1993 A. C. Nielsen Company.

alternative formats exist where time periods are used as rows. In the examples to follow, time periods will be used as columns. Report 1 is a fact trend report. A single key fact, in this case market share, is displayed across time. In the example shown, the fact is displayed for multiple products in one market so the reader can quickly spot which brands are growing or declining in the market. An alternate format might show all markets for one product in order to highlight areas where the product is growing or declining.

Competitive Monitoring

Report 2, a product profile trend, shows several facts for several brands. This report allows monitoring competitive pricing and promotional activity over time. Such reports can be prepared on an account

REPORT 3. Nielsen Scantrack®—Promotion Profile Trend
13 Weeks Ending APR2190.1
Total Calistoga
San Francisco

		Period			
	13 Weeks	**JAN 2790.1**	**FEB 0390.1**	**FEB 1090.1**	**FEB 1790.1**
Share					
Dollar basis	23.0	21.3	21.2	22.4	23.4
Share Volume (Dollars)					
Total	2596269	177934	170307	173042	186264
Total promoted volume	396738	3408	2465	36916	28424
% Promoted	15.3	1.9	1.4	21.3	15.3
W/ad only	144922	0	0	22159	17222
W/display only	164044	3408	2465	1845	11202
W/display and ad	87771	0	0	12912	0
Merchandising Info (% ACV)					
Display		12	7	22	23
Major ads		0	0	35	33
Display and ad		0	0	16	0
Coupon ad		0	0	0	0
Selling Price (per unit)					
Average retail price	1.48	1.55	1.50	1.41	1.34
Feature/display price	1.49	1.93	1.47	0.99	0.95
Non feature/display price	1.48	1.55	1.50	1.60	1.45

Copyright© 1993 A. C. Nielsen Company.

by account basis as well as at the market level, and allow monitoring of distribution, pricing, and promotional activity. Members of the sales force can use such reports to anticipate competitive threats on an account by account basis.

Report 3 shows an arrangement for many facts for a single brand, trended across time and reported for a single geography. In this last case, all the facts for extremely detailed analysis of sales performance are gathered onto a single page. With the increasing use of spreadsheet programs, hardcopy reports are generated only for simple summary forms like Reports 1 and 2, and detail reporting of facts is handled by loading fact data, as shown in Report 3, directly into the spreadsheet for further analysis.

Change Reports

Rather than monitor each time period closely, we may wish to review for differences versus year ago. In categories with pronounced seasonal sales patterns, comparison of week to week or month to month is made difficult by the combination of changes due to seasonal effects and changes representing real changes in market position. Report 4 shows a trend change analysis, where market share and volume changes are compared to changes in pricing, distribution, and promotional activity. In this case, the report shows the results for one product, with time period information absorbed into the fact set, and displays the results for multiple markets. An alternative format might show the results for one market, and all major products within the market.

Ranking Reports

If there are more than five to eight rows in the report, it becomes difficult to quickly identify the highs and lows in a column, and to visualize which other facts might follow a related pattern. Any report arranged into a cross-tabular format may have its rows reordered based on the ranking of the contents of any one column. Report 5 shows a change report that has also been ranked. The top and bottom of the report rows are easy to locate immediately, and direct attention to the items with higher than average or lower than average performance on the variable being used for ranking. Instead of all brands in a market, the report might rank all markets for a single brand.

Exception Reporting

For reviewing categories with a large number of items, the ranking report may run to several pages. In an exception report, some cutoff level for inclusion is established, and only those items that meet the cutoff are displayed. Report 6 illustrates such a report. Selection can be based on multiple rankings, such as the top items based on volume increases, the top items based on decreases in base price, and the top items based on percent of volume sold on promotional activity. If

REPORT 4. Nielsen Scan*Pro® Monitor—Topline Report
Total French Cafe Soluble Coffee
Current Period: 13 Weeks Ending FEB2490.1
Base Period: Year Ago 13 Weeks

Market	Equivalent Share	Change in Share (Point)	Change in Sales (Percent)	Change in Dist. (Point)	Change in % ACV on Deal (Point)	Change in % Volume on Deal (Point)	Change in Regular Price (Percent)	Change in Promoted Price (Percent)	Change in % Price Reduction (Point)
Total United States (over $4 million)	22.5	1.86	1.8	.0	2.9	.4	-3.9	-4.4	.4
Chicago	18.8	2.39	4.5	.4	-8.8	-11.6	-10.7	-14.5	4.0
Denver	9.5	1.64	9.8	-.1	-6.9	-16.2	-5.6	-5.7	.1
Los Angeles	7.1	1.14	5.4	.0	-3.7	-5.7	-6.3	-6.3	.0
New York	25.0	1.15	1.6	.1	-1.9	-2.5	.0	-3.4	2.6

REPORT 5. Nielsen Scantrack®—Brand Ranking Report
Category: Bottled Sparkling and Mineral Water
13 Weeks Ending APR2190.1
San Francisco

Item	$ Rank	Unit Rank	$ Vol	$% Chg vs. Ya	$ Shr	Shr Chg versus Ya	Cum $ Shr	Unit Vol	Unit % Chg versus Ya	Unit Shr	Unit Shr Chg	Cum Unit Shr
Total Calistoga	1	1	2596269	-11.1	23.0	-4.0	23.0	1752790	-11.1	20.6	-3.6	20.6
Total Vittel	2	3	60504	39.1	0.5	0.1	23.6	41067	28.9	0.5	0.1	21.1
Total Perrier	3	2	53959	-79.9	0.5	-2.0	24.1	43089	-82.6	0.5	-2.5	21.6

Copyright© 1993 A. C. Nielsen Company.

REPORT 6. Nielsen Scantrack®—Significant Item Changes
Category: Oral Antiseptics
Market: Chicago
New Items During the 13 Weeks Ending FEB2391

	Dollar Sales	Actual Change	% Change	Dollar Share	Share Change	% Promo	Pt. Chg.	Last % SS
Top Established Gainers								
Listerine Antsp Yl Oa 48 oz.	100,397	34,941	53.4	4.9	1.7	26.3	26.2	40.0
Listerine Antsp Yl Oa 32 oz.	156,161	32,058	25.8	7.6	1.6	25.3	9.5	67.0
Scope Mw&G Gn Oa 24 oz.	64,472	22,183	52.5	3.1	1.1	13.7	13.7	64.0
Top Established Decliners								
Scope Mw&G Gn Oa 32 oz.	70,338	−22,326	−24.1	3.4	−1.1	26.1	−4.3	49.0
Lmnt Mw&G/F Mt Gn Oa 24 oz.	25,025	−16,186	−39.3	1.2	−0.8	10.6	−7.8	47.0
Act F Trt Lq Cn Rd Or 18 oz.	12,656	−13,743	−52.1	0.6	−0.7	0.0	−5.7	22.0
Top New Items								
Scope Mw&G Gn −.15 Oz 12 oz.	14,483	—	—	0.7	—	22.7	—	17.0
Close-Up Lq Cn Rd Or 6 oz.	3,767	—	—	0.2	—	16.5	—	25.0
Ctl Br Mw Mt Gn 24 oz./8 oz. = 32 oz.	3,473	—	—	0.2	—	66.0	—	2.0

Copyright© 1993 A. C. Nielsen Company.

REPORT 7. Nielsen Scantrack®—New Product Highlight
Category: Bottled Sparkling and Mineral Water
Market: Birmingham
New Items During the 13 Weeks Ending JUN1690.1

Item			# Weeks Selling	13 Weeks Unit Sales	13 Weeks Sales	Max % SS	Average Weekly		Shr in Strs Selling	Avg. Price
							Sales Rate	Unit Share		
Calistoga Spkg Rasp	12	0	6	35	35	2	3.0	0.0	0.4	0.99
Per Pnt Spk	10	0	1	7	15	2	2.7	0.0	0.4	2.08
Per Sk Min Nrb Org	23	0	9	171	118	5	5.7	0.0	0.8	0.69
Calistoga Min Nrb Pch Flv	6.5	0	5	50	34	4	3.8	0.0	0.6	0.69

longer time periods such as quarters are used, both brands and markets can be combined into a single exception report reporting the largest shifts up and down in market position. Certain exception reports may be produced on a routine basis. Report 7 shows a new product review report that monitors the progress of new items introduced in the market. From reports such as this, management is kept current on the sales progress of new products, and can assess their potential impact in the marketplace.

Workstation Reporting

With the increasing amount of detail available, there is a trend toward minimal use of hard copy reports, and use of workstation software to manipulate the stored data in spreadsheet form for analysis and exception reporting purposes. Rather than define a specific format for ranking reports and exception reports, any report may be ranked and trimmed to its exceptions. Increasingly sophisticated analysis programs process the movement data against expected values calculated by models using the detail causal facts on marketing activity, and report on those results that are outside the range of values expected, given the marketing changes that have occurred. Some of these models are syndicated by suppliers, and some are built by corporate or retailer analysts based on their particular business knowledge bases, and on the integration of external data such as brand marketing plans, industry trends, and shipments to non-covered channels.

TACTICAL ANALYSIS

Reports 1 thru 7 have illustrated general comparison and evaluation reports that allow management to track the progress of a brand, identify changes in category brand list, and to identify further brand items and/or markets for further analysis. There are three key areas for further analysis: brand distribution, pricing, and promotion (both consumer and trade activity). These areas are monitored by marketing organizations with responsibility for regional or national marketing, and by the sales force with responsibility for executing marketing plans on a tactical basis with local and regional retailers. In the next section, we review some common activities and problems, and the types of reports that might be generated to support these activities.

Sales Force Objectives

A manufacturer's sales force calls on retail accounts and chain buying points to support a number of key activities. The most common and important are: (1) obtaining distribution and shelf space for products not currently carried by the account; (2) obtaining desired shelf price; (3) obtaining appropriate types of retail promotion support; (4) obtaining appropriate frequency of retailer promotion support, and (5) monitoring competitive marketing in the account—distribution,

REPORT 8. Nielsen Scantrack©—Opportunity Items
Share Basis: Bottled Sparkling and Mineral Water
4 Weeks Ending NOV1288.1
San Francisco

Item	Rate Rank	$ Rank	% SS	4Wk $ Sales	4Wk Op 100%	$ Share	Shr in Stores Selling
Ctl Br Drinking 128 OZ	1	12	31	29697	66100	1.7	5.6
Ctl Br Spring 128 OZ	4	6	54	41061	34978	2.4	4.5
Ctl Br Distilled 128 OZ	6	27	25	17193	51579	1.0	4.0
Ctl Br Drinking 320 OZ	15	26	37	17316	29484	1.0	2.7
K-S R Min W Lmnd Nrb 4P 9.6 OZ	18	32	27	10879	29414	0.6	2.4
K-S R Min W Org/Mng Nrb 25.4 OZ	22	33	27	9654	26102	0.6	2.1
K-S R Min W Org/Psfrt Nrb 25.4 OZ	28	38	24	7405	23449	0.4	1.8
K-S R Min w Lmn/Lm/Org Nrb 25.4 OZ	29	37	25	7461	22383	0.4	1.7
Villar R Min w Lm Nrb 6P 10 OZ	31	35	34	9090	17645	0.4	1.4
Ctl Br Mineral 6P 8 OZ	51	55	21	2864	10774	0.3	1.2
				152620	311908		

pricing, and promotion. An important consideration for the sales force is that the information they use for presentations is current, for the local market area, and where possible, based almost completely on sales to the account on which they are calling. Many of the reports used by sales are similar to those used by brand management, but have a more local geographical focus.

Obtaining Distribution

Report 8 is typical of the kind of information used to identify those items that are candidates for expanded distribution. The report identifies those items that do not have 100% distribution, but have high sales rates. The column labeled "4WK OP 100%" is the estimated increase in market dollar sales for the item if it goes from its current distribution level to 100% distribution, and maintains its current sales rate. The column labeled "SHR IN STORES SELLING" is useful in preparing a sales presentation for those retailers not carrying the item. If necessary, the report can be modified slightly to indicate slow moving items whose elimination would result in the least decrease in sales. Often, in order to obtain shelf space for a new item in a category, it is necessary to eliminate an existing item. The slow moving item report

REPORT 9. Sales Rate by Price Point
Product: Calistoga 12 Oz.
Market: New York
Time: 13 Weeks Ending APR2190.1

Price per Unit	Volume	Volume Per MMACV	% Total Volume Sold	Cum % of Total Volume Sold
1.09	5,365	7.76	2.4	2.4
1.14	16,784	7.47	7.6	10.1
1.19	25,476	7.14	11.6	21.7
1.24	41,619	6.61	18.9	40.6
1.27	8,075	6.48	3.7	44.3
1.29	48,231	6.45	22.0	66.3
1.33	4,142	6.11	1.9	68.2
1.34	36,347	6.16	16.5	84.7
1.37	8,653	5.76	3.9	88.6
1.39	24,938	5.80	11.4	100.0

will tell a salesperson if any of his items are candidates for delisting, or which items should be delisted in order to make space for the new items desired on the shelf. Retailers use sales rate information to expand or contract distribution of items within a chain, and to make delisting decisions.

Base Pricing

Report 9 is typical of the reports prepared to assist a salesperson in obtaining the desired shelf price for his product. Sales rates might be calculated based on absolute price (as shown), or may be shown as price differences versus a major competitor.

Promotion Frequency

Report 3, the promotion profile trend, would be used by a salesperson to compare an account's performance to a market or region. Comparisons can be made of performance across brands within the retail account, and of performance by a brand in the account versus the region. Often a "fair share" argument can be made for obtaining event frequencies at least as great as those of a major competitor, or for obtaining event frequencies at least as great as those given by major competitors.

Promotion Event Performance

Report 10 summarizes the results of a promotion event. This report could be run for an account, a market, or for a major region. The PEI results can be a very important factor in persuading an account to give desired types of discounting and ad/display support. This particular example shows that combining display with feature ads gave sales rates nearly five times those expected in a week of normal pricing and no support. Such information can be used to significantly improve the chances for obtaining in-store display support from retailers. Collecting such information across many retailers and time periods allows the construction of sales response models that predict the sales increase that might be expected on average for various combinations of price discounts and retailer ad/display support. Exhibit 2 (shown on page 213) shows a typical result of modeling expected PEI performance. The projections from such a model might be used in persuading a retailer to try promotion support combinations that it does not normally use. If cost and margin information is added to such models, projections can be made of the incremental profitability of promotion events to the manufacturer and to the retailer.

Expert Systems

The availability of such information gives a member of the sales force the possibility of anticipating problems with retail accounts, of

REPORT 10. Scan*Pro®Monitor—Event Analysis
Product: Bradford Caff Sol Coff
Market: Los Angeles
Based on Equivalized Units Sales

Description	Event December 1989	February 1990
Summary		
Duration	5	4
Incremental weeks	.6	.1
Total volume	33954	23911
Baseline volume	30502	23064
Incremental volume	3452	847
Efficiency	31.2	18.7
% Volume on Deal		
Any promo	29.6	13.9
TPR only	18.9	13.0
Any feature without display	8.5	.4
Any display without feature	.5	.4
Feature and display	1.7	.0
% ACV on deal (baseline)		
Any promo	22.7	11.7
TPR only	16.0	11.1
Any feature without display	6.0	.4
Any display without feature	.3	.2
Feature and display	.4	.0
PEI		
Any promo	145	123
TPR only	132	122
Any feature without display	157	123
Any display without feature	194	196
Feature and display	493	
% Price Discount		
Any promo	10.8	11.4
TPR only	12.3	11.2
Any feature without display	6.6	31.0
Any display without feature	3.0	1.7
Feature and display	11.2	

Copyright© 1993 A. C. Nielsen Company.

EXHIBIT 2. Marketing Response Analysis—Relationship between Marketing Activity and Sales

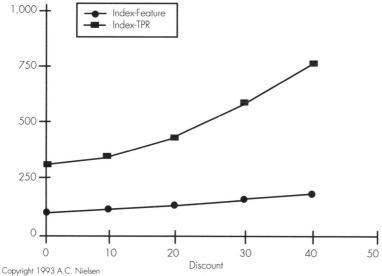

Copyright 1993 A.C. Nielsen

identifying opportunities for increasing sales, and of preparing focused presentations using a retailer's own sales data and local market data. The drawback is that a full report set on an account's recent activity may run to dozens of pages of detail information. Market research suppliers and individual manufacturers are building expert systems that sift through the data and pinpoint problems and opportunities in exception reporting forms. Other expert systems have scripts for various sales presentations and review the data to select the strongest arguments for obtaining retailer actions and may produce most of the presentation material.

BRAND MANAGEMENT UTILIZATION—STORE DATA

Monitoring Sales and Share

Brand managers will use many of the same reporting tools used by sales managers, but will usually be concerned with higher levels of geography. Trend reports, profiles, and exception reports will be run at the country level. There will be heavy use of reports comparing brand and competitive performance on a market-by-market basis.

Competitive Monitoring

Report 11, a competitive price report, compares a brand's price at regular, and on deal, across many markets. This allows brand management to review their pricing position in both absolute terms and versus key competition on both regular and deal pricing. If extreme deviations are noted, then market level profile and trend reports would be used to

REPORT 11. Scan*Pro®Monitor—Competitive Pricing Report
Product: Bradford Caff 8 Oz. Sol Coff
Competitor: French Cafe Caff 8 Oz. Sol Coff
For the 13 Weeks Ending FEB2490.1
Merchandising Condition: Any Promo Except Long Sales
Based on Equivalized Unit Prices

Market	Own Reg. Price	Own Deal Price	Own % Price Reduct	Comp Reg. Price	Comp Deal Price	Comp % Price Reduct	Reg. Price Index	Deal Price Index	% Price Reduct Diff
Total U.S. (over $4 million)	33.38	29.76	10.9	22.72	19.08	16.0	147	156	-5.1
Chicago	32.18	25.67	20.2	21.66	19.27	11.0	149	133	9.2
Denver	29.63	25.33	14.5	21.47	18.87	12.1	138	134	2.4
Los Angeles	34.35	28.15	18.1	21.99	19.43	11.6	156	145	6.4
New York	34.08	28.35	16.8	24.23	18.17	25.0	141	156	-8.2

Copyright© 1993 A. C. Nielsen Company.

identify and characterize the nature of any problems. Trend reports such as Report 1 would be used to monitor brand volume and share in order to track sales progress versus category growth, and versus brand plans. Reports 3 and 8 are used to monitor brand promotion activity and brand distribution.

Additional reports might track measures of coupon activity and TV commercial activity to round out the brand managers ability to monitor the brands marketing mix on a market-by-market basis. Suppliers of market research data have recently begun development of software that will integrate both the client's internal data such as shipments and advertising spending and external data such as coupon and media expenditures with the traditional volume and price information provided by syndicated data bases. Report 12, a marketing mix report, illustrates a report layout for reporting marketing mix activities from such data integration.

Strategic Planning

An important use of syndicated data by brand management is in the development of models relating marketing mix decisions and historical sales trends to brand sales levels. Brand managers are responsible for forecasting future brand sales and share levels, particularly when changes in pricing, distribution, or other marketing mix variables are considered. The detail data available in syndicated databases supports many analyses that are of use in the planning/forecasting process. In the simplest forms, trend reports provide a basis for projecting current rates of change in volume or share levels for a brand into a "business as usual" forecast. Sales rate reports such as Report 9 can be used to model the relation between base price and product sales during non-promoted periods. These models can then be used to provide forecasts of the probable impact of future changes in product price. Distribution opportunity reports, such as Report 8, can be used to study the potential for increasing brand distribution, and for modeling the probable impact of gaining increased distribution.

Trend reports may also be used to study the seasonal sales patterns of a brand or category. When examined at a weekly level, we frequently find that the weeks around holidays such as Easter, Thanksgiving, and Christmas exhibit extreme fluctuations in sales levels. Exhibit 3a illustrates the behavior of seasonal indices for a product around Christmas. This product category is not purchased during Christmas/New Year's weeks, although the products continue to be consumed. After the holidays are over, home inventories need to be replenished. Using the average sales indices over a four-week period will almost completely mask the detail sales behavior. For other products, such as diet aids, the holiday dip may occur without a following replenishment spike, as consumption decreases during the holiday peri-

REPORT 12. Marketing Mix Performance
Category: Bottled Sparkling and Mineral Water
13 Weeks Ending APR2190.1
Chicago

Product	Total Volume	Volume Share	Avg Base Price/Vol	ACV WT Weeks any Promo	Avg % Dsct on Promo	H.H. Grp	Coupon Circulation	Avb Cpn Face Value
Total Calistoga								
Total Vittel								
Total Perrier								

Copyright© 1993 A. C. Nielsen Company.

EXHIBIT 3. Pattern of Weekly Seasonal Sales

(a)

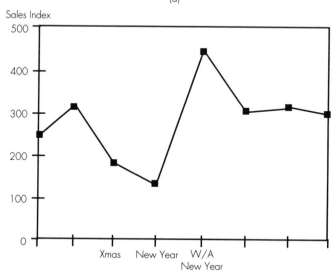

Delay Purchase until After Holiday

(b)

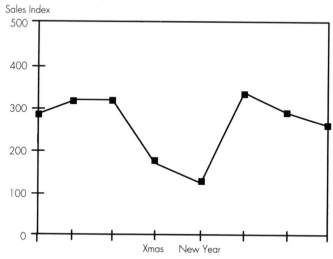

Consumption Decrease during Holiday Period

ods. Exhibit 3b illustrates such a sales pattern. Identification of such "special" sales weeks can assist the brand manager in targeting television advertising, coupon drops, and promotional activity.

When the brand manager has conducted a major marketing activity such as TV ads, print ads, coupon drops, and/or sweepstakes and contests coordinated with in-store promotional programs, then reports such as Report 10 can be used to evaluate the program's impact on national or regional sales. Detail analysis of the response of individual stores to pricing and promotional conditions will allow preparation of price/promotion response curves such as shown in Exhibit 2. These models allow the brand manager to estimate the probable impact of altering the terms offered with trade promotion allowances to retailers. If feature ads are significantly more effective than temporary price reduction only, then the brand manager might improve sales by obtaining fewer weeks of total promotion, but an increase in feature weeks over current performance. The response models should also aid the manager in determining the value of changing the trade allowances associated with promotional offers. More complex versions of the model allow assessment of the probable impact of changes in competitive pricing and promotion.

Special Studies

Availability of store level detail data permits a large variety of special studies to be conducted. If, for example, the brand manager hypothesises that certain demographic groups are more responsive to promotions on his product than to competitive promotions, then a study can be conducted in which stores are classified by the predominance of the demographic group. The response in "high" rated stores can be compared with the response in "low" rated stores. Many questions of interest to the brand manager can be studied by such store grouping techniques. If the data does not exist in the historical data base, then the brand manager can commission tests, in which elements of the marketing mix are manipulated differently across stores or markets, and the sales results compared both directly and by statistical analysis.

BRAND MANAGEMENT UTILIZATION—-PANEL DATA

Panel versus Store Data

Sales data from retail stores shows the brand's relative position in the category and the brand's sales trends, but not the reasons for such trends. In order to evaluate the brand's probable future, one needs to know if changes in sales are due to shifts in the number of brand buyers (household penetration), or in the amount purchased by each buyer (volume per buyer). The fundamental equation in panel analysis is:

$$\text{Brand Volume} = \text{Total Households} \times \text{Household Penetration} \ (\% \text{ of Total}) \times \text{Volume per Buyer}$$

Marketing mix elements often have the goal of increasing household penetration. Examples are trial-size packages, coupons, and in-store promotional activity. However, such actions may also stimulate sales by increasing the volume per buyer among existing buyers. In order to separate these possibilities, detailed analysis of the purchase behavior of individual consumers is required. When media advertising is targeted to specific groups of consumers, the analysis of panel data can determine if the objectives of the campaign are being met.

New Product Tracking

A critical success factor for new products is their ability to build a successful base of repeat buyers. When the product is initially introduced, its sales are almost totally trial sales to new buyers of the brand. As time passes, some of the initial triers return to make repeat purchases, while the trial sales decay as more and more of the potential buyers have made their trial purchases, leaving a smaller pool of potential triers. There are many examples in marketing history where strong introductory marketing programs gave strong early sales growth composed primarily of trial sales, but where lack of repeat sales among triers led to poor levels of sales after the introductory period. Several services offer tracking and modeling of trial and repeat sales for new or restaged brands.

Panel-Based Analysis Models

Brand management may use detail household purchase information to identify appropriate competitive sets for its products, assess the threat of new products, and to assess the detail impact of various marketing mix activities in consumer behavior. A number of models are available that analyze the sequence of brands purchased by individual consumers over time, and the conditions under which these purchases were made. Typical analyses include:

• *Marketing mix analysis*—Often performed by logit or similar choice modeling techniques, the impact of price, media advertising, coupon, and distribution availability are combined to generate a measure of brand "utility," which is then transformed into a choice probability for individual consumers, and into a simulated market share across consumers.
• *Coupon redemption forecasting*—Following the drop of a coupon, the use of the coupon in brand purchasing is monitored to determine usage by previous brand buyers versus new triers, and to determine at

each week of the coupon's life the percentage of total redemptions that will occur in the week.
- *Stockpiling and brand switching associated with trade promotion*— The promotional bump generated in retail stores may come from brand switchers; store switchers who would have bought your brand in other stores; and from stockpiling by a brand's loyal consumers, which reduces future sales. By analyzing detail purchase behavior, the promotional sales may be decomposed to yield net incremental effects.
- *Shopping patterns*—If consumers shop multiple stores, or if they have certain demographics or lifestyles that concentrate heavy buyers in a subset of stores, then this may imply desired distribution in only high payout stores.
- *Analysis*—Analysis of consumer shopping patterns can assist in determining the appropriate levels of brand distribution.
- *Market structure*—There are models that examine the sequence of brands purchased by individual consumers in order to determine the strength of competition among the various brands and sizes in a category. It is seldom true that all brand sizes in a category compete equally with all other brand sizes in a category. By determining the subset of items most strongly competitive with a brand, the management of that brand will know which brands to monitor most closely in the store data. In addition, knowledge of the items with which their brand does not compete may assist management in developing new products or line extensions that have minimum overlap with their existing products.

Related Data

There are some data sources that bridge the gap between panel and store data. By processing the U.S. Census data (available on a block, census tract, and zipcode basis) into store trading areas, it is possible to assign to each retail outlet the average demographic characteristics of its shopping population. While no substitute for detail individual household level data, such store level consumer data does allow comparison of brand sales and share across stores with significantly different shopping populations. This can be an important consideration for products that appeal to specific demographic groups, such as families with children under age 6, or health aids targeted toward the elderly.

SUMMARY

Since 1988, the availability of detailed weekly data at the level of retail chain and above is leading to significant changes in the way sales and brand management track market performance, identify brand problems and opportunities, and prepare forecasts of future brand performance. The trend toward faster and better price/performance in data collection, storage, and processing devices implies that scanner data will become more broadly available and will be less costly to store and analyze. Some of the trends evident in early 1993 are expanding coverage, as use of POS scanner devices grow from predominately grocery use into broad use in mass-merchandisers, drug, and convenience stores. There is increasing integration of information beyond the machine collected volume and price information, as measures of feature advertising, in-store display, coupon activity, TV, radio, and print advertising, and other marketing mix causal data are merged into the database. Use of panelist identification cards or in-home scanners permits expanded detail on shoppers and their purchasing histories.

For the manufacturer and retailer, there is a greater emphasis on fact-based selling, and creating win-win scenarios between manufacturer and retailer. Timely information on retail sales allows the manufacturer to maintain tighter controls over inventory, and to more accurately schedule manufacturing and shipment activities to minimize stockouts. Research on the impact of marketing activities on sales is establishing a better and closer relationship between the amounts spent on marketing activities and their sales and profitability results. Improved data delivery and information systems will make the data broadly available throughout the sales and brand management functions on a timely basis.

Results of current research on scanner based sales data may be found in *Management Science, Journal of Marketing Research, Journal of Marketing, Journal of Advertising Research, International Journal of Research in Marketing, Marketing Letters,* and *Journal of Consumer Research.* For general reading on market and sales research, consider the books by Churchill and Farris. John McCann gives a vision of the use of computers in marketing management. For an overview of analysis of store and panel data, the Totten and Block book should be available in late 1993. For detail analysis of store sales data, refer to the books by Blattberg and Neslin and Hassens, Parsons, & Schultz. The works by Assael, Ehrenberg, and Kamakura and Russell provide detail on some types of panel data analysis. Finally, the suppliers of syndicated store and panel sales data, such as Nielsen Marketing Research and Information Resources, Inc. are sources of leading edge analyses and applications software designed for converting the raw data into useful information for marketing decisions.

REFERENCES

Assael, Henry, *Consumer Behavior and Marketing Action*, 3rd ed. Boston: Kent, 1987.

Blattberg, Robert C., and Scott A. Neslin, *Sales Promotion-Concepts, Methods, and Strategies*. Englewood Cliffs, NJ: Prentice Hall, 1990.

Churchill, Gilbert A., Jr., *Marketing Research: Methodological Foundations*, 4th ed. Chicago: Dryden, 1987.

Ehrenberg, A.S.C., *Repeat-buying: Facts, Theory, and Applications,* 2nd ed. New York: Oxford Univ Press, 1988.

Farris, Paul W., and John A. Quelch, *Advertising and Promotion Management: A Manager's Guide to Theory and Practice.* Radner, PA: Chilton, 1983.

Hanssens, Dominique M., Leonard J. Parsons, and Randall L. Schultz, *Market Response Models: Econometric and Time Series Analysis.* Boston: Kluwer, 1989.

Kamakura, Wagner A., and Gary J. Russell, "Measuring Consumer Perceptions of Brand Quality with Scanner Data: Implications for Brand Equity," Report No. 91–122. Cambridge, MA: Marketing Science Institute, October 1991.

McCann, John M., *The Marketing Workbench: Using Computers for Better Performance.* Homewood, IL: Dow Jones-Irwin, 1986.

Sterman, John D., "Teaching Takes Off: Flight Simulators for Management Education," *OR/MS Today,* Vol. 19, No. 5 (October 1992), pp. 40–44.

Totten, John C., and Martin P. Block, *Analyzing Sales Promotion,* 2nd ed. Chicago: Dartnell (forthcoming).

Philip Kotler
S.C. Johnson & Son Distinguished Professor
  of International Marketing
Northwestern University
Kellogg Graduate School of Management
Evanston, Illinois

Philip Kotler, *Marketing Management: Analysis, Planning, Implementation and Control,* 8e, ©1994, pp. 741–766. Reprinted by permission of Prentice-Hall, Englewood Cliffs, New Jersey.

CHAPTER 14

EVALUATING AND CONTROLLING MARKETING PERFORMANCE

The marketing department's job is to plan and control marketing activity. Because many surprises will occur during the implementation of marketing plans, the marketing department has to continuously monitor and control marketing activities. In spite of this need, many companies have inadequate control procedures. This conclusion was reached in a study of 75 companies of varying sizes in different industries. The main findings were these:

- Small companies have poorer controls than large companies. They do a poorer job of setting clear objectives and establishing systems to measure performance.
- Fewer than half of the companies know the profitability of their individual products. About one third of the companies have no regular review procedures for spotting and deleting weak products.
- Almost half of the companies fail to compare their prices with competition, to analyze their warehousing and distribution costs, to analyze the causes of returned merchandise, to conduct formal evaluations of advertising effectiveness, and to review their sales-force call reports.
- Many companies take four to eight weeks to develop control reports, and they are occasionally inaccurate.

Four types of marketing control can be distinguished (Table 1). We now turn to these four types of marketing control.

ANNUAL-PLAN CONTROL

The purpose of annual-plan control is to ensure that the company achieves the sales, profits, and other goals established in its annual plan. The heart of annual-plan control is *management by objectives.* Four steps are involved (see Figure 1). First, management sets monthly or quarterly goals. Second, management monitors its performance in the marketplace. Third, management determines the causes of serious performance deviations. Fourth, management takes corrective action to close the gaps between its goals and performance. This could require changing the action programs or even changing the goals.

This control model applies to all levels of the organization. Top management sets sales and profit goals for the year. These goals are elaborated into specific goals for each lower level of management. Thus each product manager is committed to attaining specified levels of sales and costs. Each regional and district sales manager and each sales representative is also committed to specific goals. Each period, top management reviews and interprets the results and ascertains whether any corrective action is needed.

TABLE 1. Types of Marketing Control

Type of Control	Prime Responsibility	Purpose of Control	Approaches
I. Annual-plan control	Top management Middle management	To examine whether the planned results are being achieved	Sales analysis Market-share analysis Sales-to-expense ratios Financial analysis Satisfaction tracking
II. Profitability control	Marketing controller	To examine where the company is making and losing money	Profitability by: product territory customer segment trade channel order size
III. Efficiency control	Line and staff management Marketing controller	To evaluate and improve the spending efficiency and impact of marketing expenditures	Efficiency of: sales force advertising sales promotion distribution
IV. Strategic control	Top management Marketing auditor	To examine whether the company is pursuing its best opportunities with respect to markets, products, and channels	Marketing-effectiveness rating instrument Marketing audit Marketing excellence review Company ethical and social responsibility review

Managers use five tools to check on plan performance: sales analysis, market-share analysis, marketing expense-to-sales analysis, financial analysis, and customer-satisfaction tracking.

Sales Analysis

Sales analysis consists of measuring and evaluating actual sales in relation to sales goals. There are two specific tools in this connection.

FIGURE 1. The Control Process

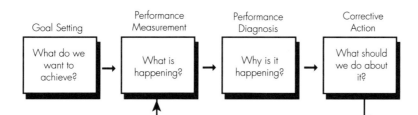

Sales-variance analysis measures the relative contribution of different factors to a gap in sales performance. Suppose the annual plan called for selling 4,000 widgets in the first quarter at $1 per widget, or $4,000. At quarter's end, only 3,000 widgets were sold at $.80 per widget, or $2,400. The sales performance variance is $1,600, or 40% of expected sales. The question arises, how much of this underperformance is due to the price decline and how much to the volume decline? The following calculation answers this question:

Variance due to price decline = ($1.00 – $.80)(3,000) = $ 600   37.5%
Variance due to volume decline = ($1.00)(4,000 – 3,000) = $1,000   62.5%
                                                      $1,600   100.0%

Almost two thirds of the sales variance is due to a failure to achieve the volume target. The company should look closely at why it failed to achieve its expected sales volume.[1]

Microsales analysis may provide the answer. *Microsales analysis* looks at specific products, territories, and so forth, that failed to produce expected sales. Suppose the company sells in three territories and expected sales were 1,500 units, 500 units, and 2,000 units, respectively, adding up to 4,000 widgets. The actual sales volume was 1,400 units, 525 units, and 1,075 units, respectively. Thus territory 1 showed a 7% shortfall in terms of expected sales; territory 2, a 5% surplus; and territory 3, a 46% shortfall! Territory 3 is causing most of the trouble. The sales vice-president can check into territory 3 to see which hypothesis explains the poor performance: Territory 3's sales representative is loafing or has a personal problem; a major competitor has entered this territory; or GNP is depressed in this territory.

Market-Share Analysis

Company sales do not reveal how well the company is performing relative to competitors. For this purpose, management needs to track its market share. If the company's market share goes up, the company is gaining on competitors; if it goes down, the company is losing relative to competitors.

These conclusions from market-share analysis, however, are subject to certain qualifications:

- *The Assumption That Outside Forces Affect All Companies in the Same Way Is Often Not True:* The U.S. Surgeon General's Report on the harmful consequences of cigarette smoking caused total cigarette sales to falter but not equally for all companies. Companies with better filters were hurt less.
- *The Assumption That a Company's Performance Should Be Judged Against the Average Performance of All Companies Is Not Always Valid:* A company's performance should be judged against the performance of its closest competitors.
- *If a New Firm Enters the Industry, Then Every Existing Firm's Market Share Might Fall:* A decline in a company's market share might not mean that the company is performing any worse than other companies. A company's share loss will depend on the degree to which the new firm hits the company's specific markets.
- *Sometimes a Market-Share Decline Is Deliberately Engineered by a Company to Improve Profits:* For example, management might drop unprofitable customers or products to improve its profits.
- *Market Share Can Fluctuate for Many Minor Reasons:* For example, market share can be affected by whether a large sale occurs on the last day of the month or at the beginning of the next month. Not all shifts in market share have marketing significance.[2]

Managers must carefully interpret market-share movements by product line, customer type, region, and other breakdowns. A useful way to analyze market-share movements is in terms of four components:

$$\begin{matrix} \text{Overall} \\ \text{Market} \\ \text{Share} \end{matrix} = \begin{matrix} \text{Customer} \\ \text{penetration} \end{matrix} \times \begin{matrix} \text{Customer} \\ \text{loyalty} \end{matrix} \times \begin{matrix} \text{Customer} \\ \text{selectivity} \end{matrix} \times \begin{matrix} \text{Price} \\ \text{selectivity} \end{matrix} \quad (14\text{-}1)$$

where:

- *Customer penetration* is the percentage of all customers who buy from this company.
- *Customer loyalty* is the purchases from this company by its customers expressed as a percentage of their total purchases from all suppliers of the same products.
- *Customer selectivity* is the size of the average customer purchase from the company expressed as a percentage of the size of the average customer purchase from an average company.
- *Price selectivity* is the average price charged by this company expressed as a percentage of the average price charged by all companies.

Now suppose the company's dollar market share falls during the period. Equation 14–1 provides four possible explanations. The company lost some of its customers (lower customer penetration). Existing customers are buying a smaller share of their total supplies from this company (lower customer loyalty). The company's remaining customers are smaller in size (lower customer selectivity). The company's price has slipped relative to competition (lower price selectivity).

By tracking these factors through time, the company can diagnose the underlying cause of market-share changes. Suppose at the beginning of the period, customer penetration was 60%; customer loyalty, 50%; customer selectivity, 80%; and price selectivity, 125%. According to Equation 14–1, the company's market share was 30%. Suppose that at the end of the period, the company's market share fell to 27%. In checking, the company finds customer penetration at 55%, customer loyalty at 50%, customer selectivity at 75%, and price selectivity at 130%. Clearly, the market-share decline was due mainly to a loss of customers (fall in customer penetration) who normally made larger-than-average purchases (fall in customer selectivity). The manager can now investigate why these customers were lost.

Defining and Measuring Market Share

The first step in using market-share analysis is to define which measure(s) of market share will be used. Four different measures are available.

- *Overall Market Share:* The company's overall market share is its sales expressed as a percentage of total market sales. Two decisions are necessary to use this measure. The first is whether to use unit sales or dollar sales to express market share. The other decision has to do with defining the total market. For example, Harley Davidson's share of the American motorcycle market depends on whether motor scooters and motorized bikes are included. If yes, then Harley Davidson's share will be smaller.

- *Served Market Share:* The company's served market share is its sales expressed as a percentage of the total sales to its served market. Its served market is all the buyers who would be able and willing to buy its product. If Harley Davidson only produces and sells expensive motorcycles on the East Coast, its served market share would be its sales as a percentage of the total sales of expensive motorcycles sold on the East Coast. A company's served market share is always larger than its overall market share. A company could capture 100% of its served market and yet have a relatively small share of the total market. A company's first task is to win the lion's share of its served market. As it approaches this goal, it should add new product lines and territories to enlarge its served market.

- *Relative Market Share (to Top Three Competitors):* This involves expressing the company's sales as a percentage of the combined sales of the three largest competitors. If the company has 30% of the market, and the next two largest competitors have 20% and 10%, then this company's relative market share is 50% = 30/60. If each of the three companies had 33% of the market, then any company's relative market share would be 33%. Relative market shares above 33% are considered to be strong.

- *Relative Market Share (to Leading Competitor):* Some companies track their shares as a percentage of the leading competitor's sales. A relative market share greater than 100% indicates a market leader. A relative market share of exactly 100% means that the firm is tied for the lead. A rise in the company's relative market share means that it is gaining on its leading competitor.

After choosing which market-share measure(s) to use, the company must collect the necessary data. Overall market share is normally the most available measure, since it requires only total industry sales, and these are often available in government or trade association publications. Estimating served market share is harder; it will be affected by changes in the company's product line and geographical market coverage, among other things. Estimating relative market shares is still harder because the company will have to estimate the sales of specific competitors, who guard these figures. The company has to use indirect means, such as learning about competitors' purchase rate of raw materials or the number of shifts they are operating. In the consumer-goods area, individual brand shares are available through syndicated store and consumer panels.

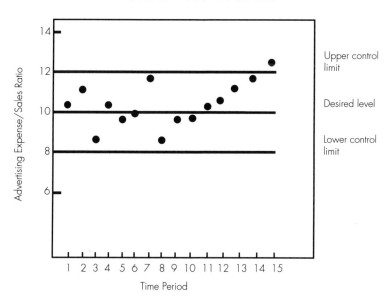

FIGURE 2. The Control-Chart Model

Marketing Expense-to-Sales Analysis

Annual-plan control requires making sure that the company is not overspending to achieve its sales goals. The key ratio to watch is *marketing expense-to-sales.* In one company, this ratio was 30% and consisted of five component expense-to-sales ratios: *sales force-to-sales* (15%); *advertising-to-sales* (5%); *sales promotion-to-sales* (6%); *marketing research-to-sales* (1%); and *sales administration-to-sales* (3%).

Management needs to monitor these marketing-expense ratios. They will normally exhibit small fluctuations that can be ignored. But fluctuations outside of the normal range are a cause for concern. The period-to-period fluctuations in each ratio can be tracked on a *control chart* (Figure 2). This chart shows that the advertising expense-to-sales ratio normally fluctuates between 8% and 12%, say 99 out of 100 times. In the fifteenth period, however, the ratio exceeded the upper control limit. One of two hypotheses can explain this occurrence:

• *Hypothesis A:* The company still has good expense control, and this situation represents one of those rare chance events.
• *Hypothesis B:* The company has lost control over this expense and should find the cause.

If hypothesis A is accepted, no investigation is made to determine whether the environment has changed. The risk in not investigating is that some real change might have occurred, and the company will fall behind. If hypothesis B is accepted, the environment is investigated at the risk that the investigation will uncover nothing and be a waste of time and effort.

The behavior of successive observations even within the control limits should be watched. Note that the level of the expense-to-sales ratio rose steadily from the ninth period onward. The probability of encountering six successive increases in what should be independent events is only 1 in 64.[3] This unusual pattern should have led to an investigation sometime before the fifteenth observation.

Financial Analysis

The expenses-to-sales ratios should be analyzed in an overall financial framework to determine how and where the company is making its money. Marketers are increasingly using financial analysis to find profitable strategies and not just sales-building strategies.

Financial analysis is used by management to identify the factors that affect the company's *rate of return on net worth.*[4] The main factors are shown in Figure 3, along with illustrative numbers for a large chain-store retailer. The retailer is earning a 12.5% return on net worth. The return on net worth is the product of two ratios, the company's

FIGURE 3. Financial Model of Return on Net Worth

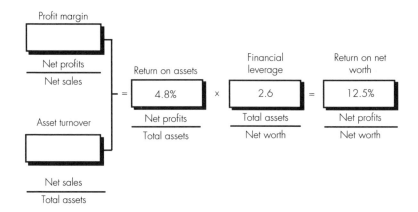

return on assets and its *financial leverage.* To improve its return on net worth, the company must either increase the ratio of its net profits to its assets or increase the ratio of its assets to its net worth. The company should analyze the composition of its assets (i.e., cash, accounts receivable, inventory, and plant and equipment) and see if it can improve its asset management.

The return on assets is the product of two ratios, namely, the *profit margin* and the *asset turnover.* The profit margin seems low, while the asset turnover is more normal for retailing. The marketing executive can seek to improve performance in two ways: (1) to increase the profit margin by increasing sales or cutting costs; and (2) to increase the asset turnover by increasing sales or reducing the assets (e.g., inventory, receivables) that are held against a given level of sales.[5]

Customer-Satisfaction Tracking

The preceding control measures are largely financial and quantitative in character. They are important but not sufficient. Needed are qualitative measures that provide early warnings to management of impending market-share changes. Alert companies set up systems to monitor the attitudes and satisfaction of customers, dealers, and other stakeholders. By monitoring changing levels of customer preference and satisfaction before they affect sales, management can take earlier action.

Corrective Action

When performance deviates too much from the plan's goals, management needs to undertake corrective action. Normally the company undertakes minor corrective actions, and if they fail to work, the company adopts more drastic measures. When a large fertilizer company's sales continued to decline, the company resorted to an increasingly drastic set of remedies. First the company ordered cutbacks in production. Then it cut its prices selectively. Next it put more pressure on its salesforce to meet their quotas. The company then cut the budgets for personnel hiring and training, advertising, public relations, and research and development. Soon it introduced personnel cuts through layoffs and early retirement. Next it cut investment in plant and equipment. The company then sold some of its businesses to other companies. Finally, the company sought a buyer.

PROFITABILITY CONTROL

Here are some disconcerting findings from a bank profitability study:

> *We have found that anywhere from 20 to 40 percent of an individual institution's products are unprofitable, and up to 60 percent of their accounts generate losses.*

Our research has shown that, in most firms, more than half of all customer relationships are not profitable, and 30 to 40 percent are only marginally so. It is frequently a mere 10 to 15 percent of a firm's relationships that generate the bulk of its profits.

Our profitability research into the branch system of a regional bank produced some surprising results . . . 30 percent of the bank's branches were unprofitable.[6]

Companies clearly need to measure the profitability of their various products, territories, customer groups, trade channels, and order sizes. This information will help management determine whether any products or marketing activities should be expanded, reduced, or eliminated.

Methodology of Marketing-Profitability Analysis

We will illustrate the steps in marketing-profitability analysis with the following example:

The marketing vice-president of a lawnmower company wants to determine the profitability of selling its lawnmower through three types of retail channels: hardware stores, garden supply shops, and department stores. Its profit-and-loss statement is shown in Table 2.

Step 1: Identifying the Functional Expenses. Assume that the expenses listed in Table 2 are incurred to sell the product, advertise it, pack and deliver it, and bill and collect for it. The first task is to measure how much of each expense was incurred in each activity.

Suppose that most salary expense went to sales representatives and the rest went to an advertising manager, packing and delivery help, and an office accountant. Let the breakdown of the $9,300 be $5,100, $1,200, $1,400, and $1,600, respectively. Table 3 shows the allocation of the salary expense to these four activities.

TABLE 2. A Simplified Profit-and-Loss Statement

Sales		$60,000
Cost of goods sold		39,000
Gross margin		$21,000
Expenses		
Salaries	$9,300	
Rent	3,000	
Supplies	3,500	
		15,800
Net profit		$ 5,200

TABLE 3. Mapping Natural Expenses into Functional Expenses

Natural Accounts	Total	Selling	Advertising	Packing and Delivery	Billing and Collecting
Salaries	$9,300	$5,100	$1,200	$1,400	$1,600
Rent	3,000	—	400	2,000	600
Supplies	3,500	400	1,500	1,400	200
	$15,800	$5,500	$3,100	$4,800	$2,400

Table 3 also shows the rent account of $3,000 as allocated to the four activities. Since the sales representatives work away from the office, none of the building's rent expense is assigned to selling. Most of the expenses for floor space and rented equipment are in connection with packing and delivery. A small portion of the floor space is used by the advertising manager and office accountant.

Finally, the supplies account covers promotional materials, packing materials, fuel purchases for delivery, and home-office stationery. The $3,500 in this account is reassigned to the functional uses made of the supplies. Table 3 summarizes how the natural expenses of $15,800 were translated into functional expenses.

Step 2: Assigning the Functional Expenses to the Marketing Entities. The next task is to measure how much functional expense was associated with selling through each type of channel. Consider the selling effort. The selling effort is indicated by the number of sales made in each channel. This number is found in the selling column of Table 4. Altogether, 275 sales calls were made during the period. Since the total selling expense amounted to $5,500 (see Table 4), the selling expense per call averaged $20.

Advertising expense can be allocated according to the number of ads addressed to the different channels. Since there were 100 ads altogether, the average ad cost $31.

TABLE 4. Bases for Allocating Functional Expenses to Channels

Channel Type	Selling	Advertising	Packing and Delivery	Billing and Collecting
Hardware	200	50	50	50
Garden supply	65	20	21	21
Department stores	10	30	9	9
	275	100	80	80
Functional expense	$5,500	$3,100	$4,800	$2,400
No. of Units	275	100	80	80
Equals	$ 20	$ 31	$ 60	$ 30

TABLE 5. Profit-and-Loss Statements for Channels

	Hardware	Garden Supply	Dept. Stores	Whole Company
Sales	$30,000	$10,000	$20,000	$60,000
Cost of goods sold	19,500	6,500	13,000	39,000
Gross margin	$10,500	$3,500	$7,000	$21,000
Expenses				
Selling ($20 per call)	$4,000	$1,300	$200	$5,500
Advertising	1,550	620	930	3,100
($31 per advertisement)				
Packing and delivery				
($60 per order)	3,000	1,260	540	4,800
Billing ($30 per order)	1,500	630	270	2,400
Total Expenses	$10,050	$3,810	$1,940	15,800
Net profit or loss	$ 450	$ (310)	$5,060	$ 5,200

The packing and delivery expense is allocated according to the number of orders placed by each type of channel; this same basis was used for allocating billing and collection expense.

Step 3: Preparing a Profit-and-Loss Statement for Each Marketing Entity. A profit-and-loss statement can now be prepared for each type of channel. The results are shown in Table 5. Since hardware stores accounted for one half of total sales ($30,000 out of $60,000), this channel is charged with half the cost of goods sold ($19,500 out of $39,000). This leaves a gross margin from hardware stores of $10,500. From this must be deducted the proportions of the functional expenses that hardware stores consumed. According to Table 4, hardware stores received 200 out of 275 total sales calls. At an imputed value of $20 a call, hardware stores have to be charged with a $4,000 selling expense. Table 4 also shows that hardware stores were the target of 50 ads. At $31 an ad, the hardware stores are charged with $1,550 of advertising. The same reasoning applies in computing the share of the other functional expenses to charge to hardware stores. The result is that hardware stores gave rise to $10,500 of the total expenses. Subtracting this from the gross margin, the profit of selling through hardware stores is only $450.

This analysis is repeated for the other channels. The company is losing money in selling through garden supply shops and makes virtually all of its profits in selling through department stores. Notice that the gross sales through each channel are not a reliable indicator of the net profits being made in each channel.

Determining the Best Corrective Action

It would be naive to conclude that garden supply shops and possibly hardware stores should be dropped in order to concentrate on department stores. The following questions would need to be answered first:

- To what extent do buyers buy on the basis of the type of retail outlet versus the brand? Would they seek out the brand in those channels that were not eliminated?
- What are the trends with respect to the importance of these three channels?
- Have company marketing strategies directed at the three channels been optimal?

On the basis of the answers, marketing management can evaluate a number of alternative actions:

- *Establish a Special Charge for Handling Smaller Orders:* This move assumes that small orders are a cause of the relative unprofitability of dealing with garden supply shops and hardware stores.
- *Give More Promotional Aid to Garden Supply Shops and Hardware Stores:* This assumes that the store managers could increase their sales with more training or promotional materials.
- *Reduce the Number of Sales Calls and the Amount of Advertising Going to Garden Supply Shops and Hardware Stores:* This assumes that some costs can be saved without seriously hurting sales in these channels.
- *Do Nothing:* This assumes that current marketing efforts are optimal and either that marketing trends point to an imminent profit improvement in the weaker channels or that dropping any channel would reduce profits because of repercussions on production costs or on demand.
- *Do Not Abandon Any Channel as a Whole but Only the Weakest Retail Units in Each Channel:* This assumes that a detailed cost study would reveal many profitable garden shops and hardware stores whose profits are concealed by the poor performance of other stores in these categories.

In general, marketing-profitability analysis indicates the relative profitability of different channels, products, territories, or other marketing entities.[7] It does not prove that the best course of action is to drop the unprofitable marketing entities, nor does it capture the likely profit improvement if these marginal marketing entities are dropped.

Direct versus Full Costing

Like all information tools, marketing-profitability analysis can lead or mislead marketing executives, depending upon the degree of their understanding of its methods and limitations. The example showed some arbitrariness in the choice of bases for allocating the functional expenses to the marketing entities being evaluated. Thus the "number of sales calls" was used to allocate selling expenses, when in principle, "number of sales working-hours" is a more accurate indicator of cost. The former base was used because it involves less record keeping and computation. These approximations might not involve too much inaccuracy, but marketing executives should acknowledge this judgmental element in determining marketing costs.[8]

Far more serious is another judgmental element affecting profitability analysis. The issue is whether to allocate *full costs* or only *direct and traceable costs* in evaluating the performance of a marketing entity. The preceding example sidestepped this problem by assuming only simple costs that fit in with marketing activities. But the question cannot be avoided in the actual analysis of profitability. Three types of costs have to be distinguished:

- *Direct Costs:* These are costs that can be assigned directly to the proper marketing entities. For example, sales commissions are a direct cost in a profitability analysis of sales territories, sales representatives, or customers. Advertising expenditures are a direct cost in a profitability analysis of products to the extent that each advertisement promotes only one company product. Other direct costs for specific purposes are salesforce salaries, supplies, and traveling expenses.
- *Traceable Common Costs:* These are costs that can be assigned only indirectly, but on a plausible basis, to the marketing entities. In the example, rent was analyzed in this way. The company's floor space was needed for three different marketing activities, and an estimate was made of how much floor space supported each activity.
- *Nontraceable Common Costs:* These are costs whose allocation to the marketing entities is highly arbitrary. Consider "corporate image" expenditures. To allocate them equally to all products would be arbitrary because all products do not benefit equally from corporate image making. To allocate them proportionately to the sales of the various products would be arbitrary because relative product sales reflect many factors besides corporate image making. Other typical examples of difficult-to-assign common costs are top management salaries, taxes, interest, and other types of overhead.

No one disputes including direct costs in marketing cost analysis. There is a small amount of controversy about including traceable common costs. Traceable common costs lump together costs that would change with the scale of marketing activity and costs that would not change. If the lawnmower company drops garden supply shops, it will probably continue to pay the same rent for contractual reasons. In this event, its profits would not rise immediately by the amount of the present loss in selling to garden supply shops ($310). The profit figures are more meaningful when traceable costs can be eliminated.

The major controversy concerns whether the nontraceable common costs should be allocated to the marketing entities. Such allocation is called the *full-cost approach,* and its advocates argue that all costs must ultimately be imputed in order to determine true profitability. But this argument confuses the use of accounting for financial reporting with its use for managerial decision making. Full costing has three major weaknesses:

- The relative profitability of different marketing entities can shift radically when one arbitrary way to allocate nontraceable common costs is replaced by another. This weakens confidence in the tool.
- The arbitrariness demoralizes managers, who feel that their performance is judged adversely.
- The inclusion of nontraceable common costs could weaken efforts at real cost control. Operating management is most effective in controlling direct costs and traceable common costs. Arbitrary assignments of nontraceable common costs can lead them to spend their time fighting the arbitrary cost allocations rather than managing their controllable costs well.

Companies are showing a growing interest in using *activity-based cost accounting* (ABC) in interpreting the true profitability of different activities. According to Cooper and Kaplan, this tool "can give managers a clear picture of how products, brands, customers, facilities, regions, or distribution channels both generate revenues and consume resources."[9] To improve profitability, the managers can then examine ways to reduce the resources required to perform various activities, or make the resources more productive or acquire them at a lower cost. Alternatively, management may raise prices on products that consume heavy amounts of support resources. The contribution of ABC is to refocus management's attention away from using only labor or material standard costs to allocate full cost to capturing the actual costs of supporting individual products, customers, and other entities.

EFFICIENCY CONTROL

Suppose a profitability analysis reveals that the company is earning poor profits in connection with certain products, territories, or markets. The question is whether there are more efficient ways to manage the salesforce, advertising, sales promotion, and distribution in connection with these poorer-performing marketing entities.

Some companies have established a *marketing controller* position to assist marketing personnel to improve marketing efficiency. Marketing controllers work out of the controller's office but are specialized in the marketing side of the business. At companies such as General Foods, Du Pont, and Johnson & Johnson, they perform a sophisticated financial analysis of marketing expenditures and results. Specifically, they examine adherence to profit plans, help prepare brand managers' budgets, measure the efficiency of promotions, analyze media production costs, evaluate customer and geographic profitability, and educate marketing personnel on the financial implications of marketing decisions.[10]

Sales Force Efficiency

Sales managers need to monitor the following key indicators of sales force efficiency in their territory:

• Average number of sales calls per salesperson per day
• Average sales-call time per contact
• Average revenue per sales call
• Average cost per sales call
• Entertainment cost per sales call
• Percentage of orders per 100 sales calls
• Number of new customers per period
• Number of lost customers per period
• Sales force cost as a percentage of total sales

These indicators raise such useful questions as the following: Are sales representatives making too few calls per day? Are they spending too much time per call? Are they spending too much on entertainment? Are they closing enough orders per hundred calls? Are they producing enough new customers and holding onto the old customers?

When a company starts investigating sales force efficiency, it can often find areas for improvement. General Electric reduced the size of one of its divisional sales forces after discovering that its salespeople were calling on customers too often. When a large airline found that its salespeople were both selling and servicing, they transferred the servicing function to lower-paid clerks. Another company conducted time-and-duty studies and found ways to reduce the ratio of idle-to-productive time.

Advertising Efficiency

Many managers feel that it is almost impossible to measure what they are getting for their advertising dollars. But they should try to keep track of at least the following statistics:

• Advertising cost per thousand target buyers reached by media vehicle
• Percentage of audience who noted, saw/associated, and read most of each print ad
• Consumer opinions on the ad content and effectiveness
• Before-after measures of attitude toward the product

• Number of inquiries stimulated by the ad
• Cost per inquiry

Management can undertake a number of steps to improve advertising efficiency, including doing a better job of positioning the product, defining advertising objectives, pretesting messages, using the computer to guide the selection of advertising media, looking for better media buys, and doing advertising post-testing.

Sales-Promotion Efficiency

Sales promotion includes dozens of devices for stimulating buyer interest and product trial. To improve sales-promotion efficiency, management should record the costs and sales impact of each sales promotion. Management should watch the following statistics:

• Percentage of sales sold on deal
• Display costs per sales dollar
• Percentage of coupons redeemed
• Number of inquiries resulting from a demonstration

If a sales-promotion manager is appointed, that manager can analyze the results of different sales promotions and advise product managers on the most cost-effective promotions to use.

Distribution Efficiency

Management needs to search for distribution economies. Several tools are available for improving inventory control, warehouse locations, and transportation modes. One problem that frequently arises is that distribution efficiency might decline when the company experiences strong sales increases. Peter Senge describes a situation where a strong sales surge causes the company to fall behind in meeting its promised delivery dates.[11] This leads customers to bad-mouth the company and eventually sales fall. Management responds by increasing salesforce incentives to secure more orders. The salesforce succeeds but once again the company slips in meeting its promised delivery dates. Management needs to perceive the real bottleneck and invest in more production and distribution capacity.

STRATEGIC CONTROL

From time to time, companies need to undertake a critical review of their overall marketing goals and effectiveness. Marketing is an area where rapid obsolescence of objectives, policies, strategies, and programs is a constant possibility. Each company should periodically reassess its strategic approach to the marketplace. Two tools are available, namely, a *marketing-effectiveness rating review and a marketing audit.*

Marketing-Effectiveness Rating Review

Here is an actual situation: The president of a major industrial-equipment company reviewed the annual business plans of various divisions and found several division plans lacking in marketing substance. He called in the corporate vice president of marketing and said:

> *I am not happy with the quality of marketing in our divisions. It is very uneven. I want you to find out which of our divisions are strong, average, and weak in marketing. I want to know if they understand and are practicing customer-oriented marketing. I want a marketing score for each division. For each marketing-deficient division, I want a plan for improving its marketing effectiveness over the next several years. I want evidence next year that each marketing-deficient division is improving its market capabilities.*

The corporate marketing vice president agreed, recognizing that it was a formidable task. His first inclination was to base the evaluation of marketing effectiveness on each division's performance in sales growth, market share, and profitability. His thinking was that high-performing divisions had good marketing leadership and poor-performing divisions had poor marketing leadership.

Marketing effectiveness is not necessarily revealed by current sales and profit performance. Good results could be due to a division's being in the right place at the right time, rather than having effective marketing management. Improvements in that division's marketing might boost results from good to excellent. Another division might have poor results in spite of excellent marketing planning. Replacing the present marketing managers might only make things worse.

The marketing effectiveness of a company or division is reflected in the degree to which it exhibits five major attributes of a marketing orientation: *customer philosophy, integrated marketing organization, adequate marketing information, strategic orientation,* and *operational efficiency.* Each attribute can be measured. Table 6 presents a *marketing-effectiveness rating instrument* based on these five attributes. This instrument is filled out by marketing and other managers in the division. The scores are then summarized.

The instrument has been tested in a number of companies, and very few achieve scores within the superior range of 26 to 30 points. The few include well-known master marketers such as Procter & Gamble, McDonald's, IBM, and Nike. Most companies and divisions receive scores in the fair-to-good range, indicating that their own managers see room for marketing improvement. Low attribute scores indicate that the attribute needs attention. Divisional management can then establish a plan for correcting its major marketing weaknesses.[12]

The Marketing Audit

Those companies that discover marketing weaknesses through applying the marketing-effectiveness rating review should undertake a more thorough study known as a *marketing audit*.[13] We define *marketing audit* as follows:

• A marketing audit *is a comprehensive, systematic, independent, and periodic examination of a company's—or business unit's—marketing environment, objectives, strategies, and activities with a view to determining problem areas and opportunities and recommending a plan of action to improve the company's marketing performance.*

Let us examine the marketing audit's four characteristics:

• *Comprehensive:* The marketing audit covers all the major marketing activities of a business, not just a few trouble spots. It would be called a functional audit if it covered only the salesforce or pricing or some other marketing activity. Although functional audits are useful, they sometimes mislead management as to the real source of its problem. Excessive salesforce turnover, for example, could be a symptom not of poor salesforce training or compensation but of weak company products and promotion. A comprehensive marketing audit usually is more effective in locating the real source of the company's marketing problems.

• *Systematic:* The marketing audit involves an orderly sequence of diagnostic steps covering the organization's macro- and micromarketing environment, marketing objectives and strategies, marketing systems, and specific marketing activities. The diagnosis indicates the most needed improvements. They are incorporated in a corrective-action plan involving both short-run and long-run steps to improve the organization's overall marketing effectiveness.

• *Independent:* A marketing audit can be conducted in six ways: self-audit, audit from across, audit from above, company auditing office, company task-force audit, and outsider audit. Self-audits, where managers use a checklist to rate their own operations, can be useful, but most experts agree that self-audits lack objectivity and independence.[14] The 3M Company has made good use of a corporate auditing office, which provides marketing audit services to divisions on request.[15] Generally speaking, however, the best audits are likely to come from outside consultants who have the necessary objectivity, broad experience in a number of industries, some familiarity with this industry, and the undivided time and attention to give to the audit.

• *Periodic:* Typically, marketing audits are initiated only after sales have turned down, salesforce morale has fallen, and other company problems have occurred. Ironically, companies are thrown into a crisis partly because they failed to review their marketing operations during good times. A periodic marketing audit can benefit companies in good health as well as those in trouble. "No marketing operation is ever so good that it cannot be improved. Even the best can be made better. In fact, even the best *must* be better, for few if any marketing operations can remain successful over the years by maintaining the status quo."[16]

Marketing Audit Procedure. A marketing audit starts with a meeting between the company officer(s) and the marketing auditor(s) to work out an agreement on the objectives, coverage, depth, data sources, report format, and the time period for the audit. A detailed plan as to who is to be interviewed, the questions to be asked, the time and place of contact, and so on, is carefully prepared so that auditing time and cost are kept to a minimum. The cardinal rule in marketing auditing is: Don't rely solely on the company's managers for data and opinion. Customers, dealers, and other outside groups must be interviewed. Many companies do not really know how their customers and dealers see them, nor do they fully understand customer needs and value judgments.

When the data-gathering phase is over, the marketing auditor presents the main findings and recommendations. A valuable aspect of the marketing audit is the process that the managers go through to assimilate, debate, and develop new concepts of needed marketing action.

Components of the Marketing Audit. The marketing audit examines six major components of the company's marketing situation. The major auditing questions are listed in Table 7.

TABLE 6. Marketing-Effectiveness Rating Instrument
(Check One Answer to Each Question)

CUSTOMER PHILOSOPHY

A. Does management recognize the importance of designing the company to serve the needs and wants of chosen markets:

    0 ❐ Management primarily thinks in terms of selling current and new products to whomever will buy them.

    1 ❐ Management thinks in terms of serving a wide range of markets and needs with equal effectiveness.

    2 ❐ Management thinks in terms of serving the needs and wants of well-defined markets and market segments chosen for their long-run growth and profit potential for the company.

B. Does management develop different offerings and marketing plans for different segments of the market?

    0 ❐ No.

    1 ❐ Somewhat.

    2 ❐ To a large extent.

C. Does management take a whole marketing system view (suppliers, channels, com-

petitors, customers, environment) in planning its business?

    0 ❐ No. Management concentrates on selling and servicing its immediate customers.

    1 ❐ Somewhat. Management takes a long view of its channels although the bulk of its effort goes to selling and servicing the immediate customers.

    2 ❐ Yes. Management takes a whole marketing systems view, recognizing the threats and opportunities created for the company by changes in any part of the system.

INTEGRATED MARKETING ORGANIZATION

D. Is there high-level marketing integration and control of the major marketing functions?

    0 ❐ No. Sales and other marketing functions are not integrated at the top and there is some unproductive conflict.

    1 ❐ Somewhat. There is formal integration and control of the major marketing functions but less than satisfactory coordination and cooperation.

    2 ❐ Yes. The major marketing functions are effectively integrated.

E. Does marketing management work well with management in research, manufacturing, purchasing, physical distribution, and finance?

    0 ❐ No. There are complaints that marketing is unreasonable in the demands and costs it places on other departments.

    1 ❐ Somewhat. The relations are amicable although each department pretty much acts to serve its own interests.

    2 ❐ Yes. The departments cooperate effectively and resolve issues in the best interest of the company as a whole.

F. How well organized is the new-product development process?

    0 ❐ The system is ill-defined and poorly handled.

    1 ❐ The system formally exists but lacks sophistication.

    2 ❐ The system is well-structured and operates on teamwork principles.

ADEQUATE MARKETING INFORMATION

G. When were the latest marketing research studies of customers, buying influences, channels, and competitors conducted?

    0 ❐ Several years ago.

    1 ❐ A few years ago.

    2 ❐ Recently.

H. How well does management know the sales potential and profitability of different market segments, customers, territories, products, channels, and order sizes?

    0 ❐ Not at all.

    1 ❐ Somewhat.

    2 ❐ Very well.

I. What effort is expended to measure and improve the cost effectiveness of different marketing expenditures?

    0 ❐ Little or no effort.

    1 ❐ Some effort.

    2 ❐ Substantial effort.

STRATEGIC ORIENTATION

J. What is the extent of formal marketing planning?

    0 ☐ Management conducts little or no formal marketing planning.

    1 ☐ Management develops an annual marketing plan.

    2 ☐ Management develops a detailed annual marketing plan and a strategic long-range plan that is updated annually.

K. How impressive is the current marketing strategy?

    0 ☐ The current strategy is not clear.

    1 ☐ The current strategy is clear and represents a continuation of traditional strategy.

    2 ☐ The current strategy is clear, innovative, data based, and well reasoned.

L. What is the extent of contingency thinking and planning?

    0 ☐ Management does little or no contingency thinking.

    1 ☐ Management does some contingency thinking although little formal contingency planning.

    2 ☐ Management formally identifies the most important contingencies and develops contingency plans.

OPERATIONAL EFFICIENCY

M. How well is the marketing strategy communicated and implemented?

    0 ☐ Poorly.

    1 ☐ Fairly.

    2 ☐ Successfully.

N. Is management doing an effective job with its marketing resources?

    0 ☐ No. The marketing resources are inadequate for the job to be done.

    1 ☐ Somewhat. The marketing resources are adequate but they are not employed optimally.

    2 ☐ Yes. The marketing resources are adequate and are employed efficiently.

O. Does management show a good capacity to react quickly and effectively to on-the-spot developments?

    0 ☐ No. Sales and market information is not very current and management reaction time is slow.

    1 ☐ Somewhat. Management receives fairly up-to-date sales and market information; management reaction time varies.

    2 ☐ Yes. Management has installed systems yielding high current information and fast reaction time.

TOTAL SCORE

The instrument is used in the following way. The appropriate answer is checked for each question. The scores are added—the total will be somewhere between 0 and 30. The following scale shows the level of marketing effectiveness:

0–5 = None	11–15 = Fair	21–25 = Very good
6–10 = Poor	16–20 = Good	26–30 = Superior

Source: Philip Kotler, "From Sales Obsession to Marketing Effectiveness," *Harvard Business Review,* November–December 1977, pp. 67–75. Copyright ©1977 by the President and Fellows of Harvard College; all rights reserved.

TABLE 7. Components of a Marketing Audit

PART I. MARKETING-ENVIRONMENT AUDIT

Macroenvironment

A. Demographic	What major demographic developments and trends pose opportunities or threats to this company? What actions has the company taken in response to these developments and trends?
B. Economic	What major developments in income, prices, savings, and credit will affect the company? What actions has the company been taking in response to these developments and trends?
C. Ecological	What is the outlook for the cost and availability of natural resources and energy needed by the company? What concerns have been expressed about the company's role in pollution and conservation, and what steps has the company taken?
D. Technological	What major changes are occurring in product and process technology? What is the company's position in these technologies? What major generic substitutes might replace this product?
E. Political	What changes in laws and regulations might affect marketing strategy and tactics? What is happening in the areas of pollution control, equal employment opportunity, product safety, advertising, price control, and so forth, that affects marketing strategy?
F. Cultural	What is the public's attitude toward business and toward the company's products? What changes in customer lifestyles and values might affect the company?

Task Environment

A. Markets	What is happening to market size, growth, geographical distribution, and profits? What are the major market segments?
B. Customers	What are the customers' needs and buying processes? How do customers and prospects rate the company and its competitors on reputation, product quality, service, sales force, and price? How do different customer segments make their buying decisions?
C. Competitors	Who are the major competitors? What are their objectives, strategies, strengths, weaknesses, sizes, and market shares? What trends will affect future competition and substitutes for this product?
D. Distribution and Dealers	What are the main trade channels for bringing products to customers? What are the efficiency levels and growth potentials of the different trade channels?

E. Suppliers	What is the outlook for the availability of key resources used in production? What trends are occurring among suppliers?
F. Facilitators and Marketing Firms	What is the cost and availability outlook for transportation services, warehousing facilities, and financial resources? How effective are the company's advertising agencies and marketing research firms?
G. Publics	Which publics represent particular opportunities or problems for the company? What steps has the company taken to deal effectively with each public?

PART II. MARKETING-STRATEGY AUDIT

A. Business Mission	Is the business mission clearly stated in market-oriented terms? Is it feasible?
B. Marketing Objectives and Goals	Are the company and marketing objectives and goals stated clearly enough to guide marketing planning and performance measurement? Are the marketing objectives appropriate, given the company's competitive position, resources, and opportunities?
C. Strategy	Has the management articulated a clear marketing strategy for achieving its marketing objectives? Is the strategy convincing? Is the strategy appropriate to the stage of the product life cycle, competitors' strategies, and the state of the economy? Is the company using the best basis for market segmentation? Does it have clear criteria for rating the segments and choosing the best ones? Has it developed accurate profiles of each target segment? Has the company developed an effective positioning and marketing mix for each target segment? Are marketing resources allocated optimally to the major elements of the marketing mix? Are enough resources or too many resources budgeted to accomplish the marketing objectives?

PART III. MARKETING-ORGANIZATION AUDIT

A. Formal Structure	Does the marketing vice president have adequate authority and responsibility for company activities that affect customers' satisfaction? Are the marketing activities optimally structured along functional, product, segment, end-user, and geographical lines?
B. Functional Efficiency	Are there good communication and working relations between marketing and sales? Is the product management system working effectively? Are product managers able to plan profits or only sales volume? Are there any groups in marketing that need more training, motivation, supervision, or evaluation?
C. Interface Efficiency	Are there any problems between marketing and manufac-

turing, R&D, purchasing, finance, accounting, and legal that need attention?

PART IV. MARKETING-SYSTEMS AUDIT

A. Marketing Information System	Is the marketing intelligence system producing accurate, sufficient, and timely information about marketplace developments with respect to customers, prospects, distributors and dealers, competitors, suppliers, and various publics? Are company decision makers asking for enough marketing research, and are they using the results? Is the company employing the best methods for market measurement and sales forecasting?
B. Marketing Planning Systems	Is the marketing planning system well conceived and effectively used? Do marketers have decision support systems available? Does the planning system result in acceptable sales targets and quotas?
C. Marketing Control System	Are the control procedures adequate to ensure that the annual-plan objectives are being achieved? Does management periodically analyze the profitability of products, markets, territories, and channels of distribution? Are marketing costs and productivity periodically examined?
D. New-Product Development System	Is the company well organized to gather, generate, and screen new-product ideas? Does the company do adequate concept research and business analysis before investing in new ideas? Does the company carry out adequate product and market testing before launching new products?

PART V. MARKETING-PRODUCTIVITY AUDIT

A. Profitability Analysis	What is the profitability of the company's different products, markets, territories, and channels of distribution? Should the company enter, expand, contract, or withdraw from any business segments?
B. Cost-Effectiveness Analysis	Do any marketing activities seem to have excessive costs? Can cost-reducing steps be taken?

PART VI. MARKETING-FUNCTION AUDITS

A. Products	What are the product-line objectives? Are they sound? Is the current product line meeting the objectives? Should the product line be stretched or contracted upward, downward, or both ways? Which products should be phased out? Which products should be added? What are the buyers' knowledge and attitudes toward the company's and competitors' product quality, features, styling, brand names, and so on? What areas of product and brand strategy need improvement?

B. Price	What are the pricing objectives, policies, strategies, and procedures? To what extent are prices set on cost, demand, and competitive criteria? Do the customers see the company's prices as being in line with the value of its offer? What does management know about the price elasticity of demand, experience-curve effects, and competitors' prices and pricing policies? To what extent are price policies compatible with the needs of distributors and dealers, suppliers, and government regulation?
C. Distribution	What are the distribution objectives and strategies? Is there adequate market coverage and service? How effective are distributors, dealers, manufacturers' representatives, brokers, agents, and others? Should the company consider changing its distribution channels?
D. Advertising, Sales Promotion, and Publicity	What are the organization's advertising objectives? Are they sound? Is the right amount being spent on advertising? Are the ad themes and copy effective? What do customers and the public think about the advertising? Are the advertising media well chosen? Is the internal advertising staff adequate? Is the sales-promotion budget adequate? Is there effective and sufficient use of sales-promotion tools such as samples, coupons, displays, and sales contests? Is the public-relations staff competent and creative? Is the company making enough use of direct and database marketing?
E. Sales Force	What are the sales force objectives? Is the sales force large enough to accomplish the company's objectives? Is the salesforce organized along the proper principles of specialization (territory, market, product)? Are there enough (or too many) sales managers to guide the field sales representatives? Does the sales-compensation level and structure provide adequate incentive and reward? Does the sales force show high morale, ability, and effort? Are the procedures adequate for setting quotas and evaluating performances? How does the company's sales force compare to competitors' sales forces?

Example of a Marketing Audit.[17] O'Brien Candy Company is a medium-size candy company located in the Midwest. In the past two years, its sales and profits have barely held their own. Top management feels that the trouble lies with the sales force; they don't "work hard or smart enough." To correct the problem, management plans to introduce a new incentive-compensation system and hire a sales force trainer to train the sales force in modern merchandising and selling techniques. Before doing this, however, they decide to hire a marketing consultant to carry out a marketing audit. The auditor interviews managers, customers, sales representatives, and dealers and examines various data. Here are the auditor's findings:

The company's product line consists primarily of 18 products, mostly candy bars. Its two leading brands are mature and account for 76% of total sales. The company has looked at the fast-developing markets of chocolate snacks and candies but has not made any moves yet.

The company recently researched its customer profile. Its products appeal especially to lower-income and older people. Respondents who were asked to assess O'Brien's chocolate products in relation to competitors' products described them as "average quality and a bit old-fashioned."

O'Brien sells its products to candy jobbers and large supermarkets. Its sales force calls on many of the small retailers reached by the candy jobbers, to fortify displays and provide ideas; its sales force also calls on many small retailers not covered by jobbers. O'Brien enjoys good penetration of small retailing, although not in all segments, such as the fast-growing restaurant area. Its major approach to middlemen is a "sell-in" strategy: discounts, exclusive contracts, and stock financing. At the same time O'Brien has not adequately penetrated the mass-merchandise chains. Its competitors rely more heavily on mass-consumer advertising and in-store merchandising and are more successful with the mass merchandisers.

O'Brien's marketing budget is set at 15% of its total sales, compared with competitors' budgets of close to 20%. Most of the marketing budget supports the sales force, and the remainder supports advertising; consumer promotions are very limited. The advertising budget is spent primarily in reminder advertising for the company's two leading products. New products are not developed often, and when they are, they are introduced to retailers by using a "push" strategy.

The marketing organization is headed by a sales vice president. Reporting to the sales vice president is the sales manager, the marketing research manager, and the advertising manager. Having come up from the ranks, the sales vice president is partial to sales force activities and pays less attention to the other marketing functions. The sales force is assigned to territories headed by area managers.

The marketing auditor concluded that O'Brien's problems would not be solved by actions taken to improve its sales force. The sales force problem was symptomatic of a deeper company malaise. The auditor prepared a report to management consisting of the findings and recommendations shown in Table 8.

The Marketing Excellence Review

Companies can use another instrument to rate their performance in relation to the "best practices" of high-performing businesses. The three columns in Table 9 distinguish between poor, good, and excellent business and marketing practice. Management can place a check on each line as to their perception of where the business stands. The resulting profile then exposes the business's weaknesses and strengths. It highlights where the company might move to become a truly outstanding player in the marketplace.

The Company Ethical and Social Responsibility Review

Companies need to use a final instrument to evaluate whether they are truly practicing ethical and socially responsible marketing. We believe that business success and continually satisfying the customer and other stakeholders is intimately tied up with adopting and implementing high standards of business and marketing conduct. The most admired companies in the world abide by a code of serving people's interests, not only their own.

The practices of business are often under attack because business situations routinely pose tough dilemmas as to what is right. One can go back to Howard Bowen's classic questions about the responsibilities of businesspeople:

> *Should he conduct selling in ways that intrude on the privacy of people, for example, by door-to-door selling . . . ? Should he use methods involving ballyhoo, chances, prizes, hawking, and other tactics which are at least of doubtful good taste? Should he employ "high pressure" tactics in persuading people to buy? Should he try to hasten the obsolescence of goods by bringing out an endless succession of new models and new styles? Should he appeal to and attempt to strengthen the motives of materialism, invidious consumption, and "keeping up with the Joneses."[18]*

TABLE 8. Summary of Marketing Auditor's Findings and Recommendations for O'Brien Candy Company

FINDINGS

The company's product lines are dangerously unbalanced. The two leading products accounted for 76% of total sales and have no growth potential. Five of the 18 products are unprofitable and have no growth potential.

The company's marketing objectives are neither clear nor realistic.

The company's strategy is not taking changing distribution patterns into account or catering to rapidly changing markets.

The company is run by a sales organization rather than a marketing organization.

The company's marketing mix is unbalanced, with too much spending on sales force and not enough on advertising.

The company lacks procedures for successfully developing and launching new products.

The company's selling effort is not geared to profitable accounts.

SHORT-TERM RECOMMENDATIONS

Examine the current product line and weed out marginal performers with limited growth potential.

Shift some marketing expenditures from supporting mature products to supporting more recent ones.

Shift the marketing-mix emphasis from direct selling to national advertising, especially for new products.

Conduct a market-profile study of the fastest growing segments of the candy market and develop a plan to break into these areas.

Instruct the sales force to drop some of the smaller outlets and not to take orders for under 20 items. Also, cut out the duplication of effort of sales representatives and jobbers calling on the same accounts.

Initiate sales-training programs and an improved compensation plan.

MEDIUM- TO LONG-TERM RECOMMENDATIONS

Hire an experienced marketing vice president from the outside.

Set formal and operational marketing objectives.

Introduce the product manager concept in the marketing organization.

Initiate effective new-product-development programs.

Develop strong brand names.

Find ways to market its brands to the chain stores more effectively.

Increase the level of marketing expenditures to 20% of sales.

Reorganize the selling function by specializing sales representatives by distribution channels.

Set sales objectives and base sales compensation on gross profit performance.

Source: Adapted with permission from Dr. Ernst A. Tirmann, "Should Your Marketing Be Audited?" *European Business.* Autumn 1971.

TABLE 9. The Marketing Excellence Review: Best Practices

Poor	Good	Excellent
Product Driven	Market Driven	Market Driving
Mass-Market Oriented	Segment Oriented	Niche Oriented and Customer Oriented
Product Offer	Augmented Product Offer	Customer Solutions Offer
Average Product Quality	Better Than Average	Legendary
Average Service Quality	Better Than Average	Legendary
End-Product Oriented	Core-Product Oriented	Core-Competency Oriented
Function Oriented	Process Oriented	Outcome Oriented
Reacting to Competitors	Benchmarking Competitors	Leapfrogging Competitors
Supplier Exploitation	Supplier Preference	Supplier Partnership
Dealer Exploitation	Dealer Support	Dealer Partnership
Price Driven	Quality Driven	Value Driven
Average Speed	Better Than Average	Legendary
Hierarchy	Network	Teamwork
Vertically Integrated	Flattened Organization	Strategic Alliances
Stockholder Driven	Stakeholder Driven	Societally Driven

Specific issues are further highlighted in Figure 4. Many were reviewed in earlier chapters. Clearly the company's bottom line cannot be the sole measure of corporate performance.

Raising the level of socially responsible marketing calls for a three-pronged attack. First, society must use the law to define, as clearly as possible, those practices which are illegal, antisocial, or anticompetitive. Second, companies must adopt and disseminate a written code of ethics, build a company tradition of ethical behavior, and hold their people fully responsible for observing the ethical and legal guidelines. Third, individual marketers must practice a "social conscience" in their specific dealings with customers and various stakeholders.

The future holds a wealth of opportunities for companies as they move into the twenty-first century. Technological advances in solar energy, home computers, cable television, modern medicine, transportation, recreation, and communication promise to change the world as we know it. At the same time, forces in the socio-economic, cultural, and natural environments will impose new limits on marketing and business practice. Companies that are able to innovate new solutions and values in a socially responsible way are the most likely to succeed.

FIGURE 4. Major Marketing Decision Areas Posing Legal or Ethical Questions

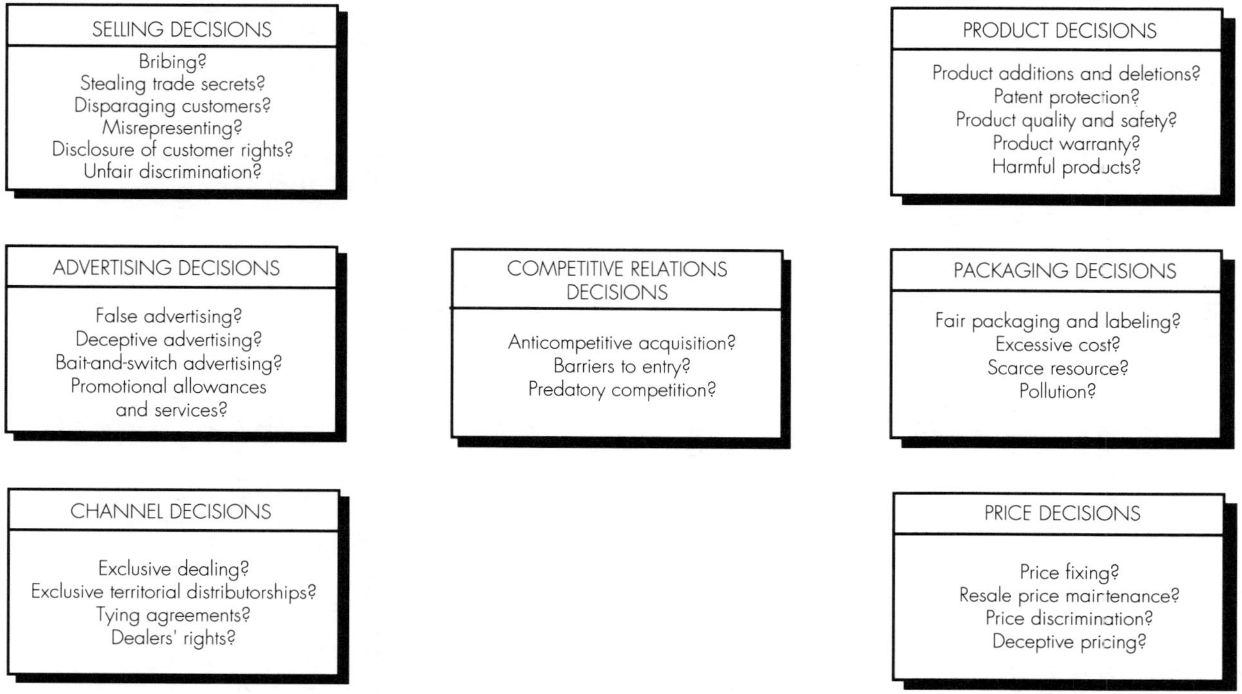

PRODUCT DECISIONS

Product additions and deletions?
Patent protection?
Product quality and safety?
Product warranty?
Harmful products?

PACKAGING DECISIONS

Fair packaging and labeling?
Excessive cost?
Scarce resource?
Pollution?

PRICE DECISIONS

Price fixing?
Resale price maintenance?
Price discrimination?
Deceptive pricing?

COMPETITIVE RELATIONS DECISIONS

Anticompetitive acquisition?
Barriers to entry?
Predatory competition?

SELLING DECISIONS

Bribing?
Stealing trade secrets?
Disparaging customers?
Misrepresenting?
Disclosure of customer rights?
Unfair discrimination?

ADVERTISING DECISIONS

False advertising?
Deceptive advertising?
Bait-and-switch advertising?
Promotional allowances
and services?

CHANNEL DECISIONS

Exclusive dealing?
Exclusive territorial distributorships?
Tying agreements?
Dealers' rights?

SUMMARY

Marketing control is the natural sequel to marketing planning, organization, and implementation. Companies need to carry out four types of marketing control.

Annual-plan control consists of monitoring the current marketing effort and results to ensure that the annual sales and profit goals will be achieved. The main tools are sales analysis, market-share analysis, marketing expense-to-sales analysis, financial analysis, and customer-satisfaction tracking. If underperformance is detected, the company can implement several corrective measures, including cutting production, changing prices, increasing salesforce pressure, and cutting fringe expenditures.

Profitability control calls for determining the actual profitability of the firm's products, territories, market-segments, and trade channels. Marketing-profitability analysis reveals the weaker marketing entities, although it does not indicate whether the weaker units should be bolstered or phased out.

Efficiency control is the task of increasing the efficiency of such marketing activities as personal selling, advertising, sales promotion, and distribution. Managers must watch certain key ratios that indicate how efficiently these functions are being performed.

Strategic control is the task of ensuring that the company's marketing objectives, strategies, and systems are optimally adapted to the current and forecasted marketing environment. One tool, known as the marketing-effectiveness rating instrument, profiles a company's or a division's overall marketing effectiveness in terms of customer philosophy, marketing organization, marketing information, strategic planning, and operational efficiency. Another tool, the marketing audit, is a comprehensive, systematic, independent, and periodic examination of the organization's marketing environment, objectives, strategies, and activities. The marketing audit seeks to identify marketing problem areas and recommends short-run and long-run actions to improve the organization's overall marketing effectiveness. The marketing excellence review helps a company grade its practices in relation to the "best practices" of high-performing companies. Finally, the company ethical and social responsibility review helps the company assess the quality of its performance along ethical and social responsibility lines.

NOTES

1. For further discussion, see James M. Hulbert and Norman E. Toy, "A Strategic Framework for Marketing Control," *Journal of Marketing,* April 1977, pp. 12–20.

2. See Alfred R. Oxenfeldt, "How to Use Market-Share Measurement," *Harvard Business Review,* January–February 1969, pp. 59–68.

3. There is a one-half chance that a successive observation will be higher or lower. Therefore, the probability of finding six successively higher values is given by $(\frac{1}{2})^6 = \frac{1}{64}$.

4. Alternatively, companies need to focus on the factors affecting *shareholder value.* The goal of marketing planning is to take the steps that will increase shareholder value. Shareholder value is the *present value* of the future income stream created by the company's present actions. *Rate-of-return analysis* usually focuses on only one year's results. See Alfred Rapport, *Creating Shareholder Value* (New York: Free Press, 1986), pp. 125–30.

5. For additional reading on financial analysis, see Peter L. Mullins, *Measuring Customer and Product Line Profitability* (Washington, DC: Distribution Research and Education Foundation, 1984).

6. The MAC Group, *Distribution: A Competitive Weapon* (Cambridge, MA: 1985), p. 20.

7. For another example, see Leland L. Beik and Stephen L. Buzby, "Profitability Analyses by Market Segments," *Journal of Marketing,* June 1973, pp. 48–53.

8. For common bases of allocation, see Charles H. Sevin, *Marketing Productivity Analysis* (New York: McGraw-Hill, 1965).

9. See Robin Cooper and Robert S. Kaplan, "Profit Priorities from Activity-Based Costing," *Harvard Business Review,* May–June 1991, pp. 130–35.

10. Sam R. Goodman, *Increasing Corporate Profitability* (New York: Ronald Press, 1982), Chap. 1.

11. See Peter M. Senge, *The Fifth Discipline: The Art & Practice of the Learning Organization* (New York: Doubleday Currency, 1990), Chapter 7.

12. For further discussion of this instrument, see Philip Kotler, "From Sales Obsession to Marketing Effectiveness," *Harvard Business Review,* November–December 1977, pp. 67–75.

13. See Philip Kotler, William Gregor, and William Rodgers, "The Marketing Audit Comes of Age," *Sloan Management Review,* Winter 1977, pp. 25–43.

14. However, useful checklists for a marketing self-audit can be found in Aubrey Wilson, *Aubrey Wilson's Marketing Audit Checklists* (London: McGraw-Hill, 1982); and Mike Wilson, *The Management of*

Marketing (Westmead, England: Gower Publishing, 1980). Also a marketing audit software program is described in Ben M. Enis and Stephen J. Garfein, "The Computer-Driven Marketing Audit," *Journal of Management Inquiry,* December 1992, pp. 306–18.

15. Kotler, Gregor, and Rodgers, "Marketing Audit Comes of Age," p. 31.

16. Abe Schuchman, "The Marketing Audit: Its Nature, Purposes, and Problems," in *Analyzing and Improving Marketing Performance,* eds. Alfred Oxenfeldt and Richard D. Crisp (New York: American Management Association, 1950), report no. 32, pp. 16–17.

17. This case is adapted with permission from the excellent article by Dr. Ernst A. Tirmann, "Should Your Marketing Be Audited?" *European Business,* Autumn 1971, pp. 49–56.

18. Howard R. Bowen, *Social Responsibilities of the Businessman* (New York: Harper & Row, 1953), p. 215.

INDEX

Composers, Authors, and
Publishers), 133
Asset turnover, 232–233
Atari, 181
Audits, retail sales, 185
Authority seekers, 35

B

Base price, 192, 211
Base volume, 192–193
"Beer Game," 187
Behavioral planning
in marketing planning process,
154–155, 160–163, 169
problems, avoidance of, 156
Benefits, buying, 177–178
Biotechnology, 178
Blanket licenses, 133–135
Borden, Neil H., 87
Brands
chemically or physically
differentiated, 69
dominance, 19–20
entry, sequential, 21
flanker, 118
loyalty to, 38, 120
management utilization
panel data on, 218–220
store data on, 213–218
preferences, perceptions
and, 69
switching, associated with
trade promotion, 219–220
volume formula for, 218
Broadcast media, for database
marketing, 52–53
Broadcast Music, Inc. v.
Columbia Broadcasting
System, 133–135
Business definition
dimensions of, 10–12

objectives and, 3, 9–10
scope and, 12–15
strategy and, 15
Business purpose. See Business
definition
Buyer. See Customer

C

Cable television, for database
marketing, 53
Carol Wright co-op mailing,
53–54
"Cash cow" products, 119
Catalogs, 55
Category dominance, 25–26
Causal measures, 199–201
Cavaliers, 161
CBS (Columbia Broadcasting
System), 133, 138
Celotex Corp. v. Catrett,
140, 141
Cereals, high-nutrition, 71
Change reports, 203
Chicago Board of Trade v.
United States, 132
Clayton Act, 131
Cluster analysis, of joint-space
coordinates, 81–83
Coca-Cola, 19
Cognitive referents, 25
Cola wars, 19
Collaborative behavior, 133–135
Columbia Broadcasting System
(CBS), 133, 138
Commercial priorities,
establishing, 178–179
Commitment
lack of, in marketing
planning, 152
to marketing change, 154

penetration, market share
and, 228–229
preferences, 19
retention, 65
selectivity, market share
and, 228–229
Customer acquisition
specialists, 63
Customer lists, 52
Customer retention
specialists, 63
Customer-satisfaction
tracking, 233

D

Data. See also Information
analysis, for market position
analysis, 74–77
panel, 218–220
related, 220
store, 213–218
Database marketing
antecedents of, 41–42
collecting/maintaining
information for, 58
computer literacy in marketing
organization, 62–63
data quantity/quality,
limitations from, 62
definition of, 44–46
economics of, 55–57
effectiveness of, 56–57
efficiency of, 56–57
emergence of computer
technology and, 42–43
expenditures, efficiency/
effectiveness of, 49–50
installed base marketing
and, 47–48
media of, 50–54
offers in, 54

one-on-one marketing
and, 48–49
organizational impact of,
63–67
package in, 54–55
programs, elements of, 49–55
relationship marketing and,
43–44
shift to, 41
statistical analyses and, 43
strategy and, 48–49
success, inhibitors to, 61–63
uses of, 58–59, 60–61
vs. conventional marketing,
46–50
Database marketing firms,
examples of, 57–61
Databases, on consumer
purchases, 191–192
Decentralization, 180–181
Deceptive advertising law, 128
Decision making
criterion for, 105, 106–110
in marketing mix process, 92
Decisions, marketing
delay, 110–111
implications, 111–112
market segmentation
implications and, 38–39
monetary measures, 107–109
nonmonetary measures, 110
Delphi technique, 176
Demand-side marketing, 173
Demographic information,
household level, 198
Demographic segmentation,
33–34, 38
Diagnostic reports, market
position and, 201–208
Direct costing, vs. full costing,
237–239

G

Geneen, Harold, 179–180
General Electric (GE), 91
General Motors, 66, 135
Geodemographic data, on
  store, 193
Geographic segmentation,
  33–34, 37
Goals
  marketing, 117
  of market planning, 151
  optimal/incremental levels
    in, 117
  vs. objectives, 4–5
Goods, marketing characteristics
  of, 37–38
Government regulations
  adversary process and,
    125–126
  awareness of, 124–125
  complexity of, 129
  for consumer safety, 128
  deceptive advertising and, 128
  frustration from, 127–128
  ineffective, 128
  need for, 123–124
  new, 127
  points of view, knowledge
    of, 125
  against predatory
    competition, 128
  stifling of competition
    and, 127
Gross rating points (GRPs), 191
Groupings, strategy, 119
GRPs (gross rating points), 191

H

Handling charges, for small
  orders, 237
Hanes hosiery, 97

Harley-Davidson, 64, 229–230
Health care networks, 135
Hewlett-Packard, 181
Household purchase data,
  sample, projection issues for,
  197–198
Hypochondriacs, 35

I

IBM, 180–181, 242
Implementation
  failure, in marketing
    planning, 153
  ownership and, 163
  strategy and, 163
Incrementalism, in market
  planning process, 152
Incremental volume sales, 195
Indiana Federation of Dentists,
  136–137
Industrial market segmentation,
  36–37
Industrial users, 35–37
Information. See also Data
  demands, in market planning
    process, 152
  direct sales, 186
  needs, identifying, 151
  from POS scanning, 220–221
Information society, impact on
  marketing mix, 98–99
Innovation-driven ventures
  corporate masters of, 180–181
  entrepreneurship and, 179–180
  evaluation of, 177–179
  researching, 175–177
Installed-base marketing, 47–48,
  66–67
Interest, lack of, in marketing
  planning, 153

264

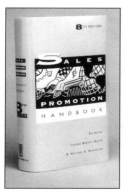